1001
Great Ideas
for Teaching & Raising Children *with*
Autism *or*
Asperger's

Ellen Notbohm | Veronica Zysk

FUTURE HORIZONS INC.
Arlington, Texas

1001 GREAT IDEAS
for Teaching & Raising Children with Autism or Asperger's

All marketing and publishing rights guaranteed to and reserved by:

721 W. Abram Street
Arlington, Texas 76013
800-489-0727
817-277-0727
817-277-2270 (fax)
E-mail: *info@FHautism.com*
www.FHautism.com

Book design © TLC Graphics, www.TLCGraphics.com
Cover by: Monica Thomas; Interior by: Erin Stark

Printed in USA.

The information presented in this book is educational and should not be construed as offering diagnostic, treatment, or legal advice or consultation. If professional assistance in any of these areas is needed, the services of a competent autism professional should be sought.

Visit the authors' websites; comments and new ideas always welcomed!
www.ellennotbohm.com, emailme@ellennotbohm.com, www.AutismDigest.com, editor@autismdigest.com

Publisher's Cataloging-In-Publication Data
(Prepared by The Donohue Group, Inc.)

Notbohm, Ellen.
   1001 great ideas for teaching & raising children with autism or Asperger's / Ellen Notbohm [and] Veronica Zysk.
-- [Rev. and exp. 2nd ed.]

   p. : ill. ; cm.

   Previous edition published as: 1001 great ideas for teaching and raising children with autism spectrum disorders.
   Includes bibliographical references and index.
   ISBN: 978-1-935274-06-3

1. Autistic children--Popular works. 2. Autism--Popular works. 3. Asperger's syndrome in children--Popular works. 4. Asperger's syndrome--Popular works. I. Zysk, Veronica. II. Title. III. Title: One thousand one great ideas for teaching and raising children with autism or Asperger's IV. Title: One thousand and one great ideas for teaching & raising children with autism or Asperger's

RJ506.A9 N68 2010
618.9289

What readers had to say about the first edition!

"Destined to become a staple for those who love, live or work with children with autism. The authors' voices are authoritative and comforting. Perhaps most importantly, they are spot on with the issues. A toolkit packed with ideas, resources, suggestions, and a good dose of encouragement, validation and yes: redemption."

JENNIFER MCCAMMON, *former publisher, Portland Family Magazine*

"A friendly voice offering parents and teachers immediately usable ideas that emphasize the practical rather than the technical. Well organized for quick reading, with major ideas preceded by helpful introductory text. A great resource that parents and teachers should keep readily available."

CHRISTINE HUNT, MS, *special education and resource teacher*

"1001 Great Ideas goes beyond a list of things to do with your child who has autism. The thoughtful comments about why these suggestions are purposeful and valuable as teaching tools make this a must have for families, childcare providers and special education professionals. The insights the authors share throughout the book put the activities into a real life focus for working with children on the autism spectrum."

NANCY SELLER, ED.S., *Vice President Early Childhood Services, Upstate Cerebral Palsy*

"Great book—couldn't put it down. So many creative ideas, and all of them detailed and easy to follow. I like reaching children through fun, so I appreciated the suggestions for games, activities and specific reading titles that we can go right to. The IEP suggestions are helpful for both parents and school staff, the authors' sidenotes about their own experiences are insightful."

KARLA MAYER, MS, CCC-SLP

"1001 Great Ideas is just that, a treasure trove of wonderful ideas and activities! This hope-filled book not only connects the reader to the world of Autism Spectrum Disorders but also provides a multitude of practical solutions to the broad range of challenges that parents and professional face each and every day. 1001 Great Ideas is a resource that both parents and professionals will continually turn to."

SCOTT TANNER, *School Psychologist*

Acknowledgements

ANY AUTHOR WHO ACCEPTS THE CHALLENGE of putting forth a book of 1001 ideas (or in this edition, nearly 2000 and all of them good, of course) knows it has to be an ensemble piece. We are indebted to the community of outstanding individuals who have enhanced our lives and our book with their expertise, their can-do, will-do attitude, and their devotion to children with autism and the broader world we all share. Through this book, we are but funnels for their collective wisdom and years of effort on behalf of countless children with autism spectrum disorders.

The fingerprints of so many exceptional educators, therapists, parents and friends are all over this book. To name only a few: Greg Jones, Mary Schunk, Julianne Barker, Veda Nomura, Nola Shirley, Lucy Courtney, Diane Larson, Sharon Martine, Marcia Wirsig, Jackie Druck, Terry Clifford, Annie Westfall, Sarah Spella, Robin Jensen, Jean Motley, Arielle Bernstein, Emily Polanshek, and Lacee Jones.

We send heartfelt thanks to the many autism professionals whose work awakened in us reservoirs of ideas we didn't even know existed. Thanks go to Temple Grandin, David Freschi, Michelle Garcia Winner, Marge Blanc, Jim Ball, Linda Hodgdon, and Lindsey Biel for sharing their knowledge and expertise in ways they might not even have imagined.

Special thanks, as always, to our publisher and friend, Wayne Gilpin, and to our editorial director Kelly Gilpin. We appreciate your unfailing enthusiasm for all our projects.

To our adored parents, whether they are with us in body or in spirit, your presence is the safe haven that gives us courage to venture forth, discover the adventures that lie beyond the edge of our comfort zone, and set that example for others. Your influence is felt daily and only intensifies as time passes.

The significant others in our lives—be they husband, children or friends—have been 150% supportive of our efforts to produce all our books. There is a squirm factor in putting your own experiences and mistakes under a microscope, and they've been there for us as cheerleaders, confidants, sounding boards, and critics. You render us speechless—we who are wordsmiths—in expressing how important you are to us.

We celebrate every person with autism or Asperger's who has entered our lives, furthering our understanding and our appreciation of their courage, their unique abilities, and their individuality.

ELLEN NOTBOHM
VERONICA ZYSK

Contents

Sensory Integration

1

Communication and Language

57

Behavior

107

Daily Living

147

Thinking Social, Being Social
219

Teachers and Learners
251

Foreword

THE FRONT COVER OF THIS BOOK PROMISES 1001 GREAT IDEAS, which is an ambitious undertaking by itself. The back cover of this second edition promises 1800. Anyone browsing autism books might question that two authors could amass this many ideas and that all of them would be "great," but I must say, this book *delivers*. It is crammed full of helpful ideas that parents and teachers can immediately put to use to teach children with autism and Asperger's.

During my childhood years my mother and teachers utilized many of the methods discussed in this excellent book. They recognized that when it came to teaching a child with autism, creativity, patience, and understanding, as well as an inexhaustible quest for ideas and strategies that made sense *to me*, were the key to helping me become the independent, successful person I am today. However, my journey from childhood to adulthood was not without its obstacles, and I'd like to share some of my experiences to demonstrate what a difference *ideas* can make in a person's life.

I was lucky to be surrounded by a supportive team of adults from almost the very beginning. Excellent educational intervention, which began at age two-and-a-half, was crucial for my success. The most important aspect of my early intervention was keeping my young brain "connected to the world." My typical day included speech therapy, three Miss Manners meals (where table manners were *expected*), and hours of turn-taking games with my nanny. I was allowed to revert to repetitive, autistic behavior for one hour after lunch, but the rest of the day I participated in structured activities.

I was nonverbal until age three-and-a-half, but even after that time, speech therapy was a very important part of my intervention. When adults spoke to me in a speedy, everyday manner, their words sounded like gibberish, so naturally I could not respond appropriately. All I heard were vowel sounds—consonant sounds dropped out. But when people spoke slowly, directly to me, I could understand what they were saying. My speech teacher carefully enunciated the hard consonant sounds in words such as "cup" or "hat" until I learned to listen for and eventually hear those types of sounds.

Playing turn-taking games occupied a major part of my day before I went to kindergarten at age five. Initially, taking turns was a real challenge for me. But daily games and other activities drilled the concept into me. Board games such as Parcheesi and Chinese checkers were a couple of my favorites. To enjoy playing them, I had to learn to wait for my turn.

Turn-taking was also taught with outdoor activities such as building a snowman. I made the bottom ball, then my sister made the middle, and then I made the head. My nanny had a box of "snowman decorations," which was full of old hats and bottle caps that could be used to make eyes and noses. We had to take turns putting these things on the snowman's head. I also had to learn to take turns in neighborhood games, such as skipping rope. Two people swung the big rope while one person jumped. I had to learn that I could not be the jumper all of the time. I had to let others jump sometimes when it was my turn to swing the rope. Turn-taking was further emphasized in conversation at the dinner table. I was allowed to talk about things that interested me, but I was taught to allow my sister and others to take turns talking.

Learning those functional life skills concepts early helped me a great deal when it was time to start elementary school. Yet I believe the structure of the classroom itself was particularly conducive to my learning style. It was an old fashioned 1950s classroom with only twelve or thirteen students per class, where everybody worked quietly on the same thing at the same time. If I had been placed in a noisy, chaotic classroom with thirty students, like too many modern classrooms, I may not have done so well.

Many other factors contributed to my success in elementary school, but there were two factors that helped me the most. First, my teachers educated my classmates about my differences. They not only explained the nature of my challenges, but they also taught my peers how to help me. The second key to my success was the close collaboration between mother and my teachers. The rules for behavior and discipline were the same at home and at school. If I had a temper tantrum at school, the penalty when I got home was no TV that night. The rules were very clear and there was no way I could manipulate my mother or the teachers to change the rules or the consequences. Be sure to differentiate between a tantrum (voluntary) and a meltdown (involuntary, usually due to sensory overload or being over-tired). Tantrums warrant consequences, but meltdowns usually indicate that accommodations are needed.

Nowadays, classroom accommodations and modifications are common, and even mandated by law. Therapists and teachers' aides have become integral to Individualized Education Programs (IEPs). There weren't any teachers' aides in my school, but if I had been put in a larger classroom, an aide would have been essential.

Some of the most common accommodations necessary for children with autism are those that address sensory challenges, and this book provides a great deal of insight into this topic. Sensory issues in autism are really variable, yet problems in these areas can cause real pain and major meltdowns. They range from a mild nuisance to being extremely debilitating. Children can have auditory, visual, and/or tactile sensitivity—or under-sensitivity in any or all of those areas. Tactile sensitivity was one of my worse problems. For example, I could not tolerate being hugged, and wool clothes felt like sandpaper against my skin.

Like many children, my sensory issues were not limited to one sense. When I was in elementary school, the sound of the school bell hurt like a dentist drill hitting a nerve. There are some individuals who have such severe sound sensitivity they cannot tolerate public places such as malls and supermarkets. Another problem with those types of places is the constant flicker of fluorescent lighting, visible only to people who are visually sensitive. Pale-colored glasses and Irlen-colored lenses have helped many children avoid sensory overload in over-stimulating places. To my knowledge, the most effective colors are pale pink, lavender, purplish brown, and pale brown.

Visual sensitivity can be equally overwhelming at home and school. To avoid harsh fluorescent lighting, it may be a good idea to move the child's desk over by a window, or put a lamp with a 100-watt light bulb next to his desk. Do not use compact fluorescent bulbs because many also flicker. Certain types of computer screens can flicker as well. LCD screens on laptops do not, so consider letting a child use an old laptop with an external keyboard and mouse instead of the school computers. Even paper can be visually offensive. If a child complains that words wriggle around on their paper, try printing the child's work on pastel-colored paper to reduce contrast. Let the child pick the color.

Throughout this book, the authors address these same areas of challenge—language and communication, behavior, functional skills—and offer countless more sensory ideas and accommodations. I found the "Adaptations at home" and "Adaptations at school" sections on pp. 30-32 to be particularly helpful. You will also find lots of good tips for promoting healthy personal hygiene. Too often these important lessons are overlooked until the child is older and hygiene problems become more noticeable. I appreciate that the authors emphasize an overall healthy lifestyle; it's a consistent theme. Getting plenty of exercise really helped me when I was a child. My mother used to say to me, "Go outside and run the energy out." Scientific research continues to reveal the numerous neurological benefits of exercise, including the great calming effect it can have on people.

It is important to address children's physical needs first and foremost to create a comfortable environment where they can learn. A child who hurts or has painful gastrointestinal issues is not able to absorb learning and benefit from treatment programs. Once those needs are met, I can't stress enough the importance of helping children develop their individual talents and strengths. My area of strength was drawing, and that became the basis of my livestock facility design business. My caregivers and educators provided me with tools to get started, such as a book on perspective drawing and art supplies, and then helped me expand my abilities through concrete lessons and remaining positive. They had that "can do" attitude reflected all through this book.

Like many other children with autism, I got fixated on certain subjects and sometimes needed prompting to try new things. For example, I loved drawing pictures of horses, but one day, my mother asked me to do a painting of a beach. She rewarded me by framing my painting. The authors of this book share hundreds of similar ways to think creatively in working with a child. To broaden children's fixations, teachers and parents must help children develop their special interests into abilities that others people value. Having a career, or even a job you're good at, can foster confidence, independence, and a lifetime of rewards.

As I was reading through this book, my mind was flooded with pictures from my childhood. So much of the wisdom of this book is timeless; some things just *work* whether it's 1950 or 2010. Simple games such as skipping stones on a pond were some of my favorite activities as a child, and I think they can become part of other children's fond memories as they grow.

In addition to the thousands of concrete ideas and activities, the authors offer genuine, commonsense advice that all parents and educators can quickly and easily use and appreciate, no matter what your level of experience with spectrum children. The advice on how to handle the dreaded trips to the doctor and the dentist is alone worth the price of the book!

1001 Great Ideas will become your go-to book as you support the child with autism in your life. Easy-to-read sections, full of bulleted tips, provide innovative solutions to infinite types of situations. The authors even carry their ideas one step further, offering extra suggestions for customizing the content to your child or student's needs.

If every school and family used even some of the ideas in this book, the possibilities for improving the lives of children with autism and Asperger's would be limitless. And that's what I call *great*.

— TEMPLE GRANDIN, PH.D.

Preface

WHETHER OR NOT YOU BELIEVE IN FATE, karma, or serendipity, an impetus greater than mere coincidence brought the two of us authors together. Veronica had been an autism professional for more than a decade, the head of a national autism organization, a Vice President for our publisher, Future Horizons, a book editor and, then and now, Managing Editor of the *Autism Asperger's Digest*, the first national magazine focused solely on autism spectrum disorders. All these things—but not a parent. On the other side of the continent, Ellen was the parent of two sons, one with autism and one with ADHD, a writer and communications consultant—but with no professional autism credentials. Forces were set in motion when Ellen submitted an article about her son's tussles with literacy to the Digest. Over the course of the ensuing year, conversation after conversation ended up in the same place: our vastly different experiences dovetailed beautifully to form a remarkable partnership. Many collaborative ideas got kicked around for months, and then came the opportunity to write this book together.

Our shared beliefs and values pervade our writing, and you won't be able to miss them because they distill down to three elements on which we are very clear.

Sensory integration is at the core of our rubric. It drives both of us berserk that some folks in the field of autism still view sensory integration therapy as an as-time-allows add-on to "real" treatments, and when we hear from parents and professionals who regard it as unscientific hogwash or teachers who never, ever incorporate it into their classroom strategy. Is it because the topic is so intensely complex that many simply turn away from it, hoping for an easier solution? Such an attitude is certainly understandable. Neurology is a very, very complicated proposition. Katharine Hepburn in *The African Queen* provides us with the definitive approach. When the German officer protests that her journey down an unnavigable river is impossible, she responds: "Never. The. Less."

Never in your parenting or teaching experience will it be more important to do whatever is necessary to put yourself in the shoes—in the skin—of another, especially one whose sensory systems are wired so differently. The child experiencing hyper-acute sensory responses to his world is in a state of constant self-defense against incessant assault from an environment that is spinning, shrieking, squeezing, and defying him at any given moment. To expect social or cognitive learning to take place under such conditions is simply unrealistic to us, thus we place major emphasis on sensory integration. You'll see it throughout the book—in just the same manner that sensory inputs pervade real life not just for children with autism or Asperger's, but for all of us. For the child affected this way, sensory therapy must be the cornerstone of any treatment program. We know this because we've seen it up close in many children. As a preschooler, Ellen's son exhibited extreme tactile, oral, aural, visual, and proprioceptive defensiveness. After seven years of focused sensory intervention, he was dismissed from both occupational therapy and adapted PE programs because his skills and sensitivities in these areas were no longer distinguishable from those of his peers. It wasn't magic. It was sensory intervention. Sustained, patient, sensory intervention.

Shoulder to shoulder with sensory intervention is the significance we place on communication and language therapy. There simply can't be any argument that a child who cannot make his needs known and thereby met is going to be a simmering cauldron of frustration and despair. Research in the early part of the decade suggested that 40% of our children with autism are nonverbal, and that a majority of these children will never develop functional language. We just don't agree, and that incites us to be vocal with parents and professionals about the importance of giving children—all children—on the spectrum a means of communication. Whatever form it takes—sign language, PECs, assistive technology, verbal language or any combination of these or other options—what is critical is that the child has what constitutes a functional communication system *for her*. Imagine going through your day unable to keep pace, comprehend, or contribute to the conversation around you, not possessing the means or the vocabulary to tell your boss or mate that you hurt or need or want, being unable to decode the symbols on a page or the sounds coming out of a telephone. As with sensory integration, when either receptive and/or expressive language is obstructed, the day becomes a minute-to-minute struggle to merely cope; no true learning can take place in such an environment. Doug Larson tells us, "If the English language made any sense, a catastrophe would be an apostrophe with fur." Any speech language pathologist or English Language Learner teacher will tell you that English is arguably the most treacherous language on the planet. For concrete thinkers like our kids with autism, the English language, with its inconsistent rules, abstract idioms, nuances of sarcasm, homophones, multiple-meaning words, and seemingly nonsensical words like pineapple (which contains neither pine nor apple) is a desperate morass. Early, intense, and ongoing language/communication therapy is crucial and, happily, it is an area where a little awareness enables adults to make a difference at every hour of the day. We've included hundreds of ideas in this area so you can do just that.

Overreaching all of this is our most heartfelt conviction that the ultimate power to live with and overcome autism lies in our willingness to love the child or student with autism or Asperger's absolutely unconditionally. Only when we are free of "what-if?" and "if he would just...," will we have a child who himself is free to bloom within his own abilities (he has many), his own personality, and his own timeline (not ours or what is "developmentally appropriate"). It is no less than you wanted for yourself as a child, and it is no less than what you want for yourself as an adult. Yes, Virginia, there *is* a magic bullet. A child who feels unconditional acceptance and perceives that the significant adults around truly believe "he can do it" has every chance of becoming the happy, competent adult we always hoped and dreamed he would be.

In the five years since we published the first edition of this book, we have between us, as authors, co-authors and editors, worked on thirteen books, some of which have risen to the top of the autism category and remained there, many winning multiple prestigious awards. In all the books we two authors have written collaboratively, the messages of this, our original book, remain consistent. The ongoing popularity of *1001 Great Ideas* coupled with five years of amassing new ideas demanded that we create this second edition—a significantly updated and expanded version of the original work. You'll find far more than the 1001 ideas the title claims, as we delve more deeply into complex subjects like social thinking, language/communication, and the adult's role in shaping a child's behaviors. We also explore topics not addressed in the original work.

Autism is an edifying experience, if you will let it be so. Each day you embrace its presence as part of your life is another day of understanding it and your child, and integrating that wisdom into your collective experience.

The gift of a rich and meaningful life for you and your child with autism or Asperger's awaits you.

Sensory Integration

There is no way in which to
understand the world
without first detecting it
through the radar-net of our senses.
DIANE ACKERMAN

O F ALL THE BAFFLING ASPECTS OF AUTISM, perhaps none is more baffling to the layperson than sensory integration. Sensory integration is the ability to process and organize sensations we receive internally and externally. Sensory input travels to the brain through our neural network, where it is interpreted and used to formulate a response. Sensory processing happens without conscious thought; it operates in the background and most people never stop to ponder how their senses function or the part they play in daily life.

There are as many as twenty-one sensory systems at work in our bodies. Most of us recognize the traditional five: sight, hearing, smell, taste, and touch. Five other senses are commonly attributed to humans: equilibrioception (our sense of balance or vestibular sense), proprioception and kinesthesia (sensing the orientation and motion of one's limbs and body in space), nociciption (pain), temporal sense (sense of time), and thermoception (temperature differences).

Through a complex series of atypical signals/connections between the sensory organs and the brain, the child with autism or Asperger's experiences sights, sounds, touches, smells, tastes, and gravity in a manner profoundly different from that of typically-developing children and adults. Every minute of daily life for a child on the autism spectrum can be a battle against invasive sensations that overwhelm their hyper-acute sensory systems. Or conversely, their senses may be hypo-active, requiring major effort to alert their bodies so that learning and social interaction can take place. Layered on top of that may be an inability to filter and process more than one sensory modality at a time.

Step for a moment inside the body of a child with sensory integration difficulties in this excerpt from Ellen's book, *Ten Things Every Child with Autism Wishes You Knew*:

> My sensory perceptions are disordered. This means that the ordinary sights, sounds, smells, tastes and touches of everyday that you may not even notice can be downright painful for me. The very environment in which I have to live often seems hostile. I may appear withdrawn or belligerent to you but I am just trying to defend myself. Here is why an ordinary trip to the grocery store may be hell for me:
>
> My hearing may be hyper-acute. Dozens of people are talking at once. The loudspeaker booms today's special. Musak whines from the sound system. Cash registers beep and cough, a coffee grinder chugs. The meat cutter screeches, babies wail, carts creak, the fluorescent lighting hums. My brain can't filter all the input and I'm in overload!
>
> My sense of smell may be highly sensitive. The fish at the meat counter isn't quite fresh, the guy standing next to us hasn't showered today, the deli is handing out sausage samples, the baby in line ahead of us has a poopy diaper, they're mopping up pickles on aisle 3 with ammonia—I can't sort it all out.
>
> Because I am visually oriented, this may be my first sense to become overstimulated. The fluorescent light is too bright; it makes the room pulsate and hurts my eyes. Sometimes the pulsating light bounces off everything and distorts what I am seeing—the space seems to be constantly changing. There's glare from windows, too many items that distract me (I may compensate with tunnel vision), moving fans on the ceiling, so many bodies in constant motion. All this affects my vestibular sense, and now I can't even tell where my body is in space.

We have said in all our books and will say it again here: sensory integration dysfunction is at the root of many of the core difficulties of autism spectrum disorders. It affects behavior, communication, nutrition, and sleep—critical functions that dictate the quality of the environment your child must live in, minute to minute, day to day, year to year. Addressing and treating sensory dysfunction should always be near the top of the what-to-do-first list.

There are two over-arching thoughts to keep in mind when considering the thousands of aspects of your child's sensory integration needs.

First, sensory training can look and feel like play. Play is the medium through which children learn. Play puts fun into functional, grabs a child's attention, and holds his interest. An engaged brain is a brain ready to learn. The wonderful thing about sensory training is that opportunities and learning moments happen all around you at any time of day, at home, at school, out in the community.

Second, your school may offer occupational therapy support, and/or you may contract with a private agency outside of school, but those hours are finite and few. Consistent, ongoing sensory integration therapy happens at home. Placing your child in the hands of a professional for a few hours a week is the beginning—an excellent beginning—but the bulk of the work will come in the home setting. If this seems daunting, go back and read the previous paragraph. It can also be playful.

All the sensory ideas in our book come with the caveat that there is no substitute for working with an occupational therapist who is well versed in autism spectrum disorders. He or she will provide the foundation of knowledge that helps you better understand how senses are impaired by autism or Asperger's, can set up a sensory diet for your child (a daily plan of stimulating and/or calming activities), and tweak the plan as you discover what works and what doesn't.

Believe—really believe—that no child wants the negative or punitive feedback he gets for his so-called "bad behavior," especially when those inappropriate behaviors are beyond his control, rooted in the dysfunctional way his sensory organs and his brain communicate. Regulating over- or underactive senses is an essential first step in helping the child master socially acceptable behavior. This achievable and worthwhile process requires patience, consistency, and an ever-watchful eye for discerning sensory triggers. Start slowly and stay the course.

Choosing the right sensory activities

Sensory integration activities should be fun for your child or student. Follow these guidelines:

- Choose activities in which your child can lead, guide, or direct the play. This is the first step in his later being able to initiate a play activity, with you or others.

- When you find something that works, share it across other venues of your child's life. Consistency between home and school enhances retention, will maximize his success, and with it, his self-confidence.

- In choosing age-appropriate activities for your child, remember that there may be gaps between his chronological age and his developmental age. The right activity accommodates his skill level and current sensory and social tolerance threshold. Example: mixing cookie dough is a great sensory activity, but having two or three friends/siblings/helpers in the kitchen at once may be too much. The activity may be successful only as one-on-one time with Mom.

- Any activity that can comfortably incorporate family members is a bonus. But ...

- Activities should not impose excessive burdens on the family budget, schedule, space, or patience. There is such thing as too much. The beauty of so many sensory activities is that just a few minutes here and there can have a cumulative effect over time.

We've amassed many ideas for sensory activities that you can incorporate easily into your child's day. Some of the ideas are appropriate for both home and school; all are designed to get you thinking beyond the traditional activities that might initially come to mind.

Twelve warning signs of sensory overload

Ideas in this book and others, as well as suggestions from your occupational therapist and other professionals, offer myriad ways to enhance your child's over- or under-stimulated sensory systems. Your child will embrace some, others not.

It is natural to want your child to engage in enjoyable sensory activities "to the max," but is more better? Emphatically no, say occupational therapists. Too much of a good thing can overload delicate senses, triggering that dreaded meltdown. Familiarize yourself with these twelve warning signs of impending overstimulation:

1. Loss of balance or orientation
2. Skin flushes, or suddenly goes pale
3. Child is verbalizing "Stop!"
4. Child steadfastly refuses activity
5. Racing heartbeat, or sudden drop in pulse
6. Hysteria, crying
7. Stomach distress: cramps, nausea, vomiting
8. Profuse sweating
9. Child becomes agitated or angry
10. Child begins repeating echolalic phrases, or some familiar non-relevant phrase over and over again (self-calming behavior)
11. Child begins stimming (repetitive, self-calming behaviors)
12. Child lashes out, hits, or bites

If any of these occur, stop the activity at once. Your child's behavior is telling you the activity is too much to handle. Resist the urge to think your child "should" be able to handle it, or handle it just a little longer. Consult your occupational therapist as to how often and how much of the activity he or she recommends, and ways to create a more appropriate sensory diet for the child.

To activity and beyond! Fifty ways to get them moving ···········

Physical activity is critical to any child's overall health, and the social interaction that takes place during such pastimes can be beneficial too. All physical activities provide your child with multi-sensory input—opportunities to retrain the brain and help their sensory systems function more as they should. With repeated practice, fine and gross motor skills will get better, even with more impaired children. Individual or group movement activities help build coordination, motor-recall, muscle-memory, control, and spatial awareness. They teach timing, predicting, following/reacting to directions, and adapting to changes. Physical and social feedback can motivate children to work through the initial awkward learning stage and experience success. When they do, you'll also see self-esteem skyrocketing.

In exploring physical activities for your child, liberate yourself from any constraints you may have as to what constitutes a legitimate sport. Although many children with autism or Asperger's enjoy soccer, basketball, and baseball, team sports are not for everyone. Myriad rules can be confusing, the jumble of bodies upsetting, the auditory and olfactory sensations overwhelming, and the expectations of team members stressful.

Some parents (not you, of course) are of the mindset, often to the detriment of their child, that Chase isn't playing a real sport unless he's on the school football team. As a concept, it simply isn't true. Our kids can excel at various activities when given the chance, proper guidance, and gradual exposure. And there is a lot to be said for seeking out the less populated sports. Many children thrive in the "big fish in a small pond" environment these sports offer. They may be much more welcoming of beginners, even offering sample courses or mini-lessons. If they don't, explain your situation and ask about it. The worst that can happen is they say no, and the manner in which they say no will give you an idea of whether or not your child will be welcomed there. So if the concept of competition is too challenging for your child, let it go for now. There is every possibility he may grow into it later, and if not, building an association of physical activity with fun has a much more profound life impact.

Where you live will partially dictate your choice of activity. Denver denizens may find surfing difficult to pursue; ditto for aspiring skiers in Miami. But it's never an excuse for the truly motivated. Remember the 1988 Olympic Jamaican bobsled team? They were the masters of adapted sports, outfitting their bobsled with wheels to practice in their tropical locale. What everybody remembers about them is their spunk and their sense of fun, not that they finished last. Six years later in Lillehammer, they in fact finished ahead of both USA teams in the four-man event.

The list below suggests many ways to enjoy sports and physical activity outside the typical arena of team sports. There is no magic about the list; it's comprised of regular activities that have been around forever.

How to choose? Before trying something new, give some thought to how an activity matches your child in the following ways:

- Interest level. Don't force your child into something that doesn't appeal to him. Start with high interest areas that will be naturally motivating and rewarding.

- Energy and affect level. A low energy child might find frisbee or yoga perfect, but basketball or tennis too upsetting for her system.

- Muscle tone and coordination. Both can improve over time with engagement, so start out at an easy pace and build from there. Take a walk around the park a few times before venturing off on a four-mile hike.

- Individual, two-person, or team activities? Your primary goal is regular movement and fun exercise. A no-stress enjoyable bike ride around the neighborhood with just you may engage her more than a dance class with several other kids.

- Fun versus winning. If your child just can't stand to lose, steer him to non-competitive, individual sports. There's no win/lose angst involved in fishing, hiking, rock climbing, etc. And keep in mind that in many children with autism or Asperger's, the concept of competition is not readily present, but must be taught. Is the angst about winning possibly coming from you?

- Use technology to create a bridge from home to outdoor or group activity. Rent a few martial arts, exercise, or dance DVDs to test them out with your child.

What we want to impress upon you here is that abundant possibilities exist and to not overlook the obvious when you're planning for physical recreation. Pursued at an individual pace, these activities may give your child more room for growth and achievement than he had before, bettering your chances for both success and enthusiasm. In the marathon of life, isn't that real success, after all?

- Water sports: swimming, swim lessons, swim team, synchronized swimming, aquacise for kids, diving, surfing/boogie boarding, rowing, canoeing, rafting, fishing

- Fun on wheels: Big Wheel, tricycle, bicycle with training wheels, two-wheeler, alley cat, tandem, scooter, roller skates, skateboard

- Racket sports: tennis, racquetball, handball, badminton, ping-pong (table tennis)

- Take-aim sports: bowling, golf, miniature golf (putt-putt), archery

- Running/walking/jumping: kids' biathlon or triathlon, jogging, trampoline, hiking, track and field events

- Snow sports: downhill skiing, cross-country (Nordic) skiing, snowboarding, tobogganing, snow-shoeing, ice skating (figure or speed), ice fishing

- Martial arts: tai chi, tae kwon do, karate, judo, aikido, kick-boxing, capoeira

- Equestrian: horseback riding, kids rodeo

- Play activities: jumping rope, hop/jump balls (handle on top), hula hoops, tether ball, pogo stick, jai-alai (scoop-toss games), or Velcro®-disk catch games, lawn or floor hockey, Frisbee

- Coordinated movement: tap dancing, ballet, hip-hop or ethnic dance, jazz or modern dance, yoga, baton twirling, gymnastic/tumbling, rock climbing. (Look for non-competitive studios that focus on fun rather than skilled competitions.)

Learning to enjoy the outdoors

Nature is its own classroom, filled with awe-inspiring sights, sounds, tactile sensations, and smells. Even though your child may have sensory sensitivities, it's important that he be exposed to new experiences to develop, grow, and even become less sensory defensive. The key is in slow and measured contact, using his reactions as your gauge.

Quiet nature settings are most conducive to your child having a good experience. Get away from the constant noise and echoes of the cityscape, the omnipresent electronics, the pervasive visual clutter and hordes of people—the sense of "ahhh" will be tangible for everyone. Go to a park in the early morning quiet, find a small babbling stream, or a field with tall grass. Look for interesting rocks to take home. Take a blanket and spend the afternoon looking for pictures in the clouds, or counting the birds that fly by. Take a woodland/nature walk: identify ten things you see, ten things you hear, ten things you can touch, ten things that are fuzzy, or hard, or bendable. Explore! (See also **A-Hunting We Will Go** in Chapter 6.)

Outdoor bracelet

Sturdy, sticky duct tape is the beginning of a neat outdoor bracelet. Tape it sticky-side-out around her wrist and let her fill it with sticks and leaves, sand and shell bits, grass and flower petals. Note: Will she melt down when you cut it off later? Make the loop big enough that she can slip it off her hand, or fold ends and secure with a paperclip on her wrist for easy undo later.

Summer fun, winter fun

Reinterpret some of your favorite summer activities for winter. A few to get you started:

- Get out the sand castle molds and make snow castles instead; packed snow behaves much the same as packed wet sand.
- Use rectangular food storage containers to make bricks for forts and igloos.

- Write messages or draw pictures in the snow with a stick. Take a photo of your message ("I love Grandma") and put it in a photo snow globe as a special gift to a loved one. (Photo snow globes are available at craft stores and photo/electronics sections of some stores, especially at holiday time.)

- Is your child a *Cat in the Hat* fan? Mix a few drops of red food coloring in a spray bottle and spray the snow pink, like Little Cats A, B, C, D, and E.

- A tire swing left over from summer is good for snowball-throwing target practice.

- Or use that tire swing to let go and land in a mound of snow.

- Practice that tennis or baseball swing with snowballs. If it splats, you know you hit it.

- Get out that slippery-slide and ice it down; use it as a bowling lane or shuffleboard alley.

Remember: Children with autism or Asperger's are frequently insensitive to temperature. Since they won't tell you when they get too cold, keep checking to make sure they are properly protected at all times.

Bring in the great outdoors

Some kids don't enjoy the great outdoors because they come in contact with so many things that, to them, are dirty or yucky. Acclimate them slowly and at their own pace by bringing the outdoors in. A small wading pool on your kitchen, bathroom or mud-room floor can be a mini-ecosystem. Dirt, sand, twigs, rocks, pinecones, nuts, seed pods, a square of sod, can all be shoveled, sorted, stacked, and otherwise manipulated from a safe spot in her inside world. She can wear plastic gloves to touch things at first. As they become more familiar to her, she may find it easier to transition to enjoying them outdoors.

Sand table

Sand play is great for stimulating the proprioceptive sense, which activates through input from joints. For variety, alternate filling the table with:

- Rice (a few drops of food coloring can add interest)
- Beans/lentils
- Kitty litter (the kind made from ground nut shells, corn, recycled newspapers or wood, other green materials)
- Potting soil or dirt
- Popcorn (unpopped or popped)
- Birdseed
- Oatmeal, bulgur, millet, other grains
- Home aquarium rocks
- Pea gravel

Sand table activities

There's more to sand table play than scooping sand, filling buckets and dumping it out again. Important sensory and motor development in eye-hand coordination, vestibular sensation, and proprioception are inherent in these activities. They offer opportunities to teach opposite concepts, such as in/out, here/there, or full/empty. Help children explore the terrain through activities that require them to push/pull/drag/dig on a repeated basis:

- Dig for hidden objects
- Combine with water play, especially to change the texture of the material.
- Play with action figures or animal figurines. They can march, crawl, jump—whatever keeps them moving through the substance.
- Play with construction vehicles—making hills and roads, and digging holes.

The not-so itsy-bitsy spider

Your little Spiderman will enjoy turning his room or playroom into a life-size web with a ball of string, yarn, kite string, or unwaxed dental floss. Wrap the string around doorknobs, dresser knobs, bed legs, chair spindles, anything sturdy. Have him crawl, climb through, and otherwise navigate the maze. At the end of the day, give him scissors to cut his way out.

A dozen things to do with a refrigerator box

Children often love the large box something comes in more than the item itself. For your child with autism or Asperger's, oversized boxes are the beginning of many wonderful sensory-therapeutic experiences. Many kiddos on the autism spectrum enjoy enclosed spaces like closets, cubbies, and hidey-holes. A large appliance box is ideal. Adapt a refrigerator box to your child's interests and needs.

- Make a quiet place. Paint the inside a calming color and furnish with pillows, books, stuffed animals, headphones, and music.
- For the outer space aficionado, cut star shapes in the top.
- For the tactile-input seeker, line the insides with favorite textured materials such as fur, corduroy, sandpaper, etc. Or fill pockets with textured items (marbles, seeds, etc.). Hang clear vinyl shoebags for inexpensive ready-made pocket space.
- Some kids bliss out on bubble wrap—imagine a whole "room" lined with it.
- Paint the interior with chalkboard paint and he can change the landscape whenever he feels like it.
- A small-screen TV or DVD player turns a simple box into a movie theater.
- A sleeping bag and flashlight make it a campsite.
- Open your own restaurant. Your picky eater may even surprise you and sample something new. Don't forget to practice ordering and paying the check.
- Install a steering wheel. He's a race car driver, a bus driver, a truck driver, fireman, or pilot.
- Staple silky fabric on the ceiling and sides, put a rug on the floor, and add some pillows. Your caravan princess can daydream to her heart's content.
- Line the inside of the box with reflective paper and hang a disco light or one of those multi-colored Christmas tree toppers from the ceiling. It's

like being inside a kaleidoscope. (Use caution if the child has strong visual impairments.)

- Language lesson: create games that teach the spatial vocabulary and concepts. This version of Simon Says emphasizes spatial terms: "Simon Says go *inside* the box. Shake your foot *outside* the box. Hide *behind* the box. Run *around* the box. Throw the beanbag *over* the box."

Bathroom sensory activities

Bath time is sensory time! Capitalize on this everyday opportunity to calm and soothe the hypersensitive child, or to give additional sensory stimulation to the hyposensitive child.

- Play with kitchen implements such as basters, colanders, ladles, funnels. An old rotary eggbeater and some liquid bubble bath, baby bath, or dish soap combine for a fun sensory exercise. Whip up a bowl of bubbles, a towering tub of suds, a wading pool full of froth, and a ferocious shark, or magical mermaid.
- Add food coloring to cups of water.
- Introduce textured items such as a bath mitt, washcloth, loofah sponge, back brush.
- If your child likes the scent of peppermint, chamomile, or other herbal tea concoctions, give her a few tea bags to steep in the tub with her.
- After the bath or shower, towel-dry him or her with lots of pressure.
- Rub body lotion on his or her arms and legs (only if the child enjoys it—and can tolerate the scent).
- Brush teeth with a battery-operated toothbrush.

Water, water everywhere (they wish!)

Many children on the spectrum are fond of any kind of water play, with its many textures, temperatures and smells. That may be good or not-so-good, depending on your child. Stay attuned to aspects that might interfere with the overall experience and make it unappealing.

- Washing dishes, especially in soapy water up to his elbows
- Playing in mud: thick and oozy or thinner and grainy
- Filling water cans and watering garden flowers
- Playing in puddles—stomping (especially with bare feet), stirring with a stick, tossing in pebbles
- Washing the car or bike or dog with bucket or hose
- Playing with a water wiggle or other toys that hook up to a sprinkler or hose
- Floating on a raft or inner tube
- Diving for objects (weighted rings, coins)

Finger painting

Most of us fondly recall this favorite childhood activity as a chance to get our hands squishily messy in an appropriate way. That good sensory feel to us might not feel so good to your child or student. Introduce finger painting to a tactile-defensive child in gentle increments. Start by letting him use a cotton swab. Then move to rubber or plastic gloves (such as food service gloves). As he becomes more comfortable, cut off the fingertips of the rubber gloves—one at a time (for instance, per week), if necessary.

> **QUICK IDEA**
>
> Commonly used sensory rewards can lose their luster quickly. Test the appeal quotient of a sensory reward often. If it no longer holds the child's interest, it's no longer rewarding.

You needn't spend major money on finger paints. You can make easy-mix, non-toxic paints from ordinary household ingredients, and your child may be more interested in the activity if he participates in creating the paint. Make a simple paint by combining equal parts flour and water, then adding food color. Or, dissolve one part cornstarch in three parts boiling water, adding glycerin for shine (monitor the temperature closely as it cools and don't let little fingers dip in until safe).

Finger painting outside can be especially fun if either you or your child worry about mess. He may enjoy painting on leaves or rocks instead of paper. As interest grows, introduce substances that differ in texture and viscosity, such as shaving cream, pudding, or bath gel. Mixing in rice, cornmeal, or grits adds another layer of sensory input.

And, think beyond fingers: paint with feet or toes or even elbows.

Tactile food fun

Even for the child who doesn't like to get his hands dirty, helping you make a snack or part of dinner might be an acceptable way to experience tactile sensations. (And it's never too early to start teaching everyday life skills.) Try these ideas:

- Mixing/patting/rolling out cookie dough by hand
- Mixing guacamole by hand, including mashing the avocado with fingers first
- Beating pudding or pancake batter with a rotary beater
- Mixing cake batter by hand with a whisk
- Churning butter in a jar until it firms up
- Creating cookie shapes in dough with cookie cutters or with a cookie press
- Kneading bread dough
- Making figures out of marshmallows or gum drops; joined by pretzel sticks or toothpicks

Bite me: Recipes for edible clay ·······························

Clay and play dough are great sensory experiences, unless you spend the time taking your child's hand away from her mouth as she tries to eat the stuff. Make her day—with edible clay.

Note: Do not use these recipes if your child is allergic to peanuts.

Recipe #1: Combine 1 cup powdered milk, 1/2 cup creamy peanut butter, 1/2 cup honey. Spray your child's hand with non-stick cooking spray and set her loose. She can eat the shapes she makes now or refrigerate for later. Adding pungent spices like cinnamon or nutmeg brings another sense to the experience.

Recipe #2: Combine 3 1/2 cups creamy peanut butter, 4 cups powdered sugar, 3 1/2 cups light corn syrup, 4 cups powdered milk.

(Recipes adapted from SurprisingKids.com)

Recipe #3: Chocolate Play Clay. Melt 8 oz. semi-sweet chocolate in a double boiler. Stir in ¼ cup plus 1 table-spoon corn syrup. The mixture will stiffen, but keep stirring until combined. Transfer to a plastic bag and refrigerate until firm. Knead pieces until pliable enough to shape (or eat). Use sparingly, as ingesting too much can bring on stomach upset in some children.

QUICK IDEA

The same daily sensory factors that affect a child—lighting, smells, sounds, colors, temperature, visual stimuli—can affect the accuracy of assessments and the effectiveness of therapy. Practitioners: Be sensory sensitive in all arenas.

Child on a roll! ·······························

Rolling can be a delightful whole-body experience for your child—up or down or across different textures. Watch for signs of dizziness, nausea, or disorientation—warning signs that sensory activity is too intense—and be ready to stop immediately. Kids can roll:

- On the grass: on level ground or down a hill, and then he can crawl back up the hill on his tummy

- On the carpet: thick and plush, sisal, or indoor/outdoor

- While inside a blanket: wool, cotton, fleece, velux, thin or thick

- While inside a large box: cut off top and bottom to form a tube

Swinging or spinning

Many kids with autism or Asperger's love to spin and swing. Occupational therapists and speech-language therapists frequently work together as language often emerges while children are swinging or involved in some fun large movement activity. Be creative with swinging and spinning.

- Regular playground-type swing

- Hammock or net swing

- Tire swing

- Platform swing (carpet- or foam-covered plywood sheet)

- Pipe/bolster swing (fabric-covered large, capped, plastic pipe) they can lie over stomach-down

- Trapeze

- Spin using any of the above equipment

- Spin in place: arms at sides/arms outstretched/arms overhead

- Spin in the pool or the shallow part of a lake

- Spin in the rain—standing in a puddle

- Spin with another person, arms outstretched with hands touching at each spin, like gears working together; how fast can you both go and still touch at each spin?

Gross motor activities ···

Many kids on the autism spectrum benefit from "heavy work" where they need to move their muscles against resistance for signals to reach their brain. Household tasks are perfect for this type of proprioceptive input, with the added bonus that your child can take pride in being part of the family and helping out.

- Carrying/dragging the laundry basket
- Pushing the lawn mower (use discretion)
- Pushing the grocery cart at the store
- Pushing the vacuum cleaner
- Carrying groceries in from the car
- Digging in the garden with a shovel or trowel
- Shoveling snow in winter
- Hammering
- Pulling a wagon or pushing a wheelbarrow
- Pumping up the beach ball or inner tube with a foot or hand pump; ditto with bicycle tire pumps
- Mopping or sweeping floors, patio, deck
- Taking turns pulling a sibling on a sheet or blanket "sled"
- Pulling a wheeled backpack or suitcase (full)
- Dragging that 10- or 25-pound bag of bird seed to the feeder and then filling it up

Simon-says games ···

Any game that gets kids to imitate can be a rich environment for sensory integration experiences. Simon Says, Follow the Leader, or obstacle courses all incorporate fun gross motor body movements. Get their whole bodies involved in:

- Crawling
- Jumping (especially in patterns)
- Hopping (two feet, one foot, holding one foot, arms overhead with hands clasped together)
- Running (forwards, backwards, sideways, in circles)
- Wiggling or slithering
- Rolling

Your Follow-the-Leader path can take the child through sensory areas in and out of your house—carpet, patio, wading pool, sandbox. Pretend you are different animals, sometimes walking on two feet, sometimes four, flying, dry swimming, meowing, cawing, and roaring.

Tip

While silly play can be fun, some literal-thinking kids with autism or Asperger's won't appreciate your silliness, at least at first. Be prepared to modify activities to suit their interests and learning styles. Remember to keep an eye out for sensory overload and know when to shift into a calming activity.

Kid-friendly contact games

All of those fun kid-contact games your parents or grandparents played with you offer great tactile, vestibular, and proprioceptive inputs. And aren't they a great way to get dads and grandpas involved? (Remember to monitor intensity carefully. For some kids, rough and tumble is too much input.)

- Horsey ride
- Piggyback ride
- Airplane ride
- Row, row, row your boat
- Trotting off to Boston
- This is the Way the Ladies Go

Fine motor activities············

For the child whose fine motor skills are underdeveloped, eating, dressing, writing, doing homework, and grooming can all be difficult to some extent. Help your child build many of the life skills needed to better navigate his day-to-day world by providing lots of fine motor activities, beginning when he is young. This will form important sensory connections between touch and function.

> ## QUICK IDEA
> Gloves are great sensory fun. Plan a class lesson around gloves. Children can put on many different kinds of gloves and try activities while gloved. Find out how gloves help or hinder writing, playing games, etc.

- Drawing or writing with a battery-operated vibrating pen: especially helpful for kids who need additional tactile stimulation
- Drawing or writing with chalk (use an easel, a sidewalk, or slate)
- Erasing the chalk using textured items—eraser, dishcloth, fingers, elbows, paper napkin, oven mitt, sock, marshmallow, cotton ball
- Using a finger to write letters or shapes on each other's back, tummy, or back of hand, and guess each one without looking
- Writing in Play-doh® or clay with pencil, chopstick, or toothpick
- Playing with glue—spreading it around the paper with a finger or a cotton swab
- Playing with wind-up toys
- Stringing beads, curtain rings, pretzel twists, buttons, popcorn or cranberries for holidays, or for your feathered friends anytime
- Hang a piece of metal sheeting (cover sharp edges and fold back) as a magnet board for letters, shapes, characters, etc.
- Puppet play—finger puppets, hand puppets, shadow puppets
- Etch A Sketch®
- Flower power—give the child a giant sunflower and tweezers to pick out the seeds. Use the seeds for crafts, art, counting, or eating.

- Have fun with the ordinary spray bottle. Squeezing the trigger helps develop the muscles in the hand needed for fine motor control:
  - Fill the bottle with water and food coloring. Spray onto butcher paper, a coffee filter or squares of fabric for instant art.
  - Fill the bottle with shaving cream or foam and create shapes, numbers or letters on sidewalk, driveway or shower/bathtub wall.
  - Fill the bottle with water and set to Stream. Fill a large tub or plastic pail halfway with water and float on it a few ping pong balls, rubber duckies, cotton balls, plastic packing peanuts or other buoyant objects. Have the child spray at the ball until he forces it out of the container. (Another outdoor or bathtub activity.)
  - And don't forget the playful nature of just squirting each other. (Note: not all kids will enjoy this. Teach siblings and friends to respect each others' preferences!)
- For the older child, combine activities into multi-sensory projects like scrapbooking, which requires working with items of various textures and handling different types of adhesives. Other ideas: simple wood-working projects using several grades of sandpaper, or introduce one-stitch knitting, spool knitting, stamped cross-stitch embroidery, or punch-card sewing projects.
- A single-hole punch with or without padded grips is a good fine-motor development tool for increasingly competent hands.

Just learning: Punch colored sheets of paper randomly to make confetti for your next party.

I'm angry: Have him work his frustrations out by giving him a picture of something he doesn't like (un-favorite food, bad guy from a movie, or just draw an angry face on a piece of paper) and letting him punch it away.

More advanced: Have him punch around the outline of a large drawing.

So all can color

Coloring is a popular activity for kids—except those with fine motor skills who struggle just to hold on to a crayon. Manufacturers have come a long way from the original box of Crayola crayons and produced all sorts of adaptations:

- Jumbo, larger-diameter crayons; the no-roll varieties even indicate to the child where to place her thumb
- Triangular pyramid-shaped crayons
- Rectangular shaped crayons
- Colorations® finger tip crayons slide right over the child's finger
- Ball-shaped crayons have a ball at the end that makes holding them easier. Kids can insert a thumb or finger into the ball for additional stability
- Crayola's TaDoodles™ First Marks give children a larger surface to hold on to while coloring, and kids love the animal shapes they come in

Fidget toys basket

The Oriental Trading Company (*OrientalTrading.com*) catalog is a great source of inexpensive fidget toys. The only caveat is that they are usually sold by the dozen, so you'll want to band together with several other parents and/or teachers to make your purchase. A fidget basket should contain items that stimulate many senses: visual, auditory, olfactory, tactile, vestibular (rhythmic items), oral-motor (blowing toys). Some suggestions: Porcupine or Koosh® balls (especially those that glow in the dark), stretchy animals, glow tubes, mini-maracas, finger puppets, squeeze toys with bulgy eyes, jointed wiggle snakes, intertwined light balls, squishy yo-yos, handheld sport ball water game, finger poppers, mini kaleidoscopes, colored sand timers, tops, sticky "buddies," whistles, hand clappers, and kazoos (check out their "noisemaker and novelty instrument assortment," fifty pieces for $12.99—2009 price), to name a few.

Homemade fidget toys

While therapy and party catalogs are full of options, you can also make simple fidget toys yourself. Get started with these:

- A balloon filled with sand or short grain rice; knotted securely
- Any small to medium sized smooth stone that can easily fit in a pocket
- A sea shell, smooth or with ridges
- An old key on a ring, or several, if sound is appealing
- Washcloths, cut in half or quarters, edged, stitched together, and filled with rice or beans
- A ball of aluminum foil
- A small pumice stone

Hair bbb-rr-uu-sss-hhh?

Many children with autism or Asperger's enjoy vibrating toys, seats, pens, and toothbrushes. Here's a less well-known item for the reluctant groomer: the vibrating hairbrush (originally designed as a scalp massager). Occupational therapists report using it successfully with children who hate having their hair brushed. Ask at a local beauty supply shop, or check online.

That sucks! Oral-motor development activities

The articulator muscles around the mouth contribute to many tasks necessary to a child's overall growth. Eating, speaking, singing, crying—even breathing and holding the head erect—all involve oral-motor development. For a child with low oral-motor tone, these everyday activities do not come easily.

Sucking and blowing are two excellent exercises that strengthen the articulator muscles. Here are some ideas for each:

- Sucking foods through a straw will give the mouth a workout. Try pudding, pureed fruit, thick milkshakes or fruit smoothies, warm pureed soups like tomato, lentil, or black bean, baby food desserts, yogurt (no fruit chunks), half-melted ice cream, sherbet or sorbet, half-congealed gelatin.

- Straws with twists and curves are fun and increase the sucking task. Pliable vinyl tubing comes in varying widths and can be loosely tied into shapes, or left as is. Cocktail straws with their tiny opening require a different sucking motion and are fun for thin liquids.

- The ultimate fun therapy with drinking straws may be the Museum of Modern Art's Convertible Drinking Straw—a set of straws with rubber connector pieces. Users can create twisting, bending multiple-straw designs including some that allow you to drink from more than one glass at the same time. Some children will find this so intriguing they may even be willing to sample new drinks this way. Visit the MoMA store online to find the set: *MomaStore.org*.

- Blowing and puffing activities can offer your child a parent-sanctioned opportunity to play with his food. Have him blow through the straw into a liquid or puree. Note together how the substances react: root beer works up a head, pudding looks like lava. Notice too how the bubbles release the scent of the food.

- Get creative with blowing objects other than food. We know one child who liked to play Babe the Pig with a straw and a handful of cotton balls. The cotton balls were the sheep and the child was Babe, winning the sheepdog competition by blowing the sheep into formation. Another child built a log jam by blowing toilet tissue tubes "downriver," then piling them up and blowing them over. Any lightweight item will do for starters: wadded-up plastic wrap, ping-pong balls, feathers, cake-type ice cream cones, inflated balloons. Items and activities can increase in weight and difficulty as the child's oral musculature improves, e.g., a dried pinecone instead of a ping-pong ball, or trying to keep the balloon aloft rather than just blowing it across the floor. More advanced: blowing up the balloons herself, blowing bubbles with bubble gum. Some of the harder types of bubble gum that start as a ball will give his jaw a workout just getting the gum pliable enough to blow the first bubble.

- Fun bubble art: mix a tablespoon of dish soap, a tablespoon of tempera paint and a half-cup of water in a pie or cake pan. With a drinking straw, blow and blow some more until the bubbles reach the top of the pan. Lay a piece of paper over the bubbles to make them pop and leave bubble art on the sheet. Repeat with more bubbles or different colors. Enjoy your bubble art as is, or add drawings or stickers, or cut into shapes.

- Make blow paintings. Trim craft paper to fit the bottom of a container with sides (disposable cake/casserole dishes are perfect). Thin down tempera paint with water or make your own: stir together equal parts of water and cornstarch, adding a few drops of food coloring to the desired shade. Dribble a spoonful of one color of paint on the paper, and using a straw, have the child blow the paint in all directions. Add additional colors, one at a time, until the painting is complete. Let dry thoroughly. Frame the paintings, fold to make greeting cards, or trim and laminate as bookmarks. (*Adapted from Education.com*)

- More blow toys and activities: whistles (conductor's whistle, slide whistle, referee's whistle, siren whistle), kazoos, recorders, harmonicas, echo microphones, megaphones, foam blow darts, inflatable toys.

- Party blowers are great exercise for the oral motor musculature around the mouth. Use them for simple games that aid speech development.

  - Target practice. Challenge your child to knock over lightweight objects, such as toilet paper tubes or a simple house of cards. Have him experiment with varying the force—blow hard, blow softly, blow one long blast, blow several short ones.

  - Set up party-blower sports: bowling (use toilet paper tubes in the 10-pin configuration), golf (coax a ping-pong ball into a hole or cup tipped on its side) or hockey.

  - Be a frog or anteater and go after tiny plastic insects or seeds.

Balloonarama

Balloons are much more than child's play for sensory and motor systems challenged by autism or Asperger's. They are terrific for gentle development of motor skills in children who are not yet ready to handle the weight of regular sports balls. Balloon activities are cheap, fun, and clean—and they work indoors or out.

How do we love balloons? Let us count the ways.

QUICK IDEA

"*A*ll kids love ..." Toss that idea right out of your head when working with kids with autism or Asperger's. What "all kids" enjoy might well be too sensory-stimulating for your child. When trying something for the first time, watch for reactions, then decide.

- Keep balloons in the air with something other than hands: blowing, tapping with a wooden spoon, pastry brush, or other kitchen utensil, fly swatter, ping-pong paddle or tennis racket.

- Tap the balloon using alternate hands (good for working the midline).

- Tap 'n' clap. How many times can you clap between taps?

- Volleyball-oon. Tape string or yarn across the room for the net.

- Basketball-oon. Anything can be the hoop, from a wastebasket to Dad's arms.

- Baseball-oon—with a foam bat, please!

- Use long balloons for spear chucking.

- Lie on the floor and keep the balloon in the air with toes only.

- Balloon balance: balance the balloon in the flat palm of the hand. Try to walk without blowing it off, then try to balance the balloon on a finger tip.

- Balloon pong. Tie a length of elastic cord to the balloon and then around the child's wrist. See how many times she can hit the balloon without missing. Then do it with the balloon overhead, or while lying down.

- Electrifying! If your child seeks tactile sensations, he might enjoy making his hair stand on end by rubbing it with a balloon. (*Warning:* some kids with autism or Asperger's will hate this.) When the balloon is electrified, see if he can make it stick to the wall. Variation: tag dodgeball-oon. Kids try to stick the balloons to each other's clothes rather than the wall.

- Some—not all—children may enjoy the goofy sounds made by blowing up the balloon, then letting the air out by pulling the neck in various ways. Bodily noises are almost always popular, but we even heard one kid produce tunes this way (Jingle Bells, Old MacDonald) by varying the speed and angle at which he released the air.

- Balloon juggling, for the advanced balloon athlete.

Once your child has mastered the skill of blowing up a balloon, it can be a great stress dissipater. Have her blow her anger, frustration, anxiety, or sillies into the balloon and pinch it shut but don't tie it. Then have her hold it aloft and let go, blowing away her troubles as the balloon zooms around the room in a burst of (ahem) fart-like noise that most children find hilarious.

Fun with bubbles

Bubbles are another great sensory item with wide appeal. Here are some off-beat ways to go beyond pulling the same old wand out of the bottle.

- Make popping them a bilateral activity. Swing a fly swatter to produce the bubbles and then attack them, alternating hands. Or, pop them by clapping.

- Soap in the eyes can be painful. Make your own non-irritating bubble liquid by mixing 1/4 cup no-tears baby shampoo, 3/4 cup water, 3 tablespoons light corn syrup.

- Use cookie cutters to make bubbles in a shape that interests your child. Numbers, animals, Halloween items, stars.

- Make your own bubble wands out of pipe cleaners bent into shapes, yogurt lids with the center cut out, plastic berry baskets, or wire whisks.

- Blow bubbles in cold weather. What does a freezy bubble look like? (It will be colorless, unlike warm-weather bubbles, which are tinged with purple.)

- Blow bubbles into a jar and trap them with a lid. How long do they last?

- Wet your hands and try to catch and hold a bubble—contact with something dry is what causes them to pop. Try to move the bubble to your other hand.

- Blow bubbles through the Musical Bubble Clown (available from Magical Toys and Products, *MagicalToysAndProducts.com*), and hear a musical tune.

The floor is so hard! ··

Little kids spend quite a bit of time sitting or playing on the floor. For the child with sensory (including vestibular) issues, it can be uncomfortable and difficult to manage. These tips can help:

- Use a back jack chair for additional postural support (many models can be found on the internet).
- Fold a blanket into quarters or use gym, camp, or exercise mats, or carpet squares for added cushioning.
- Let the child sit on a bolster or pillow.
- Be Zen and use meditation cushions or slanted wedge cushions designed to make it easier to sit for prolonged periods.

Vision and seeing ··

What do toe walking, headaches, poor handwriting, and weak organizational skills have in common? They're all signs of a visual processing problem in a child.

Just as communication involves more than words, vision is more than 20/20 eyesight. Vision is the learned developmental process of giving meaning to what we see, and it emerges from the integration of sensory input from the eyes and the body to the brain. Vision is conceptual and perceptual, and through it we learn to attend to, organize, and understand our world. (Lemer, 2009)

It is common in individuals on the autism spectrum that vision—not eyesight—is impaired, sometimes in multiple ways. Warning signs of visual dysfunction include:

- Has difficulty making eye contact
- Tilts head when observing closely
- Squints, closes an eye, covers one eye or widens eyes
- Experiences headaches, nausea, and/or dizziness
- Moves head and/or body or uses finger to track words while reading

- Frequently loses his place while reading, or can't find items in his desk, locker, or backpack
- Is fascinated by lights, spinning objects, shadows, or patterns
- Looks through hands
- Flaps hands, flicks objects in front of eyes
- Looks at objects sideways, closely, or with quick glances
- Becomes confused at changes in flooring or on stairways
- Toe walks
- Is excessively clumsy
- Pushes or rubs eyes repeatedly
- Bumps into objects or touches walls while moving through space
- Cannot spot errors in own work; does not notice details in general
- Has messy or poor handwriting; colors outside boundary lines
- Has trouble copying material from the chalkboard

If you suspect your child may have visual issues, find a developmental optometrist (enter your zip code at *Oepf.org* or *Covd.org* for referrals) and ask for a thorough vision assessment. These organizations certify and educate optometrists to work with individuals on the autism spectrum.

Adaptations at home

- Help your child see boundaries or edges of objects by adding a tactile component.
  - Add a strip of masking tape to edges of paper.
  - Use glitter glue to outline objects to be colored or mark edges with glued yarn or punched holes.
  - Use a wide black marker to thicken cutting lines.
  - Glue wooden craft sticks on either side of a straight line for easier cutting.

- Play Flashlight Follow-the-Leader. In a darkened room, the adult shines his flashlight onto the wall, and asks the child to match the spot with her flashlight. Move to another spot and repeat. Move the light around in a pattern and ask the child to follow along with her light.

- Do simple activities such as Connect the Dots (buy a book or make your own) or jigsaw puzzles that require eye coordination.

- Have fun with mazes.

  - On paper. Use store bought mazes or create your own. Have the child follow the maze with her finger, a pencil, a toy character.

  - On a sidewalk or driveway. Small or large, follow with chalk or with little feet.

  - In the snow or the sand, in a cornfield.

- The Circle Game. Cut out two matching sets of circles of various sizes and colors from felt, construction paper or vinyl. You start by placing a few circles into a pattern; the child must use his own circles to match your design. Also works with coins in a variety of sizes.

- Play picture games that ask the child to spot the differences in two similar-looking pictures to exercise visual perceptual skills.

Adaptations at school

- To reduce visual clutter on a page, mask all problems except the one being worked on. Masking templates are available that accomplish this quickly and neatly, or make your own from cardboard or paper.

- Place a thin flag-type sticky tab between words when teaching the beginning reader

- Use visual symbol sets to mark beginning and endings. For example, begin at the arrow and end at the stop sign, or begin at the green line and end at the red line.

- Glare, undetectable to us, can be a problem for the child. Cover the child's desk with black construction paper or insert a large piece of black poster board under his work.

- Give a child grid sheets to use when doing math problems or anything involving numbers or lists.

- Use a ruler or bookmark as a line-by-line guide while reading.

- To catch errors that are missed visually, teach children to read written work aloud at home before turning in homework the next day.

- Play memory games with students. Hold up a page with pictures of several objects for one minute. Remove the page and ask students to recall as many of the objects they saw as possible.

Note: Temple Grandin offers more insightful sensory adaptations in the foreword.

Did you know? The eye is one of the most nutritionally demanding organs of the body. Studies show certain nutrients have positive effects on eye health: Vitamins A, C, and E, lutein, zeaxanthin, Omega 3 oils, beta carotene, and lycopene.

Larger than life

Children with poor visual processing skills often miss parts of their surroundings. Some children's visual field is narrow, like looking through a tunnel. For others the visual field lacks depth perception, or they rely on peripheral vision to see. Magnifying glasses can open new vistas to children whose visual sense may need only a little priming. Make available to your child an assortment of magnifying tools: magnifying glasses of various shapes and sizes, telescope, binoculars. Have him explore his world bit by bit, starting with his own body.

- Have him examine the back of his hand, a toenail, his belly button. Have him look in the mirror and examine his hair, his teeth, his eyeball.

- Move on to his room. Carpet, bedspread, clock, toys, socks.

- Continue through the house. Towels, books, lettuce, hairbrush, apple, orange juice, money, lampshades.

- And on to the great outdoors. You can take it from here …
- When he shows interest in a particular object or area, expand on that interest.
  - Write a story
  - Draw a picture
  - Have him draw a picture while you hold the magnifying glass and see how tiny it is when you take the glass away.
  - Write in tiny, tiny code

Figure-ground processing

If your child seems tuned in to what children across the room are talking about, but is unaware of instructions spoken directly to her, she may have difficulty with auditory figure-ground processing. This means she cannot distinguish between foreground and background noise. A child with visual figure-ground processing dysfunction has trouble identifying the primary object in its surroundings. You'll see her having difficulties with tasks such as locating specific information on a printed page, finding a familiar face in a group of people, or finding her shoes on a floor strewn with clothes and toys.

Figure-ground dysfunction can translate into diminished sense of danger, exemplified by behaviors such as failing to stop before crossing the street or jumping from unsafe heights. Talk with your occupational therapist if you suspect your child has difficulties in this area.

Sensory survival kits

Savvy parents know the value of having favorite sensory items handy when calm begins to fade and anxiety soars. Carry that idea one step further by putting together portable sensory kits. Gather items in a box, basket, a backpack or small suitcase that is easy to grab and go. Or stash the kit in a spot easily accessible to the child for those times when relief is needed in a hurry.

- Sensory Kit for Calming and Coping: a small soft pillow, an iPod, several beanbags, a stress ball, chewing gum or chew necklace or bracelet, a lap blanket, a handkerchief and favorite aromatherapy oil, exercise bands (for proprioceptive input).

- Sensory Kit for Alerting and Energizing: a non-scratching surgical brush, squish ball, handheld video game, aromatherapy oil and handkerchief, one or two preprinted exercises that involve repetitive movements.

- Sensory Kit for Focus and Concentration: hand fidgets, tactile toys, cross-word puzzle, or games, chewing gum, or chew necklace or bracelet.

Teaching self-regulation

The Alert Program helps students understand the basic theory of sensory integration. It uses the analogy of an automobile engine to introduce its concepts of self-regulation to students. "If your body is like a car engine, sometimes it runs on high, sometimes it runs on low, and sometimes it runs just right." Alert Program leaders work in three stages, helping children identify their engine speeds, experiment with methods to change engine speeds, and regulate their engine speeds. Kids master how to change their engine levels for a variety of settings, so they can do what they want to do (learn, work, play) in the arousal state appropriate for that task.

For more information on the Alert Program, contact TherapyWorks in New Mexico: *AlertProgram.com*. Many occupational therapists are familiar with the Alert Program. If you're a parent, band together with a few other parents and ask your occupational therapist for a mini-inservice, so you know how to use the program at home, too.

Coping with painful sounds

You know the signs: your child covers his ears when he hears certain sounds, easily gets agitated when the dishwasher or the neighbor's leaf blower is running, or will absolutely, positively never return to the restaurant where the fire station alarm next door went off five minutes into your meal. Sound sensitivities cause constant anxiety, discomfort, or even physical pain, in some kids. Try a desensitizing program for the offending sound. Record the sound. Gradually introduce the sound to the child, starting at a very low volume. Allow the child to initiate and control the sound at a gradually increasing volume. Control of the sound is a big part of this process, so go as slowly as the child needs in order to build his confidence in handling the sound increases.

Headphones and earbuds, pro and con

Headphones and earbuds may help shut out distractions in a socially acceptable manner. Sounds not easily heard by others are often troublesome for a child on the spectrum. What we consider a normal amount of noise may be highly disturbing for these kids, and these sound reducing options can offer temporary relief. Also be aware that having an object wrapped around their head may be worse than the noise for certain children. Moreover, research suggests that repeated use of headphones and earbuds can impair the child's hearing, or even increase sound sensitivity. Acclimate the child to using these devices gradually and limit use to a maximum of half of the child's awake hours. (Teachers, seek parental permission.)

Toe walking

Walking on tippy toes is common in toddlers. But if your child is still walking on his tiptoes or the balls of his feet beyond age three—or begins to do so when he's older—it may be a neurological "soft sign" you should check into.

For kids with autism, toe walking can be related to difficulty processing sensory input. Your child may walk on as little of her foot as possible to avoid the feeling of a shoe or sock, or if barefoot, the feeling of the floor, carpet, sand, or grass. Your child may have an altered sense of the center of gravity or be responding to visual-spatial distortions.

Speak with your occupational therapist or physical therapist about whether you need to consult with a developmental pediatrician or neurologist about this. Meanwhile one of our favorite occupational therapists, Lindsey Biel, offers these suggestions:

- Teach your child the names of body parts, and then prompt him to walk with his heels down.

- Have your child jump on a mini-trampoline, holding your hands or a safety bar. Teach her to land with her heels down.

- Ask your occupational therapist or physical therapist to show you how to stretch your child's heel cord since calf muscles tighten up from toe walking.

- Investigate whether it helps to wear cushioned sneakers or less cushioned shoes—and try different types of socks (thick athletic socks versus thin socks, seamless socks, or inside-out socks).

- For young walkers, try Pipsqueaker sneakers that squeak when the heel strikes down. (Contact *Pipsqueakers.com* and ask them to move the squeaker back to the heel.)

- Discuss with your physical therapist or occupational therapist whether your child should have high top sneakers or an orthotic shoe insert that will help support proper alignment and hold the heel down.

What's that funky smell?

Children with autism spectrum disorders are often equipped with a hyper-acute sense of smell. Aromas, odors, and scents that the typical population may enjoy or not even notice have the potential to make your child miserable. Imagine a smell that makes you instantly nauseous, or that certain perfume that can give you a headache in five seconds flat. Now imagine that happening all day long, every day, and you might begin to appreciate how extensively the olfactory sense can affect a child with autism or Asperger's. If your child is olfactory defensive, there are many ways to make your home a friendlier place.

- Launder your child's clothes, sheets, and towels using perfume-free, dye-free, hypoallergenic laundry detergents and fabric softeners. Avoid chlorine bleach.

- Stock his tub or shower with unscented, hypoallergenic soaps.

- Burn off unpleasant bathroom smells by lighting a candle (yes, it works) or installing an exhaust fan. Scented sprays only add another layer of odor.

- Use unscented hand lotions and deodorants. Avoid perfumes, aftershaves, body gels, etc.

- Keep the house well ventilated when using ammonia, bleach and other heavily scented (such as lemon or pine) cleaning products.

- Ditto for cooking strong-smelling foods like fish or bacon. Use an exhaust fan, open the windows. Substitute raw vegetables for cooked if the odors offend.

- Store yard chemicals such as insecticides and fertilizers in a well-ventilated area away from your child's living space (i.e., so she doesn't have to walk by it every time she goes to the car, or a breeze doesn't carry the scents through her bedroom window).

- Experiment with aromatherapy to determine which scents are calming, and which are invigorating. Lavender, cinnamon, chamomile, vanilla, and patchouli are common calming scents. Lemon, basil, juniper, grapefruit, ginger, and peppermint can be energizing. Discover what works best for your child.

Did you know ...

- That our sense of smell can detect up to 400,000 odors? But noses get tired easily; that is why you can only smell a few roses at a time, or why that pool chlorine may be overwhelming when you walk in the door but fades after a few minutes.

- Babies do not discriminate between "good" and "bad" smells until they observe our responses: bakery, yum! trash can, pew!

- Women have more perceptive olfactory systems than men do.

- Most of our sense of taste is dependent upon our sense of smell.

- The part of the nasal cavity that detects and processes scents is about the size of a postage stamp.

- As you get older, your sense of smell diminishes. Young children usually have much more acute sniffers than do their parents or grandparents.

Do you smell what I smell?

To learn more about what smells your child likes and dislikes, make a game out of it. Have her close or cover her eyes and try to name smells such as orange, leather, chocolate, fish, popcorn, etc.

That's heavy!

Weighted clothing and other items can be lifesavers for children with proprioceptive difficulties. They can help keep a hyperactive child calmer and in better control of his or her senses, better able to attend, focus, and learn. Therapy catalogs offer many options, but the cost can be prohibitive. Here are some creative, budget-friendly adaptations. Note: Use a weighted item only under the supervision of an occupational therapist, who can determine the appropriate weight. Too much weight can result in over-stimulation and/or injury.

- Weighted vest. Shop thrift stores or used sporting goods stores for a small fishing vest. If you are handy with a needle, you can make or modify an existing fashion vest by adding pockets either inside or outside for the weights. Weight the pockets with zip baggies of sand, rice, birdseed, etc. For stationary weight, use clay. (Remove weights before washing.)

- Weighted blanket or quilt. Denim is a naturally heavy fabric, so gather up some old jeans. Carefully remove the back pockets, then cut the leg fabric into 6" or 8" squares. Stitch together, then sew the pockets onto the quilt top in various places. Add batting and backing. The quilt will be heavy to begin with, but adding weight to the pockets can be a fun and beneficial activity for the child. What will go in the pockets? Pennies, pebbles, marbles?

- Determine the size of the quilt based on how the child will use it. If for sleeping, you'll want a larger size. A smaller lap size pad is good for TV-watching, reading, and homework.

- Hug chair. Make two weighted "arms" (from pants leg or other fabric tube), then attach these to the arms of a chair. Weighted "arms" wrap around or drape across the child as she sits in the chair.

The human hamburger

Your little burger fanatic will love this sensory game that offers silliness in the form of deep-pressure input. You'll need two floor or sofa pillows (the bun) and a large, soft paintbrush or car wash sponge (to add the condiments). Have your child (the burger) center himself on the bottom half of the bun (one of the pillows), then ask him what he likes on his burger. Spread on the condiments using the paintbrush or sponge, using firm pressure down his arms, legs, and torso—no tickling! Then add another pillow as the top of the bun. (Do not cover the face or head.) Lean some of your weight on the "sandwich" and make chomping noises. Apply pressure to different parts of his body through the pillow. When you finish "eating" the burger—and you have told him how delicious it was—ask if he would like to be dessert now. An Oreo, or perhaps an ice cream sandwich?

It's a wrap

A child who finds deep pressure calming can crave this type of sensory input when her surroundings get aggravating. Creative moms with a sewing machine can stitch a "wrapper" shawl for the child in less than twenty minutes. Here's how to do it.

Purchase a length of lycra spandex fabric (usually sold in 60" widths) equal to your child's chest measurement, plus 8–10" (allow extra if tying knots as described below). Fold the selvage edges of the fabric together and sew the edge. Turn inside out.

To use: wrap the shawl around the child, criss-cross the ends in front, have the child grab one end in each hand and pull as needed for a calming "hug."

Tip ....

To prevent material from slipping through little hands, tie each end into a knot so the child has something to grab before pulling.

Hideout ....

Children seeking proprioceptive input sometimes enjoy tight spaces. Create a spot for them in a closet or closet-like area (under the stairs, other cubby-type spaces in the house) as a calming place to self-regulate, read, or do homework.

Bean bags ....

For great sensory integration fun, make a bean bag family from tube socks filled with beans, bubble wrap, nut shells—anything that has a distinct texture or makes a sound. Seal the end of the sock by tying a knot or stitching across. Make faces on the socks with paint or marker pen if that tickles your child.

- Bigger bean bags—use the sleeve of an old sweater or sweatshirt; stitch the ends shut.
- Even bigger bean bags—use a pant leg from sweatpants; stitch ends shut.

Comfort first when it comes to clothes ....

While many children delight in new clothes, your tactile-defensive child may find them torturous. Hand-me-downs or clothes purchased at consignment shops, thrift shops, or garage sales have the advantage of already being broken in. They've been laundered several times, are softer, the sometimes smelly and scratchy factory-applied chemical sizing is gone. The garment has already shrunk to its true size, and won't end up pinching or binding after one washing. Remove all tags that may scratch, or search for clothes with thermal-applied labels—no tags.

Hand-me-downs (call them something else if you prefer—hand-overs or hand-offs, or just "the sweater that came from Jenny") from a favorite sibling or cousin may carry special association for the child with autism or Asperger's, whose social connections are sometimes limited.

Clothing preferences—both sides now

A textured button here. A hidden zipper there. For the child who seeks tactile input, being able to inconspicuously access a favorite sensation can be calming when her sensory system is acting up. Or it can help her focus when quiet or attention is appropriate (during a test, library time, or silent reading time). Add simple embellishments (hidden or not) to your child's clothing as a way for her to access her favorite tactile sensation.

- Sew one half of a Velcro patch (the rough side) to the inside hem of a shirt or T-shirt.
- Line a pocket with smooth silk, soft fleece, or fur.
- Thread several beads, buttons, or metal charms on one or more leather or fabric cords and attach to dangle from a button, the pocket on a vest, or from the waistband on a skirt. Cute while providing appropriate finger-fidget sensation.

What one child finds calming, another may find stress-inducing. Many children with autism or Asperger's find clothing embellishments and fasteners invasive and uncomfortable to the point of distraction. That can include buttons, snaps, zippers, collars, cuffs, French seams, appliqués, tags, beads, sequins, ribbon, or embroidery.

> **QUICK IDEA**
>
> For the child who needs constant tactile input to help him stay calm, on task, or to self-regulate, use Velcro® to attach a surgical brush or other textured item (piece of fur, sandpaper) to the bottom of his desk.

Snug leggings or tights, ace bandages or a close fitting vest may calm a child seeking proprioceptive input (deep pressure). Other children who are tactile sensitive might choose shorts year round, because the less clothing touching their legs the better

The easiest way to discern clothing needs and preferences is to *ask for your child's opinion*. He may not be able to tell you, but if he is, you may be in for a stiff surprise. We know a mom who was mortified to discover her son hated the jeans she was buying him to wear to school. They were extremely uncomfortable to him, stiff and heavy, but she had assumed he would want to wear what the other kids wear. When she asked why he never told her he didn't like them, his answer was, "You never asked." Mom learned through her son's occupational therapist that he wanted to wear soft sweatpants and T-shirts—which was fine with her. The boy's teachers reported a noticeable decrease in his general agitation level following the shift to softer clothes.

Always ask and honor your child's preferences for comfort over style or fashion. It can ward off sensory problems and empower children by giving them choices.

More on clothes

If overstimulated visual perception is a problem, your child may prefer clothes in muted solid colors, free of stripes, patterns, plaids, logos or prints. If you think he is not able to tell you, offer clothing choices and notice what he selects.

Be aware of fabrics. If your child is chemical-sensitive, he may be more comfortable in natural fibers like cotton. Wool and linen are natural but can be scratchy. Polyester (including fleeces), rayon, and nylon are synthetics and retain heat more than cotton.

Windy weather can be, literally, hair-raising for your child, causing unpleasant sensations that can make him anxious or angry. Make sure he leaves the house with a suitable hat or cap on those breezy days, whether balmy or brr-r-r-r.

Sleep on it ·····················

Of all difficulties associated with autism or Asperger's, sleep problems are among the most vexing. These children may have atypical proprioceptive and/or vestibular issues contributing to their sleep difficulties. Here are some tactics that take those characteristics into account.

- Pajamas. Long-john type pajamas, with their gentle all-over pressure, may be comforting. Loose pajamas, nightgowns that ride up, fabrics that scratch or pill, buttons, ribbons, or embroidery that scratches or produces bumps, and elastic around ankles, waist, or neck, are all possible irritants.

- The sleeping space. Is the sleeping space so big he might not feel boundaries? Downsize it with a tent, canopy, or hanging curtain around the bed (á la Harry Potter, or a hospital room). A mummy-style sleeping bag or weighted blanket (consult an occupational therapist before using this) might also help.

- Taking a "lovey" to bed is a common childhood practice, but the usual teddy bear or dolly may not be your child's lovey of choice. However odd, accommodate his preference, as long as it's safe. We know one child who adored his whisk broom and took it to bed with him every night.

- Rubbing your child with lotion before bed can be calming, but beware of perfumes and scents that may bother him as he tries to go to sleep. Be especially aware of competing scents, e.g., soap, shampoo, lotion, and toothpaste, all from the bedtime routine, that combine for a nauseating effect.

Sleep tips for road trips ·····················

Going to sleep, especially in a place other than home, can be hard if hypersensitive ears pick up all those sounds that typical people push into the background and easily disregard. The uncertainty of not knowing when and how often an unfamiliar sound might arise, especially one that might be painful, can be a source of constant anxiety for these children.

Talk with your child about what kinds of sounds he might hear at night in another house or hotel. For some kids, making a game of listening to and identifying sounds might lessen the anxious feelings. Before he goes to bed, listen for: traffic noise such as sirens, buses, or trains, footsteps or voices in the hall or overhead, various plumbing noises, crickets, birds, dogs, or other animal sounds, elevators whooshing up and down, food carts rattling up the hall, sounds from an ice machine or vending machines. Knowing what the sounds are and that they are okay can help a child relax.

Tip

When booking a hotel room, tell them you are traveling with a special needs child and request a room in a quiet area. That is, not near the elevator, vending machines, or over the kitchen, and away from the main avenue or street. And not booked onto the floor with the all-night wedding or sports celebration going on!

Pre-event strategy

Crowded, noisy places such as parties, shopping malls, amusement parks, and popular beaches, parks, and playgrounds are almost sure to be sensory challenges for your child. Plan a three-step entry for your child when visiting these venues so he is not thrust into the thick of the activities without the opportunity to acclimate. Offer a sensory-calming activity before the event, such as squeeze ball, chewing gum, weighted lap pad and/or soothing music in the car on the way over. Arrive early and designate a corner, room, or other area away from the main action where he can play and organize his sensory needs before joining the rest of the group. Let him decide when—and if—he is ready to do so.

If he's not ready, don't force him. Whether the activity is fun or duty, forcing will only increase his resistance. Fun cannot be forced anyway. Instead, read what your child's resistance is telling you, take steps to address it for next time, and trust that with teaching and maturity, your child will enlarge his circle of enjoyable activities when the time is right for him.

Sensory diet for low arousal levels··

The squeaky wheel gets the grease, right? In autism-speak, that means our kids' hyper-acute senses usually draw our attention first. Children make it known through their behavior when things are too loud, too bright, too yucky, too crowded, too many things going on at once. Hands over ears, spitting out food, running away. Developing calming strategies for overwrought senses can be an ongoing part of life with autism or Asperger's. But there's a flip side to hyper-acute senses, and it gets much less attention.

> **QUICK IDEA**
>
> Do the flamingo! Standing on one foot is a great proprioceptive exercise. It builds core muscle strength and helps kids get a better sense of their arms and legs. Tree pose, in yoga, or tai chi, are other good options.

Some children live with hypo-acute sensory function, meaning their senses do not detect normal levels of input. When sensory arousal level is continually low, we may see the child as lethargic, unresponsive, or withdrawn. As they seek greater sensory stimulation, some children engage in odd activities, ranging from self-talk or eating non-food items (pica) to more serious behaviors such as skin-picking and head banging. We want to add alerting rather than calming components to the routine of the hypo-sensitive child.

Let's go through a child's day with suggestions for providing alerting input. Bear in mind that a child's arousal level can change and shift during the day. A child who experiences low arousal in the morning may wake up by late afternoon or evening and give you the opposite problem at the other end of the day—over-stimulation. Keeping an hour-by-hour chart of his activities and response to them can help you pinpoint where and when these shifts seem to occur.

- Waking up a sleepyhead. We've heard parents report that their child has such low sensory perception that he falls back to sleep throughout the morning routine: while getting dressed, in the bathroom, at the breakfast table. Alerting strategies can help counteract the sleepiness:

- Experiment with alarm clocks or wake-up devices. He may respond to his favorite music while ignoring a conventional alarm clock. For the younger child, a noisy device in the form of a favorite character may be the ticket. If your older child has a cell phone—well, show us the tween or teen who ignores a cell phone call.

- A shower can be invigorating/alerting with a pulsating showerhead. Install a hand-held one with several settings and let him choose. A sharply-scented soap, if (and only if) he can tolerate it, is also alerting, as is applying soap foam, gel, or liquid with a nubby washcloth, mitt, or loofah sponge.

- Have him dress standing up in front of a full-length mirror. Sitting on the bed to dress is too tempting for the sleepyhead. The mirror gives him colorful visual input. It also helps him see the appearance he presents to the world, an important social awareness skill.

- Breakfast is essential and breakfast should be foods he likes. But within that sphere, some foods are better than others. Crunchy foods are alerting (choose the granola over the oatmeal—same food, different delivery), as are foods with sharp tastes, such as sour or spicy.

Don't assume your child prefers sweet foods. Ellen's son Bryce goes for the tartest grapes, rejects the reddest strawberries as too sweet and soft, and insists on green-tinged bananas for their sour edge. Grapefruit juice, anyone?

- Incorporate movement into his trip to school. If he takes the bus, can he walk to the next stop past his usual one (with supervision as necessary)? If you drive him to school, can you drop him a block away? Can his paraeducator, teacher, or peer buddy walk him to class the long way, or take a few turns around the gym or playground with him before settling down?

- During the school day (and homework time)

  - Children seeking proprioceptive input need opportunities for movement and change of position during the day. They will not get it by keeping their backsides in a chair for long stretches. Equip your classroom with options for them to do their work in many positions: at their desk, standing at a podium or counter, lying on a mat or carpet, sitting on a fitness ball or in a rocking chair or swiveling office chair.

- Some children seek alerting input through oral activity. Crunchy foods are good choices at meal times, but in between, a water bottle with a straw (sipping cold water and even chewing on the straw) can be effective. A chew necklace (sanitary non-toxic rubber object on a lanyard) can go anywhere with him. Blowing bubbles or chewing gum during breaks from the classroom can help.

- When planning classroom activities, bear in mind that repetitive or linear activities are calming while activities that incorporate change and movement are alerting.

- Never take away recess or PE time as a penalty or behavior consequence. Movement is what the child needs; taking away opportunities for movement only exacerbates whatever problem you are trying to address. Wherever possible, redirect with *more* movement: emptying the trash cans, shelving books, wiping tables or counters.

- **Cautions**
  - Children with low sensory perception levels may seek tactile or oral input by putting objects in their mouths or close to their mouths. Or they may press their hands on other people in an exploratory (not threatening) way.
  - They may have trouble holding on to small, light objects. If using a picture card system, attaching the picture to a weightier object such as a book, block, or smooth stone may help.

> **QUICK IDEA**
>
> If balance is a problem, have the child do a movement in slower motion. This gives his body time to adjust to the movement. Another idea: give him a fixed object to look at during the movement, similar to the way a dancer "spots" during a turn.

- They may not notice objects or people around them as they move through their environment, hence unintentionally bump into classmates, furniture, or other things.

Distinguishing between needs and rewards

Rewards or reinforcers can be an important part of teaching the child with autism or Asperger's at home or in the classroom, and for children with sensory issues, sensory rewards can be motivating. The trick is to distinguish between a sensory *need*, the fulfillment of which should not be withheld based on behavior, and a sensory *preference* (favorite activity, object, food, or other choice).

Sensory need

- The classroom is too noisy for the child. Allowing him to wear headphones, earmuffs, a stocking cap, or use an iPod, is not a privilege, rather it helps him manage the level of sound input so he can self-regulate and attend to his work.
- He needs movement. Allowing him to run errands to the office, move chairs around the room, or restack books is not a privilege. It supplies the proprioceptive input his system needs to stay focused, alert, and organized.

Sensory reward

Nearly all children will respond to rewards if the proper reward is identified. That's an important if. A reward is effective only when and as long as it continues to be meaningful to the child—this is not a "forever and ever" relationship. Consider all the child's senses when constructing sensory rewards. A reward can be:

- Something to play with, such as a favorite fidget toy
- Something to look at, such as a book, water fountain, traffic, animals
- Something to eat
- Something to smell
- Something to do (ball pit, sand table, other sensory experience)

Note: A critical part of the successful use of reinforcers is the question of how much is enough, how much is too much (satiation). If you let him play with the marble tree, will he willingly give it up after the reward period, or will taking it away seem like punishment? Use a variety of reinforcers; mix them up. Set clear guidelines from the beginning: we only play with the marble tree as an earned reward, and we play with it for three minutes—we set a timer and when it goes off, marble time is over. And for this same reason, we strongly advise against using food as a reinforcer. First off, food reinforcers are seldom healthy (lucky you, if your child will accept grapes or baby carrots as reinforcers over candy, chips, or crackers). Second, what do you do after he's just had breakfast or lunch and he's full? Where is the line between how many fish crackers or chocolate chips are motivating, or how few are just frustrating?

Hands-on learning

Build opportunities for tactile and visual learning into all curriculum areas:

- Science labs

- Math manipulatives in many textures, shapes, and colors, gathered from nature or from the child's special area of interest.

- Dioramas for history, literature, and science subjects (have kids bring special interest figures, animals, rocks, etc. from home to personalize).

- Take apart or deconstruct items to see how they are made: dissect a broken appliance or toy, unstitch a book or shirt. Lay the pieces out and sequence its construction.

Deep pressure inputs for desk time

Develop a menu of several deep pressure exercises your student can do at his desk during times when it is inappropriate to be moving around the room. Attach small visuals of each activity to the desk so you can point to one as needed. Such movements might include:

- Squeeze toys or other noiseless fidgets
- Passing a heavy stone, beanbag, or theraputty back and forth from hand to hand
- Pulling on a fitness rubber band
- Chewing on rubber tubing or water bottle with sport top or straw
- Isometric exercises such as pressing chin into fist, lacing fingers together and trying to pull them apart (pull and release, repeat), placing hand on knee and pushing down with hand while pushing up with knee (release and repeat).

Please remain seated

A weighted lap blanket may help your child remain seated longer, but be sure to rotate it—twenty minutes on, twenty minutes off. Other adaptations might include:

- A bungee cord strung between the legs of a chair
- A saddle bag filled with sand
- Having the child straddle a large bolster in lieu of a more traditional seat
- Putting a piece of an egg-crate mattress pad on the chair for extra sensory feedback

You are now free to move about the classroom

If your student has difficulty staying in his seat for desk tasks, he may be a movement seeker, needing that sensory input to self-regulate. Designate a second desk or work area for him. This gives him somewhere constructive to move toward, rather than simply moving to fill the need to move.

Teachers often place fidgety students at the front of the classroom where she can more easily establish eye contact and verbal exchange, but the opposite strategy might work as well. Place the child at the back of the room and allow a certain amount of spontaneous movement, provided it does not disrupt the rest of the class. Some teachers have even found that a restless student absorbs auditory information more readily when performing a small physical task such as feeding the class pets, watering the plants, passing out supplies.

Building physical movement into classroom lessons can be beneficial for all kids, not just your special needs student. Be creative. Play stand-up, sit-down games while learning nouns and verbs, odd-even numbers. Simon Says lends itself to many true-false learning situations as well. Bunny-hop your arithmetic tables or spelling words.

Dealing with "stims" in the classroom

Certain stims (self-stimulating behaviors) such as hand-flapping, rocking, or fidgeting are a symptom of the child's disordered vestibular sense seeking motion. Trying to eliminate the stim misses the point: There's a function to the stim that needs to be recognized and replaced with a socially appropriate behavior. Incorporating movement-seeking activities into the child's day at every opportunity can help significantly.

At school, give the student an outlet to self-regulate: let him take the attendance or lunch count to the office, bring out the PE equipment, clean the chalkboard or erase board, stack chairs, carry books, pull on a piece of rubber tubing attached to his chair or backpack, rub a worry stone, climb or swing on playground equipment, hit a tether ball, play drums in music class, or during classroom songs.

Sensory goals on the Individualized Education Program (IEP)

Sensory needs change over time. When writing IEP goals keep any reference to an adaptive device written in generic language. Replace "Monica will remain in her seat for fifteen minutes during story-telling time using a Movin' Sit wedge" with "Monica will remain in her seat for fifteen minutes during story-telling time using an adaptive device." That way the device can change as needed (e.g., using a vibrating pillow instead) while the IEP goal stays current.

That back to school smell

If your student with autism or Asperger's gets queasy or antsy when strong scents invade his space, ask the principal about the types of cleaning products, paints and other materials used to prep and clean classrooms for back to school in the fall, and on an ongoing basis. Many schools are moving toward using green cleaning products, but if yours isn't, staff should be made aware that the smell from harsh industrial chemicals can linger for days or weeks, interfering with the learning process of chemically-sensitive kids. This includes visually-sensitive students. That shiny just-waxed floor can cause sharp (and painful) reflections from sunlight and overhead lighting.

Your child's other classrooms

As awareness of autism increases, we are thrilled to be getting more and more inquiries asking how to successfully include our kids in classrooms other than day school: Sunday school or religious classrooms, after-school art classes, playgroups, Scouts, and other social groups. Many of the accommodations for these classrooms should be the same—visual supports, a quiet retreat corner, prescribed routine, visual boundary for circle time, transition alerts. In addition, this short list of sensory-friendly suggestions will help your student feel more at home in his other classrooms.

- Teachers, start the class or meeting with an organized multi-sensory activity that kids can readily join in as they arrive. Unstructured free play can be intimidating for children with autism, who have a hard time with initiating social contact and transitioning from one setting to another. Parents, suggest activities your child likes that fit this bill. Most teachers will be happy to have this input; they want your child to be successful.

- If your student has a comfort toy, allow Spiderman to participate. He can jump in the clay, make feet prints in the paint, glue himself to the leaf collage, and get his face painted with (washable) markers.

- If the class or activity meets only once a week, a class photo with class-mates' names labeled will help your child learn more quickly and remember from week to week.

- If projects or knowledge must carry over from week to week, written and visual instructions and reminders that go home with the child are essential.

- Give the teacher a list of warning signs that indicate your child is approaching sensory overload (hands over ears, humming, biting himself, running around or out of the room, agitated language or noises, repeated words or phrases). She can then direct him to the quiet corner or per-haps have him leave the activity under the supervision of another adult.

- Children with autism generally have difficulty processing auditory-only information delivery. Add visuals to story-telling time, especially three-dimensional visuals. Old Playmobil or Lego people and objects are great for acting out stories. Blue plastic wrap makes great fake water, and noth-ing beats real dirt, stones, twigs, a broom, or blanket as realistic props.

- Changing activities frequently (with appropriate transition warnings) will keep the child with autism from zoning out. Have several tables or stations in the room so activities can rotate. The same for circle activi-ties—they don't have to be in the same corner of the room every time. Moving around at intervals appropriate to age and attention span is good for all kids, not just those with autism.

Unsafe, inappropriate, or just annoying?

Once you understand how greatly your child's sensory integration difficulties affect him, prioritizing his needs can feel overwhelming. As always, start by knowing that helping your child learn to live comfortably with his autism is a process—a long, long process wherein you have plenty of time.

Deciding what to address first will become clear when you break his challenges down into three categories: behaviors that are dangerous to him-self or others, behaviors that are not physically dangerous but are socially inappropriate and isolating, and behaviors that are quirky or annoying but have no life-threatening consequences. Here are some examples of each:

- Dangerous to self or others—consult an occupational therapist at once
  - Seems oblivious to pain (critical to address, as pain is the body's natural warning system) or cold—refuses appropriate outdoor clothing even in winter
  - Jumps from heights—playground equipment, stairs, furniture, trees
  - Handles glass items roughly—bangs on or throws mirrors, glasses, framed photos or artwork.
  - Engages in head banging
  - Bites himself or others
  - Engages in excessive masturbation or handling of genitals
  - Exhibits fascination with fire
  - Exhibits fear of or fascination with bodies of water
  - Bolts from undesirable situations or, in general, is a "runner"
  - Has oral or feeding difficulties—trouble chewing, overfills mouth, tries to swallow food whole, spits, or regurgitates food
  - Eats or puts non-food items in mouth
- Socially inappropriate or isolating, or posing health risks over the long term—consult an occupational therapist, speech-language therapist, dentist or other professional as indicated
  - Handles feces, his own or animal
  - Sniffs or smells other people or things obsessively
  - Eats only a few things, may be limited to certain textures, food groups, or colors
  - Resists hygiene tasks such as teeth brushing, nail clipping, shampooing, handwashing, showering, toileting
  - Exhibits low threshold to pain, dizziness, light, touch

- Walks on tiptoes—address immediately as this can cause shortening of the tendons and make normal flat-footed walking difficult (see **Toe walking** earlier in this chapter)
- Takes off clothes in public
- Shows obsessive interest in touching or licking certain body parts. One child we knew loved to touch women's legs: family, friends, even strangers.
- Hugs and/or kisses everyone—even strangers—at first meeting. (This might be cute at four, but dangerous at fourteen.)
- Has difficulty with transitions: between activities, between home and school, between waking and sleeping, between seasons.
- Exhibits low tolerance for frustration, gives up easily
- Has difficulty with balance, trouble with running, riding a bike
- Displays inconsistent eating habits, alternates between ravenous and not eating at all
- Quirky and/or annoying, but no real physical or life skill consequences
  - Prefers to wear underwear inside out
  - Needs favorite items arranged in a specific pattern
  - Doesn't like foods touching each other on his plate
  - Can't stand so-called fashionable clothes
  - Shows no interest in animals
  - Clings to benign narrow or obsessive interests

Communication *and* Language

The limits of my language mean
the limits of my world.
LUDWIG WITTGENSTEIN

ONSIDER FOR A MOMENT HOW EASILY typical kids capture our attention with eye contact and pointing. With a slight turn of the head or a small finger raised, they communicate, they connect without words or language. They tell us how they feel about their world and what attracts their attention in it. Most kids with autism, however, have difficulty indicating interest. Their over- or under-sensitive sensory systems can interfere with visual processing, their impaired social thinking can hinder their ability to know what to reference, and their motor systems can't plan, coordinate and execute in a way that produces the spontaneous gaze or gesture.

Bottom line: we can't rely on what kids with autism or Asperger's do or don't do, from either a movement or speech perspective, as an accurate gauge of their interests, inner thoughts and feelings, or an indicator of their desire to communicate.

In the absence of a point or eye gaze, we must look for other clues that signal interest and communicative intent. It might be a glance in the direction of an object, a mouth puckered, arms thrown wide or pulled in, a squeal of delight, or a particular part of a DVD the child plays over and over. It can be as simple (and silent) as a turn of the head every time something of interest is mentioned. When we become careful observers and listeners, we will see our children's attempts to communicate and be able to uncover the clues that tell us what to acknowledge, respond to, and teach.

The words we use are only a small part of all that comprises interpersonal communication. Yet as a society, we value speech over all other forms of communication. "Please, teach my child to talk." This global focus on "using our words" is so prevalent that every day our children with autism reach out to us in ways so slight we miss their attempts to connect. Sadly, when those attempts go unnoticed, their motivation to communicate with us fades.

Our job, as the communication-proficient adults in our children's lives, is to break down this complex landscape of communication into smaller, more manageable parts, and give them a meaningful, reliable, and functional communication system, *in whatever form it may take.* We no longer believe that 40% of children with autism will never develop speech, as the literature told us as little as five years ago. We've learned our children are far more adept at communication than we give them credit for, and that targeted and intensive intervention can give them the tools needed to express themselves. Whether that expression comes through spoken language, or picture cards, a communication device, or sign language matters not—it's all communication. All children have something to say to us. It's our responsibility to listen in a manner that allows them to be heard.

Inquiring minds ask ··

Ellen well remembers the day her barely-verbal four-year-old son came home from preschool (a supported integrated social communication classroom) and asked an important question.

> *"You wan' know someting?"*
> *"Yes, of course," I responded, delighted that it appeared he was going to spontaneously offer something he had learned at school.*
> *"You wan' know someting, Mom?"*
> *"Yes! Yes, I want to know something," I enthused.*
> *"You wan' know someting?" This went on for several more exchanges with me starting to wilt around the edges because I clearly wasn't giving the right response. Finally he said, with a great deal of pride:*
> *"Well, you wan' know someting, just axsk me!"*

We forget to "just ask" the child with limited language, perhaps under a partially misguided assumption that he can't tell us, or worse, doesn't have an opinion or preference.

Just ask—the student with autism learns in ways that may not be typical or common. Teachers, let him help you teach. Ask him how he feels he learns best, and listen to the response (which may not be verbal). Is it through reading or writing? By working with a peer? Through field trips, or through hands-on activities like science experiments, art projects, or board games?

By asking the child to think about how he learns and what helps him learn, he takes a step toward accepting some responsibility for his own learning. Such awareness is empowering.

Ask in reverse

When your usual questioning methods aren't working, ask the question in reverse. Instead of "what do you want to do for a birthday party?" ask "what do you *not* want to do for your birthday?" You may be surprised to find that she hates candles, bowling, the birthday song, any place that requires her to dress up, or having more than five people in the house at a time.

Use this reverse psychology to both educate and entertain. Have your child tell you ten bad things about the dog and you might find out he adores Buster but neglects feeding him, not because he forgets but because he hates the smell of the dog food.

Five important words: "I am here for you."

Raising a child with autism can seem like a vise of minute-by-minute management: engineering the strict structure he needs, the visits to professionals whose expertise we need, our own need to feel that we are doing everything we can, or at least doing enough—these needs frequently dictate all the minutes of our days. Structured, professional help and self-evaluation are necessary—but not to a slavish degree. Do you live by the clock? If so, it's important to take a giant step back and reflect upon how your child learns and grows. Yes, he learns by doing—but long before he can do that, he learns and responds to his environment in the context of *how it feels to him*. We all know from personal experience that emotions can and do sometimes overtake logical thought or action.

"Being emotionally available (to your child) may be as,
if not more, important than what activities you do."

These wise words come from Jennifer Rosinia, PhD, OTR/L and president of Kid Links Unlimited, Inc. Strong, stable relationships with the primary adults in his life form a child's potent front line against stress and anxiety during the long process of learning self-regulation. Dr. Rosinia advises us to "be as much in the business of being as of doing."

Does he hear what you hear?

When language impairments exist, a child's hearing should be tested to rule out physiological problems. The child with autism may have difficulty with the typical school-administered test, wherein the student is asked to raise his hand in response to pitched tones. He may not understand the instructions, taking visual cues from the other children around him, raising his hand when they do, or doing so randomly in an attempt to give the expected response.

You may wish to consult a pediatric audiologist, a specialist in assessing hearing loss in children. Audiologists may be MAs or PhDs, and go through a similar credential process as speech language pathologists. Look for certifications from the American Speech Language Hearing Association (CCC-A) or Fellows of the American Academy of Audiology (F-AAA).

Testing is based on the child's developmental and chronological age. The audiologist can work with your doctor, teacher, and speech language pathologists to determine appropriate tests. Behavioral response tests like the one described above can be modified for children as young as infants. Auditory brainstem response (ABR) testing or otoacoustic emissions (OAE) testing measures nerve response in the ear. Tympanometry measures eardrum movement and is useful in detecting problems such as fluid behind the ear.

First things first: get his attention

As adults, we often forget to establish contact with a child before we begin speaking or initiate conversation. Words fly out of our mouths and we expect our kids or students to understand that we're talking to them. Children with autism generally lack social referencing skills, making it imperative that we get their attention before initiating conversation.

- Physically move to the student's level. Walk over to the child, sit, bend, or squat to get your face at the child's eye level.

- Establish attention. Get physically close, if tolerated. Put yourself in the child's line of vision, even if it means moving his or your seat. Watch for the student to orient to you—that doesn't necessarily mean eye contact. Be animated. Use visual props.

- Let the child know that what follows merits her attention. This could be a simple verbal or visual cue: a tap on her shoulder or arm, saying the child's name or a preparatory word or phrase, such as "listen," "watch," or "look at me."

- Use gestures and body language meaningfully. Avoid waving your hands around in the air while you talk; use gestures and body movements in a slow, pronounced way so the child has time to make the association.

Jump right in

Often children with autism can be so engrossed in their thoughts that they start conversation mid-stream, making it difficult for a listener to follow: " … and there was a girl in a green dress, so pretty, and then a frog came in!" It's common for a child with autism or Asperger's—even one we label as "smart"—to lack the ability to attribute ideas, beliefs, intentions, likes, and dislikes to himself and others, and to appreciate that these may differ from person to person. Our kids don't perceive that other people's thoughts are not the same as their own. They assume the listener already knows what he is thinking and can fill in the blanks.

We need to probe—at length and with patience. Ask him, "What are you talking about? What happened? Is it a book, is it a movie, is it real? Did it happen yesterday or today?" Have the child go back to the beginning of the thought. This may be frustrating for him; he may not want to take the time to go back to the beginning or he may not know where the beginning was.

You can help him by verbalizing your own thoughts throughout the day. Ask him: "See that little girl at the swing? She has such a big smile—what do you think she's thinking?" Then contrast his answer with your own, or offer other options he may not have considered. Give him lots of opportunities to learn that people are thinking all sorts of things at any given moment.

Your child or student can't discern what his listener does or doesn't know. Resist the temptation to say or think, "Okay, whatever," and move on. Recognizing "other minds" is a social processing skill necessary for him to learn to see the things from the perspective of another and be able to appreciate the thoughts and opinions that others hold. Don't let him get away with substituting random thoughts for comprehensible conversation, at any age.

> ### QUICK IDEA
> Play a vocabulary game in a semi-darkened room. Give the child or children a flashlight and have them find and illuminate objects or words as you call them out.

Feed language in

Here's a scenario that may be familiar to many parents and teachers. A child can articulate the first and last word of a sentence, but everything in between is unintelligible, such as "The cat ah-do-nee-durn-nee-bont the fence" for "The cat ran and jumped over the fence." Or, even more simply, "I ah-ah go ah-ah-ah store," for "I want to go to the store." In both cases, the child knows that more words are needed but can't come up with them, so she inserts a marker. When this happens, feed the language in: "Oh, you want to go to the store!"

When speech gets stuck

Speech is a complicated affair, and speech is only part of language and communication. The Communication Development Center in Madison, Wisconsin specializes in physically-supported speech and language services for children with autism spectrum disorders. Director Marge Blanc, MA, CCC-SLP, shares this information about the relationship between speech, language, and communication.

Speech is movement. It is "motor," or muscle behavior. It is not language. As a motor behavior, it is complex. It involves: (a) breathing, specifically exhalation; (b) voice, or vocal production at the level of the larynx, or voice box; and, (c) as it develops, coordination with sequenced movement of the jaw, tongue, and lips (articulation).

Dyspraxia is a disorder of muscle coordination that affects unique motor "plans," not automatic muscle sequences. When a child screams out of distress, this is automatic. If he tries to repeat this vocalization, on purpose, it is a plan. The latter would be difficult, if not impossible, for a child with severe dyspraxia. (Blanc, 2006)

Building the foundations for breathing, voice, and articulated speech is a bottom-up process achievable through an eight-level hierarchy of supports. Each level builds on the previous one, starting with the nonverbal child who does not yet have the muscle tone to produce vocalizations, and building to purposeful speaking at level eight. Parents and therapists alike can use this successful protocol to help a child find his voice.

Hierarchy of practical supports for helping children with autism or Asperger's find their words

Level 1—Deep breathing/exhalation. The child at this level makes no utterances or vocal attempts to communicate, or those that are produced are very weak and unsustainable.

Level 2—Voice/vocal production. The child uses his voice—but not necessarily words— to communicate during play: "zoom, zoom" when playing with his toy car, squeals of glee going down the slide, humming.

Level 3—Intonation. The child's utterances lengthen enough to have variations in tone, with the voice rising and falling, quiet or animated.

Level 4—Starting, maintaining, and stopping sound. At this level, the child's sounds and verbal utterances are reliable forms of communication that he can start, stop, and maintain.

Level 5—Vowel sounds. A child's sustained verbal utterances, combined with occupational therapy as needed, strengthen the child's tongue and articulator muscles so that "uh" now becomes "ah" (which requires more muscle control) and other vowel sounds emerge. At this level, kids now sound like they're "talking."

Level 6—Consonant sound development. Like vowels, consonants are the by-product of differences in mouth shape; however, the hard "edge" of many consonants requires additional supports and exercise of the mouth muscles to develop. (See Temple Grandin's comments about this in the foreword.)

Levels 1-6 are strengthened with fun activities that elicit giggles and squeals of delight. These levels are not about purposeful communication, but giving children lots of opportunity to exercise their voice through appropriate physical supports: taking big breaths, involuntarily laughing, and making a variety of sounds. Once children are confident and know they "have a voice," teaching can move into the early stages of speech:

Level 7—Sequencing sounds. Using sounds, repeating sounds in a specific order.

Level 8—Purposeful speaking.

Beyond single words

Shelley speaks in one-word sentences such as "Cup." To help Shelley move beyond these single word utterances, model the full sentence, "I want the cup," and have the child echo it back to you.

Activity: Choose a photo to talk about. It can be one of yours, or one from a book or magazine. Have the child describe something in the picture. Take turns adding more and more detail. The conversation might build something like this:

Boy.
Boy with a ball.
The boy's ball is black and white.
The boy is playing soccer with the black and white ball.
The boy is going to kick the soccer ball.
The boy kicking the ball is wearing a green shirt.

The green shirt is because his team is called the Dragons.
He is number 3 on the Dragons.
The Dragons are playing outside.
It is a sunny day.
His face is happy.

Start a card file of pictures and photos from which to choose. Return to each photo more than once to build on previous conversations. And be patient. The process of going from the original one-word description to a full paragraph may be months or even years.

Don't sweat temporary lapses

A child's language development is not a straight line. Illness or injury, embarrassing situations, and emotionally driven clashes can all affect a child's ability to express himself. Despite your most careful planning and management, you will not be able to shield your child from all such experiences, nor should you. Do not overreact to temporary lapses in language. Move on with a positive attitude.

Visual strategies

Most children with autism or Asperger's are visual learners, that is, they more easily understand what they see than what they hear. However, the majority of our educational and social interactions take place through verbal communication, resulting in numerous daily opportunities for communication breakdowns to occur.

Supplementing verbal communication with visual tools can help. Linda Hodgdon, visual strategy expert within the autism field, defines a visual tool as anything the student can see. Visual schedules, choice boards, communication strips, classroom rules, step-by-step written directions, even body movements, can all make a significant difference in a student's ability to participate successfully at school or at home. Visual tools assist students in processing language, organizing their thinking and remembering information. They can help students learn appropriate social interaction and positive behaviors.

Visual schedules and calendars are the most common visual tools used for children with autism or Asperger's. They range from simple to complex and can be used within all environments (e.g., classroom/gym/music room, in occupational therapy or speech therapy, at home or church, etc.). The benefits of using visual schedules are many:

- Visual schedules clarify that activities happen within a specific time period and help children understand the concept of sequencing.

- They alert the student to any changes in the daily routine.

- Visual schedules are effective in helping a student transition independently between activities and environments by showing where he is to go next.

- They lessen the anxiety level of children with autism, and thus reduce the possible occurrence of challenging behaviors, by providing the structure for the student to organize and predict daily and weekly events.

- Visual supports can also increase a student's motivation to complete less desired activities by strategically alternating more preferred with less-preferred activities on the student's individual visual schedule.

- Social interactions can be incorporated into a daily schedule: showing completed work to a teacher, saying hello and goodbye, asking a peer to play, etc.

- For non-verbal students, a visual schedule can be a way to introduce symbols that the student can eventually use as an alternate form of communication. Through the consistent use of the schedule, the student can begin to pair the symbols presented with the activities that are occurring.

How to create a visual schedule

1. Decide who will use the schedule: several people (i.e., a general schedule) or a single child?

2. Divide the day or the activity into segments and name each segment.

3. Choose the visual system you will use, based on the child's level of representation (object, photo, drawing, word).

4. Think about how and when the schedule will be used, and select an appropriate format. An individual schedule for a single child might be desk sized or even smaller, to fit into his notebook and carry with him. A schedule for many students will be larger and posted on a wall.

5. Select appropriate visuals that pertain to the activity or the day and create the schedule.

A minimum of two scheduled items should be presented at a time. This helps the student understand that events and activities happen in a sequential manner, not in isolation.

6. Walk through the schedule before introducing it to the child to make sure it is clear, sequential, and that no parts are missing.

7. Teach the student how to use the schedule. Confirm that she understands each visual representation used.

8. Refer to the schedule often for information about what is happening, what is changing, and anything else he needs to know.

Before using that visual schedule

Using visual schedules for a child with autism can alleviate stress in even a more advanced-functioning child. (Think of the comfort level your Daytimer, PDA, or activity calendar brings you.) However, an effective visual schedule is more than just pictures placed in a sequence.

● Have your speech language pathologist or autism specialist determine your child's level of representation. What is meaningful—photos, drawings, words? A child may need little toys or objects attached to the schedule if his level of processing is at this stage.

● Then, have an occupational therapist assist in determining how your child best tracks the visual. Is it top to bottom, or left to right?

- How many items should appear on the schedule? Three may be the maximum for some children; others may be able to handle six or more.

- What type of visuals might be included? Safety pictures (danger, stop, hot), emotions (happy, sad, tired, angry), food (favorites and staples), daily routines (mealtime, bedtime, bath time), favorite characters (SpongeBob, Thomas, Dora)?

- Account for visual or physical impairments that may impede use of the schedule.

- Is the schedule portable? Can it travel along with the child to daycare? Can it go in the car or along on vacation, or to the holiday celebration at Aunt Jennifer's house?

When do we use a visual schedule?

Often! Visual schedules can be used as part of an individual activity or lesson to provide additional help with sequencing, or to supply predictability. Whole day schedules give the child a picture reference of what will happen throughout the day. It can include information about when work or play starts and ends, alert the child to changes in routine, and it can serve as a visual representation of work accomplished. Weekly and monthly schedules can help with planning and organization, and are useful at home as well as school. Use a whole year schedule to teach seasons, mark holidays, and show the start/end of long-term events, like attending school, or moving to a new home.

Visual crutches?

Your student with autism is using a visual schedule to manage his day at school and you've seen his self-esteem and independence skyrocket. Things are going so well, in fact, that you think the schedule may no longer be needed.

Visual schedules are not temporary aids to be faded out. View them instead as management tools that help students stay organized, calm, and functioning efficiently. If the child's representation skills change, so should the format of the schedule, from photos, to drawings, to words. But for the student with autism, the consistent use of a visual schedule is an important lifeline, one of the keys to increasing independent functioning throughout his life—at school, home and in the community.

Fit the language support to the child's learning style

Visual language supports help children with autism be successful in school, but before adding that Velcro communication strip to his desk, think about his learning style. Does he do most of his work at his desk? If so, securing the visual tool there is perfect. But what if she's a student who moves often, does work in places other than her desk? She needs the support to travel with her—perhaps request cards laminated and attached to a metal ring, or a support posted in more than one area of the room.

Tips for using your visual schedule

Oh, unhappy day: despite your careful attention in creating a visual schedule for your child or student, it just doesn't work. Time to check again for comprehension: does the child understand each of the components used? Has she been taught (and does she understand) how to reference and use the schedule? It's not enough to show her the schedule; you must teach her how to use it.

- Put a red stop sign at the end of the activity card. Knowing when to start and stop is often difficult for kids with autism or Asperger's.
- A clock face next to each picture or schedule item can be a reminder of an upcoming activity, providing some children with advance warning of a transition so they can internally prepare, or it can be an opportunity to match the clock picture to the real time.
- Combine words with pictures for the child with emerging language skills. In times of frustration, retrieving a word or its meaning may be difficult. If you switch to words only and the child's skill level starts to backslide, return to pictures and try again later, after more training.

- Just as we get a warning that the traffic light is going to turn red, we can insert a caution sign into the activity card on the schedule and follow it up with a verbal cue.

- Add a "finish" ritual to your schedule. Once the activity time is over place the visual symbol of that activity into a "finished" box or container on the schedule.

- It's the end of the school day; what comes next? Indicate things like getting on the bus and going home, attending an after school activity, or waiting for mom or dad. If the child gets anxious about the next school day, create an end-of-day ritual. Sit down one-on-one with the child and place the pictures for the next day's routine on the schedule.

Expressive or receptive?

While a visual schedule is a receptive communication tool that helps the student comprehend messages coming from others, choice boards, by their definition, require an expressive response.

A choice board is a visual two- or three-dimensional representation of choice possibilities using photos, text, or tangible objects. Choice boards are effective because they give the child an extended opportunity to reply. Under normal circumstances, a verbal choice, "Do you want juice or milk?" is over in a couple of seconds. Supplementing the verbal message with a graphic representation gives the child additional information with which to process the message and be successful in responding.

Give your child whatever extra time she needs to answer. Listening, comprehending, and then speaking, is a complicated communication process and does not always happen within nanoseconds, as it may for typical kids. Don't rush in to repeat the question or comment, or finish her sentences for her.

> ### QUICK IDEA
>
> Homemade picture cards are easy to make. Cut out pictures from magazines, catalogs and weekly grocery ads. Glue to index cards, then print the name of the object below the picture. Laminate if desired. Make portable sets by punching holes in one corner and stringing sets together by topic.

If you're relatively certain she knows the word but can't retrieve it, you can feed in the language by offering a choice: "Were you saying that you wanted the turkey sandwich or the peanut butter sandwich?"

Assistive technology (AT) is more than a keyboard

It is a service available within the Individuals with Disabilities Education Act (IDEA) that helps students achieve goals and outcomes that might previously not have been attainable because of their limited language/communication abilities. Giving a student access to an AT item, such as a communication board, a computer, or a DynaVox is a tool, not an educational goal in itself. Tools enable the larger task, which is the development and implementation of a relevant and meaningful support strategy that covers all facets of the child's life.

What type of strategy and technology might be helpful to a particular student? According to *ClosingTheGap.com*, a useful website on various AT issues, professionals evaluating a child and a particular activity for AT might ask themselves the following questions:

- What are classmates expected to do in this activity?
- What is the student with autism expected to do?
- What are the learning goals for this activity?
- How can this particular student best access the information, i.e., what's his learning style?
- How can we check that learning has actually taken place?
- What are the student's strengths and how can we use these strengths in this activity?

If you think AT would benefit your child or student, ask school administrators for an Assistive Technology evaluation to determine the supports and systems that could best help him succeed within the educational environment.

Environment impacts speech development ·······················

We learn much of our speech imitatively, and a child not frequently exposed to other speaking people will develop speech more slowly. Self-contained special education classrooms may limit opportunities for typical-peer language modeling. Parents and language professionals should actively seek settings where a child will be exposed to typically-developing kid talk. Write peer-appropriate conversation goals into the child's IEP. As children age, this should also include the slang being used. "Nicole will learn to use peer-appropriate slang during informal conversations with her fellow students during lunch and breaks." Siblings are another source of typically-developing kid talk. They can also identify for the child with autism the words and phrases that are currently "in" and those that are "out."

Maintaining a language-rich environment ·······················

One of the best ways parents and teachers can nurture speech and conversation development day to day is to keep meaningful, understandable language flowing. Here are a few simple ways to do that.

- Send your child's teacher or speech language pathologist a note each Monday listing three things your child did over the weekend. Ask that they engage the child in conversation about these things.

- Answer your child every time he speaks to you, letting him know you value everything he has to say. Look at him when you speak to him. Do this for the nonverbal child as well. A paraeducator's story: "I worked with a child who made non-word sounds over and over. Shushing cues didn't work. So I tried repeating his sounds. He looked at me and stopped. I asked specialists if they thought this was making fun of his sounds, and they quickly assured me that it wasn't. He most likely thought I was listening to him and acknowledging that I had heard him. I hope so. It often helped."

- For the child who asks a continuous stream of questions, parroting the question back to him may break the cycle, especially if he already knows the answer. Child: "Are we going to PE?" Adult: "Aaron, are we going to PE?" Child: "Yes!"

- Or break the stream of questions with a visual: Draw three simple squares/boxes on a piece of paper. Tell the child, "You get to ask me that question three times." When she asks, "Are we reading Charlotte's Web today?" respond with, "Yes. Now that's once you have asked," and show her you are crossing off one square. When you get to three, tell her, "Okay, that is three times and now we are not going to talk about it again." Then change the subject.

- Singing is speech. If your child learns songs easily, use that strength to enhance his language skills. Talk about any new words in the song he may not understand. Distinguish nonsense words from real words.

- Don't correct grammar or pronunciation. Just model the correct way. Child: "He didn't wented to the store." Adult: "That's right, he didn't go to the store."

The two-minute rule for conversations

Being put on the spot to generate conversation can be very stressful for your child. Practice a two-minute/two-minute rule. Tell him you'd like to talk about his day at school or a subject of his choosing. Give him two minutes to gather his thoughts, then converse for two minutes. Observing manageable parameters removes the performance-anxiety factor.

And instead of asking the same question every day—what did you do at school?—try asking *how* his day went. This gives him a chance to explore his feelings, not just his actions, and gives you a wider window on his experiences of the day.

The two-second pause for responses

Many families converse at a rapid-fire pace that leaves the child with autism unable to keep up. To slow the overall pace of exchanges and give your child a better chance to participate, observe this rule: wait two seconds before responding.

Snack time: It's not just about the food

Preschool snack period can be a great time to teach communication skills. Kids are generally motivated to make their wishes known during this part of the school day. Two skills to teach are getting a peer's attention and requesting an item. Each day, assign a child the job of juice helper. Teach students to get the juice helper's attention by doing three things:

- Tap your friend on the shoulder
- Look her in the eye
- Say her name
- Ask. "Katie, I want juice please."

Model the steps yourself, and surreptitiously coach peers to ignore improper requests. Then prompt, "Katie didn't hear you. Tap her on the shoulder." Many children with autism will not respond unless you add this gentle physical prompt.

Generalize this skill to the dinner table at home by manipulating the meal to where everyone needs something. Maybe it's cheese for the pasta, butter for the bread, or something to drink. One teacher cheerfully calls this "sabotaging the environment to create teachable moments out of everyday, functional activities."

Note: using food as a teaching tool won't be motivating to the child unless it's something he likes. If he hates raisins, he won't use his language to ask for them.

Time to say goodbye

Saying goodbye puts an end bracket on a conversation. In our culture, merely walking away at the end of a sentence is considered rude or awkward. Teaching your child how to say goodbye doesn't have to mean using those exact words. Goodbye can be "See you later," "Hasta la vista!" or "It was nice talking to you." For the not-yet verbal child, it can be a wave, a nod, a smile. Brainstorm with your child the different ways of saying goodbye and then practice often.

Wordless books

Narrative, non-fiction, or conceptual in nature, wordless books are remarkable tools for introducing or stimulating book enjoyment, for building both oral and written language, and for developing vocabulary and critical thinking. Wordless books allow children to create stories as they go along, and because there are no words, their interpretations are the right ones. They control the story—a boon for developing self-esteem alongside other skills. And there can be more than one right way to tell the story, if they choose. To get started:

- Preview a book before you share it with your child, to confirm that the content is appropriate for his age level, life experience, attention span, and interests.

- For younger children, familiar themes are best, such as cars or pets. As the child grows older, you can introduce less familiar themes such as science topics and foreign cultures.

- Use the age recommendations on these books only as the loosest of guides. They are a gauge for typically-developing children and may or may not have any relevance to your child.

Suggested reading:

The Patchwork Farmer by Craig McFarland Brown.................................All ages

The Mystery of the Giant Footprints
   by Fernando Krahn.................................Ages baby-preschool

Beach Day by Helen Oxenbury.................................Ages 18 mos.-3 years

Tabby: A Story in Pictures by Aliki.................................Ages 2-5

Do You Want To Be My Friend? by Eric Carle.................................Ages 2-5

I Can't Sleep by Philippe Dupasquier.................................Ages 2-5

Moonlight by Jan Ormerod.................................Ages 2-5

Mouse Numbers by Jim Arnosky.................................Ages 3-6

Amanda's Butterfly by Nick Butterworth.................................Ages 3 and up

Truck by Donald Crews ....Ages 3-6

Pancakes for Breakfast by Tomie DePaola ....Ages 3-6

A Boy, a Dog and a Frog by Mercer Mayer........................Ages 3-6

Picnic by Emily Arnold McCully...Ages 3-6

Look! Look! Look! by Tana Hoban.......................................Ages 3-7

10 Minutes till Bedtime by Peggy Rathman ....Ages 3-6

Dinosaur! by Peter Sis ....Ages 3-6

You Can't Take a Balloon Into the Metropolitan Museum
    by Jacqueline Preiss Weitzman ....Ages 3-8

The Bear and the Fly by Paula Winter...............................Ages 3-6

The Bear by Raymond Briggs ....Ages 4-8

Building by Elisha Cooper ....Ages 4-8

Good Dog, Carl by Alexandra Day ....Ages 4-8

Shrewbettina's Birthday by John Goodall.........................Ages 4-8

Good Night, Garden Gnome by Jamichael Henterly .....Ages 4-8

Changes, Changes by Pat Hutchins ....Ages 4-8

Rain by Peter Spier ....Ages 4-8

Look-Alikes by Joan Steiner ....Ages 4-8

Time Flies by Eric Rohmann..Ages 4-9

Flotsam by David Wiesner..Ages 5-8

Anno's Journey by Mitsumasa Anno....................................Ages 5-9

Free Fall by David Wiesner..Ages 5-9

The Crocodile Blues by Coleman Polhemus.....................Ages 5-12

Magpie Magic: A Tale of Colorful Mischief
    by April Wilson..Ages 6-10

Why? by Nikolai Popov...Ages 7-9

The Arrival by Shaun Tan..Ages 8 and up

Our House on the Hill by Philippe Dupasquier ....Ages 8-10

The Red Book by Barbara Lehman..Ages 8-10

A Day, a Dog by Gabrielle Vincent ....Ages 8-14

Ocean Whisper by Dennis Rockhill ....All ages

The Yellow Balloon by Charlotte Dematons...All ages

Zoom by Istvan Banyai...All ages

The following authors have published multiple books in the wordless or nearly-wordless format:

Mitsumama Anno
Peter Collington
Alexandra Day
John Goodall
Tana Hoban
Mercer Mayer
Emily McCully
Peter Spier

Eight ways to enjoy wordless books with your child:

1. Look at the cover of the book and make a prediction as to what the book will be about. Look at each page and ask the child questions about how the pictures in the book relate to him.

2. Ask "wh" questions—who, what, when, where, why. Phrase the questions beginning with "I wonder." I wonder why he is scared? I wonder what is going to happen after she opens the door? I wonder what he is saying to her?

3. Have your child make up a story to go with the pictures (use answers to the "I wonder" questions as a basis), then write the story down to read back later. Older children can write the story themselves, with greater attention to detail.

4. Have your child make up names for the characters.

5. If the book is a narrative story, introduce sequencing: What happened first? What happened next? What happened last? Talk about how the story has a beginning, middle, and end.

6. Explore feelings and emotions. Ask your child how he thinks the characters are feeling by looking at their faces and body language. Build a vocabulary of emotions: happy, sad, anxious, scared, proud, disgusted, angry, shy, disappointed, excited, confused, etc. Keep the list age-appropriate.

7. Most of these authors have released multiple books; if your child enjoys one, explore them all.

8. Check your library or bookstore for video versions of some of these books, and other wordless stories. Here are a few:

   The Red Balloon
   The Remarkable Runaway Tricycle
   A Boy, A Dog and a Frog / *Frog Goes to Dinner* / *Frog on His Own*
   Raymond Briggs' *The Bear*

> ### QUICK IDEA
> A child who shows no interest in typical children's books may be interested in reading or listening to his own material. Have him write out his stories or narratives, or dictate them to you. Read them back together.

Jump-start literacy for concrete thinkers

You may have discovered that perennial childhood favorites like Peter Rabbit or Winnie the Pooh get no response from your young one. Stories that revolve around animals who not only talk, but wear clothes, drive cars, and keep house can be incomprehensible and disturbing for some literal-minded children with autism. When typical children's literature doesn't make sense, another approach is required. Your child may enjoy books more if they have these characteristics:

- Books with photographs, not drawn illustrations
- Books about real-life things that a child can correlate with his own life, such as construction equipment, babies, ice cream, farms, the zoo, or parks
- Books about people (especially children)
- Books about the child himself. Window books have a cutout in each page. Tape your child's photo to the back page of the book and his/her face appears on every page. *Hey, Look at Me!* from Merrybooks is one

such series. Or create your own book, using family photos as illustrations. Write about a past event ("My 5th Birthday Party") or a familiar routine ("Thanksgiving at My Grandma's House").

Scout the library's nonfiction section for fact-based books with strong photographs about things that are interesting to the child. There are literally thousands of photo-essay books for kids. Here are just a few:

- Scholastic's Let's Find Out series: big, bright photographs of kids learning about things like bicycles, toothpaste, and money.

- Dorling-Kindersley Books (DK) offers literally thousands of nonfiction titles. *Jobs People Do* features children in grown-up attire as doctors, fishermen, photographers, chefs, etc. A related series: A Day in the Life of … a Dancer, Police Officer, Lifeguard, etc.

- Baby animals may intrigue. DK's series See How They Grow acquaints kids with *Puppy*, *Kitten*, *Foal*, *Duck*, *Lamb*, *Chick*, and many more. Compass Point Books' Animals and Their Young series has titles like *Bears Have Cubs*, *Pigs Have Piglets*, *Cows Have Calves*.

- Tana Hoban's dozens of photo-illustrated books introduce children to many concepts around them, such as *Colors Everywhere, Is It Rough? Is It Smooth?*, and *Shadows and Reflections*.

- *From Wheat to Pasta, From Plant to Blue Jeans*, and *From Wax to Crayon* are representative of photo-essay titles from the Changes series published by New York Children's Press.

- Our Neighborhood is a people-based series including *The Zieglers and their Apple Orchard, Exploring Parks with Ranger Dockett, Learning about Bees with Mr. Krebs.*

- Mr. Rogers books cover many potentially difficult situations, from "first experiences" (*The New Baby, Going to the Doctor, Making Friends*) to tough transitions (*Moving, When a Pet Dies, Divorce*).

- For the 3rd to 5th grade child, The Grandmothers at Work series is irresistible. *Meet My Grandmother: She's a United States Senator* as told by Dianne Feinstein's six-year-old granddaughter: "When a bill Gagi has written gets passed … Gagi goes to a meeting with the President." Equally charming is *Meet My Grandmother: She's a Supreme Court Justice* as told by Sandra Day O'Connor's granddaughter.

Once your child makes the connection to books, keep the momentum going:

- When you find a book that works for your child, exhaust the series, the author, the genre.

- If a favorite among the library books emerges—buy it. Nothing is more discouraging to a budding reader than to discover his beloved new "friend" has been returned.

- Don't waste energy bemoaning that young Peyton doesn't like *Frog and Toad* even though you did. With time and acclimation, that may change. It's a short leap from reading about construction equipment to reading *Mike Mulligan and His Steam Shovel.*

Repetitive-language stories

Children with autism love predictability. Stories with oft-repeated lines can give children a sense of competency, whether they are actually reading, or just reciting the story from memory.

Especially good are stories whose recurring words are language the child can apply to real life. Example: "Not by the hair on my chinny chin chin!" repeats throughout the Three Little Pigs story, but is not likely to come up in everyday conversation. By contrast, Pat Hutchins' *The Doorbell Rang* uses phraseology and a situation common enough for even small children to relate to in real life.

QUICK IDEA

Ask your speech language pathologist for a set of activities related to your child's IEP goals that you can do at home.

Here are some ideas for using repetitive language books.

- After the first couple of readings, tell your child you will be taking turns reading the story. You begin, and when you get to the repetitive phrase, stop and indicate that it is her turn to finish the sentence or fill in the blank. Use a visual or tactile prompt if necessary, such as pointing to her or patting her hand.

- Your child may memorize entire books and "read" them back to you. Applaud this as you would real reading. It is a key piece of literacy skill development.

- Choose books whose repeated language is relatively simple, at least at first. Cumulative repeated language stories such as *The Old Woman Who Swallowed a Fly* may be too fanciful, frightening, or confusing.

Suggested reading:

Who Sank the Boat? by Pamela Allen
Do You Know What I'll Do? by Charlotte Zolotow
King Bidgood's in the Bathtub by Audrey and Don Wood
The Doorbell Rang by Pat Hutchins (and other titles by this author)
Something from Nothing by Phoebe Gilman
A Dark, Dark Tale by Ruth Brown
The Important Book by Margaret Wise Brown
It Looked Like Spilt Milk by Charles G. Shaw

Make reading fun

Despite the ability to read, many children with autism struggle with decoding, interpreting characters' emotions, and comprehending the theme or message. When reading is work, it takes the fun out of the experience. Michelle McConnell, homeschooling mom of four kids, offers these suggestions to bring them to the joy of reading from a fresh angle.

- You be the narrator. Choose books with a lot of character dialogue, with mom reading as the narrator, and the child reading anytime someone is speaking. The Boxcar Children series fits this method wonderfully.

- Audio books. Series are great here, because familiarity with the characters maintains interest. Listening to a story first may progress to your child choosing to read those same books on her own, in time. The Magic Tree House series is a good starting choice.

- Book clubs. Select clubs with smaller numbers of kids, matched to the child's social and reading level, not his or her age. Look for clubs that are reading funny stories or will be reading books of high interest to your child. Check with your local public library for clubs in your area.

Raise a reader: What parents can do at home

Many, many teachers tell us that reading to your child at home is the single most important element in developing literacy. One teacher even told us that it is more important than anything they do at school. If you aren't currently reading to your child on a regular basis, start now.

- If reading every day seems overwhelming, start with two days a week and work up from there.

- It's common for children with autism to have as much as four grade levels discrepancy between their decoding skills (ability to read single words in isolation) and their comprehension skills (ascertaining meaning). Decoding is an essential element of reading, but decoding without comprehension is merely a recitation of syllables. When reading to your child at home, emphasize content and comprehension more than error-free recital of words. Correcting every little error discourages enjoyment in reading by turning it into work. So:

- Overlook errors. Teachers say, let us deal with that at school.

- If you must correct, do it in a way that doesn't sound like criticism. Just repeat the word the correct way in a positive tone of voice as if you didn't even notice it was wrong, and move along quickly.

- Probe for comprehension by asking questions. "How do you think the Little Engine feels? Have you ever felt like that?" But keep interruptions infrequent so the child doesn't lose the story line.

- If your child's teacher requires twenty or thirty minutes of home reading each night, remember that it doesn't have to be all at once. Two ten-minute sessions or several five-minute sessions may be infinitely more manageable. The cumulative effort is no less valuable than at a sustained sitting.

- Reading doesn't have to be in a chair or a bed. If you like reading in the bathtub, your child might, too.

Say what you mean, mean what you say

To become an effective communicator with kids with autism or Asperger's, keep in mind two basic tenets about their thinking style and architecture: 1) they think in literal, concrete ways, and 2) they tend to think specific to general, rather than general to specific. Help them better understand the world around them by becoming cognizant of the ambiguities that regularly fill our conversations. Sloppy talk is confusing for a child who is analyzing your every word to get the full meaning of your conversation. Speak plainly, speak in concrete terms, speak in complete thoughts, and speak in the positive.

SAY:	RATHER THAN:
This is a picture of a dog.	This is a dog.
Put the flowers in the vase.	Put these in there.
It's a red sweater.	It's red.
After you finish your math, you can go to recess.	If you don't finish your math, you can't go to recess.
Please walk to the classroom.	No running in the halls.
Put your hands in your pockets.	Keep your hands to yourself (a figure of speech. He's thinking: where else would they be?)
We are going home now.	Let's get going.

You loved the movie—now read the book

A lot of wonderful classic literature may be beyond the reading comprehension level of your child. But if a movie version exists, it can serve as a wonderful introduction to the story and may even motivate your child to want to read the book or have you read with him. Go beyond Harry Potter and discover *20,000 Leagues Under the Sea, Treasure Island, In Search of the Castaways, Heidi, Tom Sawyer, The Secret Garden, Anne of Green Gables, The Wizard of Oz, Moby Dick, The Jungle Book, Black Beauty.*

Beware of idioms

An idiom is a phrase made up of words not used in their literal sense. "That's the way the cookie crumbles" means "that's the way it happens." Daily English language is littered with thousands of idioms, many of which you may not even be aware you are using. To a child with autism, with his concrete, literal way of thinking, these idioms are incomprehensible. The visual picture he creates upon hearing "It broke my heart" or "You're playing with fire" may be quite disturbing.

Idioms fill entire books, but here are some more common ones to help you become aware of how prolific they are in conversation:

- Animal idioms: a little bird told me, you're in the doghouse, cat got your tongue?, the early bird catches the worm, buzz off, running around like a chicken with its head cut off, a bird in the hand is worth two in the bush.

- Body idioms: costs an arm and a leg, it made my blood boil, so hungry I could eat a horse, you're pulling my leg, break a leg, eyes were popping out of his head, keep your eye out, shake a leg, go hand in hand, I've got your back, shooting himself in the foot, put my foot in my mouth, butt out, egg all over your face, go belly up, have a frog in the throat, give the cold shoulder, hate his guts, make no bones about it.

- Clothing idioms: at the drop of a hat, off the cuff, birthday suit, below the belt, putting yourself in another person's shoes, zip it, wear the pants in the family, caught with pants down, hats off, dressed to kill, ride the coattails.

- Color idioms: feeling blue, green with envy, looks black-and-white to me, tickled pink, seeing red, green thumb.

- Heart idioms: big heart, broken heart, by heart, lose my heart, from the bottom of my heart, with all my heart, wears her heart on her sleeve.

- Initials: ASAP, PDQ, IOU, FYI, TTFN.

- Medical idioms: dose of his own medicine, go under the knife, running a temperature, take a turn for the worse, be under the weather.

- Money idioms: burn a hole in one's pocket, chicken feed, cheapskate, deadbeat, dime a dozen, feel like a million bucks, put in your two cents' worth, day late and a dollar short, turn on a dime, not worth a plugged nickel.

- Number idioms: looking after #1, two heads are better than one, six feet under, dressed to the nines.

- Situational idioms: behind the eight ball, blend into the woodwork, connect the dots, get on board, go with the flow, you're in hot water, making a mountain out of a molehill, on the fly, slam on the brakes, two-way street.

Idioms are frequently the last language element new or struggling language learners understand, yet they are commonly used in conversation. Learning devices are available to help acclimate your child or student to idioms, but in the meantime, strive to minimize them in your conversations.

Go fish for idioms

A creative way to teach idioms (age 9 or so and up) is to make your own version of the "Go Fish" game.

Materials Needed: index cards, marker, list of idioms and meanings

1. Write idioms on one index card and the matching meaning on a second card

2. Make an answer key to be used during the game

3. Laminate the pieces for durability

4. Store pieces in a manila envelope. Write the instructions for the game on the outside.

Some suggested idioms to use in the Go Fish game (you can find thousands more on internet sites and in books):

- Kick the bucket—die
- On cloud nine—extremely happy
- Know the ropes—understand what to do
- A wolf in sheep's clothing—a mean person who is pretending to be nice
- Stick out one's neck—do something risky
- Through thick and thin—always a friend even if things get bad
- Look a gift horse in the mouth—be ungrateful in response to a kind action
- Out of the frying pan and into the fire—going from a bad situation to something even worse
- A piece of cake—doing something that is very easy
- A chip off the old block —acting or looking like one's parent
- Let the cat out of the bag—tell a secret
- Eager beaver—a person who is anxious or excited about doing something
- Jump the gun—starting something before you are supposed to
- Pull the wool over one's eyes—trick someone
- Mind one's Ps and Qs—being sure to behave properly
- One-horse town—very small town
- Being chicken—afraid to do something
- A green thumb—able to make plants grow and look beautiful
- To split hairs—being extra picky about what is done or said
- Go out on a limb—doing or saying something that could end in trouble

Game instructions

This can be played one-on-one or with multiple players.

1. Deal five cards to each player.

2. The person to the right of the dealer goes first.

3. Each player asks someone else for a card to match either the idiom or the meaning.

4. A player must surrender the matching card if he or she has it.

5. If there is no match, a card is drawn from the deck and play moves to the next person.

6. Pairs of cards are laid on the table when there is a match.

7. At the conclusion of the game, the answer key is used to check for correct matches.

Phrasal verbs

Like idioms, phrasal verbs can evoke disturbing or confusing associations for the child with autism. Instead of "I wish you hadn't brought that up," say, "I don't want to talk about that right now." Instead of "I said he could go but I had to take it back," say "I said he could go but then I had to tell him no." "Pass it off" means pretend or fake, "put it off" means stall or procrastinate. "Nod off" means fall asleep, "fall through" means not happen. Remember: keep conversation simple and concrete.

Homophones

Words that sound the same but have different meanings (pale and pail, bear and bare, allowed and aloud) can be utterly confusing and frustrating to your child. Patient repetition over time may be the only solution. You can offer a book like *The King Who Rained* by Fred Gwynne, wherein a girl imagines such incongruous sights as "a king who rained for forty years," "the foot prince in the snow," "bear feet," and "fairy tails." If the child appears disconcerted by it, put it away for a while. Many typical children aren't ready for homophones until age nine or so.

Flash cards: Pros and cons

Because many children on the autism spectrum are visual learners, it might seem to make sense that using flash cards to teach and increase vocabulary would be an effective strategy. But while flash cards are useful for labeling, being able to articulate a word doesn't equate to knowing what it means and using it in an appropriate context. The production of speech is a motor process. Understanding what a word means involves semantics, and the appropriate use of the word involves context-driven social pragmatics. Flash cards don't cover this. Next time you reach for that flash card, think about what you want to teach and try an alternate strategy, or augment the flash card routine with the additional teaching that promotes comprehension, not just rote repetition.

> **QUICK IDEA**
>
> When language therapy is listless, get away from "the table." Go explore the attic, see what's hidden away in an overstuffed closet or go for a walk through the neighborhood! Any change of scenery can re-energize the motivation to communicate.

Not just for tiggers: Trampoline fun

Speech language therapists, occupational therapists and many parents recognize the benefits of a trampoline in helping our children regulate their sensory input, decompress when needed, and even stimulate voice development and language. There's so much more to do on that bounding mat than just jumping. Check out our suggestions, then go on to create your own fun and educational variations:

- Draw letters and/or shapes on a trampoline with regular sidewalk chalk. Jump from letter to letter to spell out a word.

- Jump from one shape to another in a preplanned order, or spontaneously as the therapist or child shouts it out.

- Print words on the trampoline. Jump from word to word to create a phrase or a sentence.

- Practice patterning and sequencing with a simple game of Follow the Leader.

Profanity

Children with limited means of verbally expressing themselves may be quite intrigued by the reaction they get when using cuss words or toilet talk. Many of these words have become endemic in the media culture; kids are exposed to them constantly through television, movies and internet outlets, and many toss them around casually without any inkling of their meaning or the severity of their inappropriateness in social conversation. If your child is imitative or echolalic, there's a good chance he has no concept of the meaning of the words themselves. Here are some common sense ways to deal with the situation.

- Intercede at first incident. Calmly state, "We do not use that word in our family" and explore what might have provoked its use.

- If it came from anger or frustration, give your child a slate of suitable alternative expressions. Especially with younger children, humor may work wonders in this area. Some families come up with their own personal expletives: "Oh, crudmuffins!" or "Oh, shitake mushrooms!" or "Oh, pluck a duck." Ellen's four-year-old son astonished more than a few adults in his day by bellowing "Abomination!" when frustrated. Older children can invent their own personal word.

- A visual behavior chart may help in getting the problem under control, illustrating the child's progress in decreasing the cussing.

- Older children will be unmoved by explanations of social etiquette. But they may respond when the reasoning affects them directly. Cussing in front of his friends' parents may cause them to limit their child's time with him. Using profanity in conversation with customers can cost him a job. Swearing during sports activities affects how Coach sees him.

- Set the tone by monitoring your own language. Avoid using expletives as shorthand for expressing difficult emotions, even though one word in *that* tone of voice and everyone understands what you mean. But in frequent usage, it's no substitute for talking to your child in language that helps him understand how to convey his thoughts and emotions. Many families have had success with a Cussing Cup or jar. Each offense requires a 25¢ donation. When the jar is full, the family decides upon a deserving charity. The fine is intended to create awareness, with the intent that it translates into behavior change.

- To use the cussing cup with a child, give him ten dimes (or twenty pennies or something else he likes) at the beginning of each week. Each potty word requires a donation to the cup. He gets to keep whatever is left over at the end of the week

- Decide whether you will take a zero tolerance approach or if you will allow some words in some contexts, such as, never at school, church or friends' homes, but occasionally in the privacy of your own home.

- Be clear with your child which words are off-limits. Beyond George Carlin's infamous "seven words you can never say on TV" are the borderline cuss words like ass, crap, and piss. Will you allow some words while banning others?

Almost as easy as 1-2-3 ·

For the child with autism or Asperger's, learning to write requires mastery of fine motor skills that you may take for granted. Executing a mature pencil grip and applying the proper amount of pressure from pencil to paper are tasks that do not come naturally or easily to many autism-challenged young people. Arduous though it may be for them, there is yet another element equally essential: motivation.

Pushing themselves to conquer the difficult task of writing may seem pointless if they cannot assign any relevance or significance to the abstract numerals, characters and shapes on a page you are asking them to reproduce. (Most of us resent being asked to perform complex rote tasks when we do not see any end value in it.) Children with autism have a pronounced need for relevance. So, first break down the mechanics of writing into understandable pieces. Then, give him a reason to write.

To help your child or student learn to write, use a three-step method:

- You write, for instance, his name (or other word or phrase interesting to him) lightly on lined paper and he traces over it.

- You write the name or phrase and he copies it on the line below or beside.

- He writes it independently.

Motivate him to write by having him trace, copy, or write you a note when he wants something special: "Can we go to the _____ today?" or "I would like _____ for my birthday" or "May I have _____ for dinner?"

Such notes may not cover the entire alphabet, but you may find him more willing to work on alphabet drills once he sees there is something in it for him.

Blueprint his work

You can help a child communicate her process (whether drawing, writing, or creating or accomplishing a physical goal) by documenting it through words and drawings by either you or the child. Eight-year-old Jamie had constructed a block ramp much like the other children were putting together, but with fewer blocks. Before he took it apart and put the blocks away, his paraeducator drew the way the blocks had been put together on a piece of paper, and had Jamie write about it. Jamie wrote: "The ramp is a tunnel ramp. The two trucks don't fit in the tunnel ramp." He tried to build it taller, but time ran out, and the activity ended for the day. The drawings were a blueprint for being able to come back to the activity another day and try again. A copy of the blueprint went home to Mom and Dad as an update on Jamie's school projects for the day.

Crossword fun

So easy to do! Visit *www.crosswordpuzzlegames.com/create.html* to create a crossword puzzle tailored to your child. You make up the words and the clues, so it will always be at his ability level. High interest is guaranteed when you use words that pertain to his interests, his family members, his experiences. Create a small book of puzzles as an extra-special gift for your child or student.

When out of reach is a good thing

The ability to ask for help, even recognizing that he needs help, is a huge issue for your child and an important life skill. Putting desired objects out of reach can be a clever way to elicit communication. (Always oversee carefully, to avoid safety issues and/or frustration.)

- Place a toy or book on a shelf so he has to ask for it, either with words, pictures, gestures, or whatever manner of communication you are developing.

- Put his favorite juice on a top shelf in the refrigerator, prompting him to ask in order to get it.

- Put a desired object in a jar and screw on the lid too tight. He will have to ask for help opening it. (Note: do not do this with rewards, as you are interrupting the action-response sequence with another step he must perform to get the reward.)

The talking stick

Talking in a group, even informally, can be an anxiety-laden activity for kids with autism or Asperger's. Knowing when to talk, what to say, and how to say it involves not just speech, but complex mental processing and a strong foundation of social thinking. Reduce some of that anxiety by using a brightly colored stick or other object, passed from child to child, as a visual indication of whose turn it is to speak.

I spy a conversation game

The popular old car game "I Spy" is perfect for practicing back and forth conversation and social thinking skills. One player starts by giving a clue, "I spy something that begins with the letter 'p'." Other children take turns trying to guess the item by asking yes or no questions. After each player guesses once, another clue is added. "I spy something that begins with the letter 'p' and is yellow." (Answer: pencil)

Language in motion

Outdoor therapy is a hit with most young children learning language and communication. Play equipment such as swings, slides, jungle gyms, and teeter totters are perfect for working on basic concepts such as in/out, under/over, up/down in both verbal and sign language. Physical movement gives kids the sensory feedback they need for speech to flow more easily.

- Practice repetitive language phrases, such as "1, 2, 3!" and "Ready, set, go!" while a child is swinging.
- Teach the child to say or sign "more please" to keep the activity going.
- Teach the child to say or sign "stop" or "all done" when she's had enough.
- Use outdoor props like bubble wands to teach contrasting concepts like big/little or temporal concepts like before/after.
- Do creative ball tossing activities to practice language, social referencing, and turn taking. Use large plastic beach balls, marked off in 4-6 sections. In each section, write words, phrases or sentences, draw pictures—whatever you want to teach. Toss the ball back and forth; wherever the child's finger or hand falls is the language to be repeated. Or practice eye contact—to know when to catch the ball or from whom.

At the movies

Watching movies at home is a fun and engaging way to observe and practice social communication. Watch old favorites with your child and have him look for:

- How characters greet each other: casually, formally, with a handshake, with a rude remark
- How characters start a conversation: greeting, interrupting, asking a question, asking for information, extending invitation to an activity

- How characters use gestures like nodding, winking, waving

- How characters use body language to convey feelings: cringing/fear, crying/ hurt, smiling/happy, hugging/love

- How characters use rejoinders and interjections during conversations to indicate interest, disinterest, agreement, disagreement ("Really!" "Who cares?" "You don't say!" "Whatever …")

- How characters use appropriate or inappropriate tone of voice or volume

- How characters use similes, metaphors, sarcasm, idioms (older child)

Dribble this kind of learning out casually. Or, occasionally make it into a game where you watch the movie and keep score to see how many instances you can identify. Just don't overdose on teaching; keep movies fun, not work.

Night and day

Temporal concepts (references to time) are difficult for many children with autism spectrum disorders. To help your child or student, relate temporal terms to familiar activities and verbalize them frequently. Morning is the time we eat breakfast. Nighttime is when it is dark outside and we get ready for bed. In the summer, it is hot and we don't go to school. In the winter, it's cold and we wear coats and mittens.

> **QUICK IDEA**
>
> Turn on the closed-captioning while your child is watching a DVD. It reinforces spelling, word recognition and comprehension.

Communication objectives for an IEP

Knowing what goals or objectives to include on an IEP is complex, especially if your school is less than cooperative or not fully knowledgeable about the IEP process. Virtually all children with autism spectrum disorders require some degree of adaptive communication. Don't be placated by assertions that the child's language skills are fine because his enunciation is clear. Diction is only one component of the complex science of language and communication. Here are thirty suggestions for short-term objectives in the area of speech communication for the child who already is verbal. Short-term means the goal is achievable within the course of one school year. Remember that each IEP goal must include measurable, quantifiable criteria as well as method(s) of evaluation and frequency. For example, using the first suggestion below:

Short-term objective: Child will answer when, how, why (because …) and whose (your, my, mine) questions.

Criteria: Four or five opportunities, with 90% accuracy

Evaluation method: Speech-language pathologist and teacher, by observation and probing for mastery of objectives

Schedule: Quarterly or end of each grading period or ongoing

1. Child will answer when, how, why (because …) and whose (your, my, mine) questions.
2. Child will answer comparative questions (heavier/lighter, slower/faster).
3. Child will describe a two-step or three-step procedure (First I … , then I …).
4. Child will arrange three pictures in sequence to tell a story about a person, an action and an object.
5. Child will accurately use spatial terms: under, over, behind, in front.
6. Child will accurately use temporal terms: first, last, yesterday, tomorrow.
7. Child will accurately use pronouns in conversation: I, they, he, she, his, her.
8. Child will describe attributes of objects: size (bigger, smaller, long, short, tiny, huge), texture (rough, smooth), color.
9. Child will describe functions of objects (I use this to …).
10. Child will describe parts of an item (It has a red handle and a round wheel.).

11. Child will comprehend four new vocabulary words for each new classroom theme (tides/crustacean/ocean/gills, veins/skeleton/organ/muscle).

12. Child will learn to protest appropriately ("Not now please.").

13. Child will follow instructions that require math vocabulary: more, fewer, less than.

As the child progresses in his abilities, IEP goals should acknowledge the deeper levels of communication (expressive and receptive) and introduce the social nature of language and communication (pragmatics). Depending on the initial level of perspective taking and the social thinking ability of the child, not all of these goals will be achievable within one year.

14. Child will stay on topic for (3, 4, 5) exchanges with a conversation partner.

15. Child will learn to make appropriate small talk in varied settings (formal, informal) and with varied groups of people (family, close friend, acquaintance, stranger).

16. Child will identify basic emotions (angry, frustrated, sad, excited) in self and others.

17. Child will verbally respond, in an appropriate manner, when recognizing the emotions of others.

18. Child will retell a story or answer questions about what he has read, to include character, setting, and main events in sequence.

19. Child will learn to give spontaneous compliments (see **With my compliments** in this chapter).

20. Child will give appropriate verbal feedback in conversation, including comments and rejoinder questions.

21. Child will ask for help, clarification, or repetition when he doesn't understand or remember what is said.

22. Child will describe how two events, objects, or people are alike and how they are different.

Tip Use subject matter relevant to the child to teach concepts. If Sam is a movie lover, ask him to compare how Shrek and Shrek 2 are alike and how they are different.

23. Child will describe why he does or doesn't like a story.

24. Child will learn to recognize the need for, and make, repairs to a conversation.

25. Child will learn to recognize and use nonverbal cues commonly used in communication.

26. Child will learn to use intonation and tone of voice that matches the communication environment.

27. Child will learn to feign interest in a conversation topic, as is needed to maintain communication with a partner or in a group.

28. Child will understand and accurately use ten homonyms (antonyms, synonyms) from his reading material.

29. Child will understand ten common idioms.

30. Child will use irregular past tense verbs accurately (ate instead of eated, drew instead of drawed, rode instead of rided).

Reduce your student's performance anxiety

Teachers, there is much you can do to reduce anxiety-creating performance pressure on the student who has difficulty with language. Avoid calling on students in alphabetical or numerical order, which can create countdown-type tension as he awaits his turn. Conversely, neither should your student be called upon to read or present to the class without allowing him adequate preparation time; don't call on him "by surprise." Enlist the aid of the school speech language pathologist in preparing for oral reports.

Help peers understand language difficulties

Under no circumstances should adults or peers tolerate teasing of a student or sibling who communicates differently. In the classroom setting, a visit from the school speech language pathologist can help classmates better understand the student who has speech and language difficulties. She can discuss the various parts of our bodies involved in speech, obstacles some children encounter, and ways peers can help. This discussion can take place with or without the child with language challenges in the classroom.

Why we talk

We talk for reasons that go far beyond a functional means to communicate our wants and needs. Yet, for many individuals with autism or Asperger's, the primary reason for talking is to request something desired, or to acquire additional information that feeds their specific interest(s), or to help them achieve more control of their surroundings. It's important that we continually reinforce that we talk with others for reasons that extend beyond "learning or teaching":

- To create or maintain emotional connections with others
- To share personal news that may be of interest to another
- To express concern, love, support, empathy
- To share observations about our surroundings
- To warn another of impending danger or possible harm
- To entertain others
- To seek comfort
- To persuade, or call to action
- To intimidate

Asking questions and making comments ·······················

Without these two mainstays of conversing with others, exchanges become tediously one-sided. Does this sound familiar?

"How was school today?"

"Okay."

"Did anything new happen?"

"Nope."

"Did you get your math test back?"

"Yup."

"How did you do?"

"Fine."

Frustrating, isn't it? Within all conversations there's an underlying, unspoken expectation that each partner will do their part to keep conversation flowing and satisfy the purpose of the communication. When we do that, we're considered a good communicator; when we don't, people may have odd or negative thoughts about us.

Children with impaired social thinking skills need to be taught social language, concepts, and strategies, just as we would teach them math or science skills, beginning with the two communication basics: asking questions and making comments.

Why ask questions?

- To demonstrate interest in others. We are all expected to have some degree of social curiosity about others—to show we're interested in what others are thinking, saying, or doing. This makes others around us feel good about communicating with us.

- To verify our assumptions or perceptions. Unless we ask questions, we never know for sure if what we think about others is accurate or true.

- To clarify or gain new information. We learn new things and expand our personal education through asking questions.

Why make comments?

- To let people know their thoughts and viewpoints have been heard. It makes them feel valued.

- To agree or disagree

- To offer additional information about a topic

Offer your child or student repeated practice in both formal and informal settings (i.e., within structured teaching sessions and in real life situations). Here are additional thoughts to get you started.

Asking questions

Many children on the autism spectrum do not know how to ask a question, and even when they master the art of formulating their thoughts into intelligible questions, it may take an unfathomable amount of courage to get that question out in front of a group. Teach the art of questioning from a young age.

- Games like Lotto ("Who has the bear?"), Go Fish ("Do you have any threes?") or Guess My Name ("Are you an animal? Are you a food?") are good starters.

- Build guessing games into your daily routine. If you bring home a bag of groceries, have your child guess what's in the bag. Is it for breakfast? Is it for dessert? Is it cereal? Is it eggs? Is it oatmeal? Is it cornflakes?

- For classroom or home: make a Mystery Box. Children have to guess what's inside, gradually narrowing down the choices. Start with the category: Is it animals, clothes, food, or toy? Then get more specific: Is it brown, is it white, or is it red? Do you wear it on the top part of your body or the bottom? Do you wear it at night or during the day? Winter or summer? And so on.

- With a very young child, take turns playing "What is it?" with a picture book. Point to an object on the page and ask "What is it?" Turn the page and now it is the child's turn to ask you, "What is it?" This builds vocabulary and reinforces the habit of asking a question if there is something they do not know or understand.

In social situations, questions help us find a way to connect, to find something in common with our conversation partner.

- Environment ("What do you like to do best at this park?" "What's your favorite ride?")

- Shared purpose ("What flavor of ice cream are you getting?" "Is this your first time at chess club?")

- Prior history ("When did you get back from vacation?" "What movie did you and your family see this weekend?")

- Shared activities ("Did you like the fireworks?" "Do you have the homework assignment for math ready?")

Use the "w" words (and one "h" word) to form basic questions:

- Who were you with?
- What did you do?
- When did you do it?
- Where did you do it?
- Why did you do it?
- How did you do it?

Making comments

Supportive comments are the connectors of a social conversation. We use them to:

- Acknowledge the feelings of the speaker: "Lame!" "Awesome."
- Add our own impressions: "I like that too!" "Yuck!"
- Let the person know we can take their perspective: "Dude, that sucks."

Children with autism or Asperger's must be consistently taught that words themselves are not enough: tone of voice and facial expressions need to match, too. For instance, a child who says "bummer" with a smile on his face would be perceived as either joking or insincere.

With my compliments··

Giving and receiving compliments are social skills that add immeasurably to our enjoyment of life. Start young, teaching your child to identify opportunities to issue compliments, and to graciously accept compliments that come his way.

- Teach your child that there are many kinds of compliments, give examples of each, and model the giving of compliments throughout your day.

    - Personal compliments: "Thank you for holding the door for me; you are very polite."

    - Skills/talents compliments: "Wow, you sure are a fast runner," "I like the way you played that last piece on the piano," "You have beautiful handwriting."

    - Achievement compliments: "Great job setting the table / finishing your math / singing in the school program."

    - Appearance compliments: "You look great in that red sweater."

    - Secondary compliments involve saying something nice about something connected to the person: "It's neat how your bedroom is painted like a jungle" or "Your cat is very playful."

- Motivate your child to look for opportunities to give compliments by having an informal quota each day. Did we give a compliment (or two, or three) today, to a classmate, a sibling, a parent, or teacher? Impose a quota on yourself too, actively looking for things about your child to compliment.

- Role-play situations in which your child might identify opportunities for compliments: in class, in the gym, at the dinner table, or at a friend or relative's house.

- Watch a favorite movie or DVD with your child. Look for and pause to discuss instances where characters give each other compliments.

- Teach and role-play appropriate and inappropriate responses to compliments.

- Compliment: "You look great in that red sweater."
- Appropriate: "Thank you."
- Inappropriate: "I hate this sweater. My mom made me wear it because Grandma gave it to me," or "I'm only wearing this because nothing else was clean today."

The four steps of communication

Scattered throughout this chapter and the chapter on social skills is material pioneered by Michelle Garcia Winner, a brilliant, forward-thinking speech language pathologist who has the uncanny ability to break down the complex world of social thinking and social communication into components that can be discussed and taught. Her work is thought-provoking and entertaining, and throws a spotlight on the assumptions and ingrained perceptions we adults often hold toward communication and what it means to "be social." We recommend that anyone not familiar with her work visit her website, *SocialThinking.com*, (a wealth of free information), read her books, and be prepared for some amazing insights about teaching language and communication.

Winner breaks the intricate act of face-to-face communication into four definable components that unfold in an organized progression. Interestingly, language only comes into play during the last step. Communication first involves thinking about other people and establishing a physical presence. Winner calls this progression "The Four Steps of Communication."

Step 1: Think about the person(s) with whom you will communicate or who are sharing physical space with you. Consider other people's thoughts, emotions, motives, intentions, belief systems, prior knowledge, experiences, and personality, to better establish successful communication.

Step 2: Establish a physical presence. We do this by physically approaching those we wish or need to communicate with and orienting ourselves toward them, using body language and gestures to establish, nonverbally, our intent to communicate.

Step 3: Use our eyes to: watch what other people are looking at as clues to what they may be thinking about, consider how people's body language and facial expression supports (or doesn't support) their words, evaluate the motives or intentions of our communication partner(s), explore the environment for additional cues to add meaning to what is being said. We also use our eyes to show people what we are thinking about, and to demonstrate to other people that we are paying attention.

Step 4: Use language to relate to others and demonstrate our interest in them and what they are saying. We do that by asking questions, discussing topics that are of interest to them, making related comments, and adjusting what we want to say based on how we think other people will respond.

> ## QUICK IDEA
>
> Simon Says is a versatile game and can be used in all sorts of incarnations; use it acclimate your child to the multiple ways we express emotions. Simon Says act mad. Simon Says act happy. Silly but instructional.

Recommended reading (both by Michelle Garcia Winner)

Think Social! A Social Thinking Curriculum for School-Age Students
Thinking About YOU Thinking About ME

Behavior

Strong reasons make strong actions.
WILLIAM SHAKESPEARE

BEHAVIOR IS COMMUNICATION. We repeat: Behavior is communication. All behavior, whether appropriate or inappropriate, is a message about how a child perceives his relationship with his environment at that moment. Happy, sad, fussy, or content, behavior is an outward expression of an inward state. As a society, and as individuals within it, we assign both global and personally subjective labels to what constitutes appropriate and inappropriate behaviors within specific contexts. The quiet child is thought of as "good" while the rambunctious child is labeled a "handful" or a "problem child." It's acceptable to tell jokes and laugh aloud at home or in a circle of friends, but that same behavior elicits stern frowns when displayed at church or a funeral. We each have our own interpretations of what is good and bad behavior.

Perhaps nowhere will those assumptions about behavior be tested more severely than within the array of behaviors exhibited by children on the autism spectrum.

Inappropriate or negative behaviors interfere with a child's learning process at school, at home, and in social situations. Extinguishing these behaviors is not enough … is *never* enough. *Exchanging* negative behaviors with appropriate alternatives that fulfill the same function must happen before real learning—social, cognitive, or emotional—can flow. If this idea is new to you, sit up and take notice, because it tops the list of behavior principles and is possibly the single best strategy you will ever use to help your child.

Your child or student truly does want to interact appropriately with people and the world around him. When inappropriate behavior occurs, it is a response to something affecting him internally and/or externally. Unacceptable behavior occurs because the child becomes overwhelmed by disordered sensory systems, cannot communicate his wants or needs, or doesn't understand the situation or what is expected of him. Throughout this chapter, we'll be elaborating on five guidelines:

Look for sensory issues

- Resistant, troublesome, questionable, problematic, baffling, aggressive, overwrought behaviors—all can have their root in sensory issues.
- Look beyond the behavior to identify and eliminate its source.

Never assume anything

- He may not know or understand the rules.
- She may have heard the instructions but not understood them. She cannot comply if she doesn't comprehend.
- Maybe he knew it yesterday but can't retrieve it today.

Establish a functional communication system—in whatever form it may take.

- Picture cards, choice boards, sign language, gestures, keyboarding— without a functional way to express their wants and needs, the only communication option left to children is their behavior.
- This goes double for children who are nonverbal or have limited verbal skills.

Behavior occurs for a reason

- Common triggers include sensory overload, emotional overload (frustration, anger, persecution, fear), sleep deprivation, food sensitivities, hunger, dehydration, physical pain, avoidance or resistance to unpleasant tasks, any unmet need.
- Distinguish between "can't" and "won't." It's the difference between "I am not able to" and "I choose not to." Our kids can't do or know what they have not been taught.

- Honor behavior as an attempt to communicate in the only way they know how at that moment. Believe, truly believe, if they could access their words or act upon your direction or exhibit the self-control you seek, they would.

Your own behaviors are part of the equation

- The behavior equation that governs your child's life is: you + me + environment = behavior. Your own behaviors are a major influence on his environment—social, emotional, physical, temporal.

- Children can sense when someone is truly supportive and when they're just getting lip service. Even well-intentioned parents and professionals can unknowingly reinforce the very behavior they're working to change in a child. Do a periodic reality check of your own behavior, particularly when your efforts to change your child's behavior are not working. It may be your behavior that needs to change first. Here's a small story that illustrates this great truth:

> In a nice kindergarten in a nice town in the United States in the mid-2000s there was a classroom with two teacher's aides. One had some training in autism and one did not. In the class was a girl named Addie who had autism, and one day when the children came in from recess, Addie had a hard time turning off the fun and settling down to seat work. Around and around the classroom she ran, with one of the aides in hot pursuit, shouting, "That's enough! That's just enough, young lady! Do you hear me, missy? I said that's enough!"
>
> The other teacher's aide, who had been out of the room, returned. She took one look at the situation, stepped in front of the little girl and calmly said, "Addie, go sit in your seat. It's time for silent reading." Addie slipped into her desk chair and took out her book.

Strengths and weaknesses

Keep near you at all times a list of your child or student's strengths and talents. Reframe challenging traits as positives: He is energetic (hyperactive), steadfast (stubborn), spontaneous (impulsive), or observant (watches without joining in). She has a great singing voice, is responsible with pets, keeps her desk tidy, dislikes soda, and can name 800 species of flowers. Reminding yourself of your child's strong suits at those moments when his behavior is most trying will help you refocus on his positive qualities and capabilities, and help you maintain your own self-control and equilibrium.

Don't ask why

In most instances the child with autism or Asperger's does not understand why she does the things she does. Her behavior may stem from sensory issues; it might feel good to her; something about the situation may be reinforcing. Yet, our first response in most cases is to probe, "Why did you ... ?" (Or, "Why didn't you ... ?") The pressure to come up with a response can lead to making excuses, fabricating reasons, or shifting blame to others.

Toss that three-letter word out of your vocabulary when discussing behaviors with your child or student. Instead ask the following four questions that give a child the opportunity to explore her behavior in a more constructive framework:

1. What did you do?

2. What are you going to do about it?

3. We don't want this to happen again. What should we do now to make sure it doesn't?

4. If this does happen again, what consequences should apply?

What we "miss" in misbehavior ···

Georgia is "misbehaving" again and your nerves are stretched thin. You've tried every behavior management strategy you can think of, all in vain. You're tired, frustrated, and at your wit's end. Why does Georgia behave like this and what new miracle technique don't you know?

Many of the behaviors we label problematic are symptoms of the child's physiology, biology, and neurology. Acting out, noncompliance, disrespectful words or actions may arise more from inadequate communication skills, a challenged motor planning system, sensory sensitivities, or social thinking impairments than deliberate disobedience. Effective behavior modification (not just management) requires that you understand and accept that in many—perhaps most—situations, the key to a child's appropriate behavior is you and your perspective. When loving or working with a child with autism, misbehavior means misunderstood.

Before assuming misbehavior, pause and ask:

- Is it his problem or mine? Is his behavior negatively affecting him or others, or just me? Whose behavior needs addressing? Should it be mine, as the adult in the situation?

- Are your expectations reasonable for his skill level in this situation? Many children need to be taught appropriate behaviors in increments, breaking a larger skill down into step-by-step components. Have you done this?

- Has he mastered this behavior and can he use it consistently in different situations? If Paula has learned to ask for help at home with her jacket, has she generalized that skill to other situations, or have we assumed the knowledge would transfer? Generalization needs to be taught.

- Is the child capable of modifying his own behaviors under all or most circumstances? Children with autism or Asperger's strive to do the right thing, but environmental influences can wreak havoc on the best of intentions. Teaching an appropriate behavior, even mastery of that behavior within a defined situation does not automatically mean he can control behavior under times of added stress, added sensory invasiveness, routine changes, or surprises (even positive ones).

- Are you sure the problem is not language/communication-based, or that it doesn't stem from social thinking challenges? Have you taught the prerequisite communication or social skills needed to be successful in this situation? If the student hasn't been taught such skills, it's likely he doesn't know them.

- Are accommodations or supports missing? Did she forget her daily planner, or did you take down the classroom rules and forget to put them back up?

- Is there a possible medical reason for the behavior? Children with limited communication abilities cannot usually tell us if their throat hurts, their stomach aches, or their head is pounding. Be alert for physical ailments that may produce negative behaviors.

Behavior and personality: Consider both

So often we ask children to respond to our behavior requests according to a timeline—one that we set up and that works within our own day. "It's time to go to the store" (because this is the time you've chosen as convenient). "We have to leave now to pick up Justin at baseball practice" (because of the practice schedule). "It's play therapy time" (because of a preset appointment).

Take into account your child's personality and how your requests—especially home or clinic-based appointments—match his basic nature. And consider your own too.

- Do you function more like turtles (slow and steady) or rabbits (fast paced, in constant motion) by nature?

> **QUICK IDEA**
>
> According to the American Optometric Association, 80% of learning occurs through the visual system. Children who have executive functioning/ organizational difficulties should be checked for an underlying visual processing dysfunction.

- Is your child an A.M. person—most alert and engaged before noon—or a P.M. person, needing to ease into a day for a while to get his engine primed and ready for learning?

- How much time do you each need during the day to recharge and refuel before tackling another event? Can your child handle back-to-back functions or does he do better with just one formal-learning event per day, mixed in with other fun, less structured engagement time?

- Think about the unspoken message communicated when scheduled therapies, tutorings, and activities are nonstop: You are broken. You need fixing.

- All children need downtime, especially school-age children for whom the demands of the school day can be draining. How many breaks does your child need to function with a manageable degree of behavior control and compliance?

Slow down the rushing from one activity to the next and insert some break time into your daily schedule. Overloading a child's day with therapies, appointments, household chores, and errands can often result in a burned-out, demoralized child, and can even exacerbate some of the very problems you are trying to address. Maintain a moderate schedule and trust that your child will progress in a healthy manner when allowed to do so at the pace that best suits his character.

(Pssst … there's no such thing as "doing nothing." What seems like "doing nothing" to you is fostering the creative thinking so many kids miss in today's over-scheduled lifestyles. Think of it as re-filling a well that has been pumped dry. You're going to find that you like it.)

Collaborative discipline

Whether at home with an individual child or in a classroom of twenty-five students, establishing a system of collaborative discipline is beneficial to all and can diminish behavior problems significantly. With collaborative discipline, the family or class discusses their wants and needs and draws up a reasonable set of rules by which everyone abides. The child or children then also decide upon reasonable penalties for broken rules. (Teachers, listen closely here—you may get a startling glimpse of your student's home life.) Adults retain final approval over rules and consequences. Interestingly, children may continue to break their own rules, but under collaborative discipline, they have been given a voice in their own social environment and the consequences are of their own making.

Consequential learning

The terms *consequence* and *punishment* are sometimes used interchangeably but they are not at all the same thing. Consequences are either natural or adult-applied results of actions or words. Punishment is retributive, intended to hurt or shame. Consequences are valuable life lessons in accountability, teaching the child the role of self-control in making good choices. Punishment attempts to squash behavior without addressing the source, and through means that too frequently foster anger, hatred, and humiliation, none of which are conducive to furthering social awareness and encouraging emotional connection with others.

> ## QUICK IDEA
> Respond to "I can't" with "Yes, you can. I am here to help. I have lots of ideas. We will try until we find one that works."

Natural consequences remove you as the instrument of unpleasantness. Some examples of natural consequences: he refuses to eat his dinner; he's hungry later. She won't wear her boots in the rain; her feet are wet by the time she gets to school. He doesn't put his ball back in the bin; the puppy chews it to bits. The natural consequences of these three actions may be powerful motivators for behavior change. Just keep in mind:

- Natural consequences will not result in behavior change if you sabotage the consequence. If you let him eat later, if you bring dry socks to school for her, if you buy him a new ball, not only has the child not learned the natural consequence of his behavior, but you have reinforced the careless behavior by accommodating it.

- Never permit natural consequences of a dangerous nature to transpire. Take the knife away before he slices his finger off, ditto for the matches before he burns his fingers, or worse.

Applied consequences are those you impose when natural consequences aren't present. Most of us are familiar with *positive consequences*, the idea of a reward or reinforcer for appropriate behavior or performance, and *negative consequences,* the removal of a privilege or other desired circumstance for unacceptable behavior or performance. Another form of applied consequence is the *logical consequence,* and for our concrete-thinking kiddos, it may be the most effective applied consequence. The logical consequence ties the consequence to the unacceptable action: if he throws his toys, he has to put the thrown toy plus another one in toy jail for two days. If she screams and hits her brother to get the TV remote, she doesn't get to choose a program that night. If he doesn't do chore X, he either does double chores next time, or forfeits part of his allowance. (Ellen says: if your child values his money, you will not believe how effective this is!)

Tips for presenting consequences effectively:

- Formulating effective consequences takes effort and planning. Give thought to your child's behaviors and plan how you will address them as they come up.

- Consequences that are too harsh or too lenient will not be effective. Calibrate the consequence to the crime.

- Don't bother imposing any consequence that you will not be able to follow through with consistently. You know how rigid and routine-bound your child is. Ignore the behavior once, and you may be back at square one. For this reason, all adults involved must be aware of the consequence and willing to enforce it.

- Give it time. Changing behavior is a process, not an event. It's unrealistic to expect behavior to change overnight or at the first imposition of consequences.

- Give a consequence with empathy, not anger. Speak directly to your child in a calm tone of voice. Meting out your consequence with anger, disappointment, dismay, or shock shifts the focus from his actions to your feelings, and to how your feelings make him feel.

- Check for comprehension—make sure he understands why the consequence is being imposed, and what he can do next time to avoid it.

- Keep it short and to the point. Your child will tune out after mere moments. Don't sermonize, bring up past episodes, compare him or a sibling or peer, generalize, or berate personally.

- Consequences must be relevant. You can threaten to take away her new shoes if she wipes boogers on them, but if she doesn't care about the shoes to begin with, the consequence has no meaning.

- Offer refresher or practice time if it seems regression has set in: "You know dirty clothes go in the laundry basket, not the closet floor. The next time you show me you have forgotten this, we will have practice time." Post a written set of house rules to help him become independent and avoid negative consequences.

- Before vocalizing the rule, be sure you have your child's attention. Calling out from a room away, "It's time to set the table" isn't effective behavior management.

- If you choose to give warnings, one is sufficient, unless you have reason to believe your child did not hear you or did not understand you the first time. Too many warnings send the message you don't mean what you're saying.

"I'm angry!"

Teaching children of any communication skill level an acceptable way to express powerful feelings like anger and frustration goes a long way in alleviating negative or troublesome behaviors. Recognizing the need is the first step. Head banging, hitting or kicking, stubborn resistance, and verbal insults are all signs of frustration.

Start by choosing a physical outlet that is acceptable to you, such as punching a pillow, screaming in a closet for thirty seconds, jumping, or stomping feet.

Next, create a social script that talks about being angry or frustrated. It can be simple and brief:

1. Everybody feels angry sometimes.
2. It is okay to feel angry.
3. When I get angry, I can punch pillows in my room.
4. Soon I will feel better.
5. When I am done being angry, I will feel happy again!

Use words, pictures, photographs, or a combination of visuals that are meaningful to the child, such as a photo of the child's face when she's angry and when she's happy. Some kids may respond to a small story booklet produced with words and drawings. Introduce the social story/booklet to the child when she is calm. Read it more than once and discuss ideas as needed to match the skill level of the child.

Give the story/booklet to the child the next time she is angry or frustrated. Remind her of the action she can take to quell her anger. Fade the prompt to just a cue card reminding her of acceptable ways to release her anger, then a hand signal or just one word ("Pillow!"). Reinforce the child when she makes a good choice.

Sign language: Not just for baseball

Ever notice how baseball coaches communicate with their batters and runners through a series of hand signals? Develop a similar set of discreet cues to let your child know when a behavior is inappropriate. Putting a finger on your chin might mean, "You are interrupting." Lacing your fingers together might mean, "You are monopolizing the conversation; let someone else talk now."

Accentuate the positive

Think through your responses to inappropriate behavior to ensure that you are modeling appropriate behavior and not unwittingly furthering negative behavior. A child may respond to punitive consequences by lying, cheating, or trying to shift blame to someone else. A willful child may also win this game by developing a tolerance to the penalty. What, then? Do you escalate the penalty? If you do, where does it end?

A better overall approach is to constantly reinforce appropriate behaviors and interactions, no matter how small the increment. Discuss infractions at a time when both you and she are calm, not at the height of the battle.

Construct a visual barrier

Teachers in a classroom that was half below ground had a problem with a child continually jumping from the wide windowsill that sat at ground level. His art-savvy paraeducator stopped the behavior by creating an earth-to-sky mural on the lower wall, then disguised the ledge with paper clouds. End of behavior.

Two-step redirect

Many kids are easily distracted (frequently by tantalizing sensory inputs), and once distracted will find it nearly impossible to redirect themselves back to the primary task without firm intervention. Use concrete stop-do instructions. Get his attention, then label the behavior you want him to stop, followed by telling him what you want him to do: "Alex, stop spraying water on the mirror. Get your toothbrush out and brush your teeth."

Fear of bathroom = Fear of the dark

Problem: a student who would not use the restroom at school. The restroom was windowless, and the child was eventually able to tell teachers that some students had teased him by turning off the lights while he was in there, leaving him alone in the dark. Solution: providing him with a large flashlight that could be set on the floor inside the stall. The child was resourceful enough to come up with a reply to students who asked why he took a flashlight into the restroom: "In case the power goes off!"

Resistant/avoidant behaviors

These can strain even the most patient of parents and teachers. Remember your guidelines—behavior is communication; assume nothing—and proceed with these proactive tactics:

- Identify the source. Keep a journal detailing what happened or was happening immediately before the meltdown. Note people involved, time of day, activities, settings, sensory issues, foods. Over time a pattern may emerge. If you can identify the antecedent (trigger) to the behavior, you can avoid, eliminate, or address it.

- Phrase requests in the positive rather than the imperative. "You are tracking mud all over the house!" may not spur your child to remove his shoes. You've made a statement of fact, and his literal-thinking brain isn't able to infer the action you're requesting. "Please take off your shoes by the back door" may be met with more cooperation. Verbalizing the behavior in the positive form presents your request clearly and at the same time reinforces appropriate behavior. It removes the uncomfortable guessing game the child must play if he is to figure out what he should do.

- Does the child know how to do what is being asked of him? If he suddenly needs to run to the bathroom every time he's asked to set the table or do a math sheet, maybe he doesn't know how, or fears his effort will draw criticism. Stick with him through enough repetitions of the task to where he feels competent. Most kids with autism or Asperger's will need more practice to master tasks than will their typically-developing counterparts. Patience is everything; results *will* come.

- Does the child know the rules? You can't be certain unless you ask him. Does he understand the reason for the rule (safety, economy, health, etc.)? Is he breaking a well-known rule because there is an underlying cause? Maybe he is pinching forbidden snacks out of the fridge because he was worried about finishing his art project, didn't eat his lunch, and is now famished. (Establishing a communication check-in each day with your child's teacher or assistant is helpful in avoiding such incidents. The teacher would have reported that he didn't eat his lunch.)

- Give the child a break for self-regulation before the behavior gets out of hand. Frame it as positive regrouping time, not jail. The purpose of the break is to help the child learn to take responsibility for her own self-regulation. At a time when she is calm, pre-designate a spot she can go to for a few minutes when she is overwhelmed. Ask her what items might be good for this spot. A favorite book or plush animal, pillow or chair, headphones with favorite music? Make

> **QUICK IDEA**
>
> To break perseverative behavior, change the scenery. Send the child on an errand; walk to the office, the rest room, the mailbox, the back yard.

sure those items available to her during her break are readily available at other times of the day, and in other settings. Otherwise, she will come to view them as rewards for behavior that will give her access to these favorite items.

Be careful that you do not frame these breaks as punishment or a consequence for inappropriate behavior. Because the spot will be pleasant to the child, you may inadvertently reinforce the negative behavior and see it escalate (so the child can get the break more often).

Locate the break area in a place where she can smoothly reintegrate to the flow of home or classroom. Sending the child to her room or the hallway may be too far physically removed to allow this.

- Keep your behavioral expectations reasonable and age-appropriate. Church services, restaurants, concerts, or other events requiring long quiet sits are set-ups for conflict. Arrange movement breaks at reasonable intervals, or abbreviate or skip the activity until she is older and better able to handle it.

- Timing is everything. Of course he would rather play with his cars than go to pick up his sister at dance practice, but a little respect goes a long way. Give him a five-minute warning and a two-minute warning—and build a few extra minutes in on your end to compensate for resistance or dawdling. This holds true for asking him to interrupt any pleasurable activity (play, TV, or reading) to perform a less pleasurable one (chores, errands, or unwanted appointments).

- If nagging has become the norm in your house, you may have noticed it is ineffective and irritating to all parties. One definition of insanity is doing the same thing over and over and expecting a different result. Brainstorm with your family about better ways to accomplish what needs to get done. Depending on his age and ability, your child may or may not be able to verbalize suggestions, but you will have given him the respect and the opportunity to be part of the solution. If he can verbalize he may tell you that when he gets home from school he likes to run around the backyard for a while before settling down to homework, or that the toothpaste you've been buying tastes horrible to him so he avoids brushing his teeth.

- Set up visual schedules and charts that you can discreetly point to as gentle reminders of what he needs to do. If your child is a visual learner, his auditory channel may shut down in times of stress. Your child can refer to these visuals as concrete reminders of what he should do, especially when anger or irritation is creeping in.

- Reality check: Is your love for your child whole-hearted and without reservation, or does it feel conditional? If the vibes she picks up tell her your love depends on a tidy room, good grades, or perfect behavior, she may feel defeated enough to not even try.

Hostile or aggressive behavior

Hitting, biting, scratching, shoving—these tough and sometimes baffling behaviors may seem to erupt out of nowhere, or may be wearyingly ongoing. Meeting them with logic rather than emotion is surely difficult—and surely worth it. You can make major headway if you:

- Focus on what is happening to him, not your reaction to it. Remember: his behaviors are rooted in his sensory and/or social impairments (or even underlying medical causes such as acid reflux, constipation, or other aches and pains). He is not doing it to provoke you, embarrass you, or make your life miserable. He is not an inherently unkind, cruel, malicious, or evil individual. He is feeling frustrated, fearful, threatened, tired, unable to communicate his needs, or otherwise unable to cope. Let your response spring from this understanding.

- Respond at the first infraction. Don't wait until the third or fourth time he's swung a fist to see if "he figures it out" from the other child's reaction. He needs a crystal-clear directive from you that such behavior is not acceptable, period.

- Respond in the same manner every time, in word, action and consequence. It may take many repetitions to imprint. Your consistency is essential for his comprehension.

- Do not respond in kind. You are trying to get him to change an inappropriate behavior and you must teach by example. Answering aggression with aggression (verbal or physical) will only confuse him in ways he cannot possibly process: it's not okay to hit other children, but the same aggressive behavior is okay if you are the bigger person? The horrifying long-term consequence of this is that he may not tell you if, in the future, another adult behaves aggressively or abusively toward him.

  - Impose natural consequences, not punishment. Punitive consequences for noncompliance or inappropriate behavior are the least effective behavior strategies you can use with a child on the spectrum. Without an understanding of cause and effect, your intent will be lost on your child and succeed only in lowering his self-esteem. Accentuating the negative does not help him understand what to do differently next time. Focus on helping him understand the natural consequences of his actions. (See also **Consequential learning** in this chapter.)

  - Evaluate where aggressive messages are coming from in his life. Children with autism are famous for concrete thinking, and your child may have great difficulty distinguishing fantasy from reality. Know what television shows your child is watching and what video games he's playing—watch or play with him. It may be worth weaning him off television programs and computer games that portray violent or anti-social behavior in entertaining or unrealistic ways.

- If you do decide to ban a show or game, ease the transition by gradually reducing the time allowed, rather than yanking it cold turkey. Week 1: He may play Cosmic Combat for thirty minutes. Week 2: reduce time to twenty or twenty-five minutes. Week 3 and beyond: continue reducing time until it is eliminated. You can also gradually reduce the number of days on which you allow him to play it: every other day, every third day, etc. until eliminated.

- To be upfront about it or not? Your call—your child. If you gradually reduce time, will he notice? Or will he be better off if you are straightforward in your explanation: "This program/game shows people being hurtful to each other. This is not okay and we are not going to watch it/play it."

- Offer replacement programs or games that will truly interest him, not just lame time-fillers. (These may take some homework on your part to find.)

- Praise appropriate social behavior and do it often. Just as he does not hit out of innate nastiness, neither may he understand that waiting his turn (and other examples of self-control) is good.

Game plan for meltdowns

A child or student's meltdown is a stressful experience for everyone involved. Having a working plan put together ahead of time can alleviate some of the stress and allow you to respond calmly.

Follow these six guidelines for effective behavior management during a meltdown. You'll find the episode is over more quickly for everyone.

1. Never try to teach during a meltdown. It won't work. Ask yourself how open you are to learning when you are angry, terrified, overwrought, over-anxious, or otherwise emotionally disabled.

2. The more stressful the situation, the more reduced and concrete your language should be.

3. Set a rule that once a situation gets out of hand, one previously designated person communicates with the child one-on-one. Everyone talking at the same time will only escalate the situation for the child.

4. Rehearse your behavior plan ahead of time. Many plans that look good on paper are just not effective in practice.

5. Time-outs are good—for both of you. When your child has danced on your third nerve for the tenth time since lunch, don't blow. Tell her: "I am angry right now and I can't be around you. I am going to my room to calm down for a few minutes, then I will come back and we will talk about it." Modeling self-control will help your child begin to understand how she can manage her own behavior too.

6. Choose only battles with significant consequences. Yes, she must wear her seat belt in the car and she must wear a helmet when riding her bike. But are books on the shelf upside down really an issue? Establish a list of nonnegotiable have-to items (taking her medicine, going to school, wearing sunscreen at the beach, using seat belts and bike helmets) and be as flexible and creative as you can about everything else.

From bad to worse:
How to avoid escalating a skirmish

We are all human and despite our supposed adult maturity, we sometimes make bad decisions in the heat of the moment. A child in full meltdown is an unhappy situation for any classroom, but teachers (and parents at home) must take care not to prolong the episode by responding with inflammatory behavior of our own. Beware of specific behaviors that perpetuate rather than resolve a crisis:

- Raising the pitch or volume of voice (yelling, shrieking)
- Presenting threatening body language, such as clenched fists, narrowed eyes, towering, or advancing posture

- Mocking or mimicking the student, using sarcasm, insults, or humiliating remarks, attempting to embarrass the student out of the behavior

- Attacking the student's character or personality

- Making unsubstantiated accusations

- Rewarding unacceptable behavior, bribing

- Nagging or preaching

- Invoking a double standard

- Comparing the student to a sibling or other student

- Referencing previous or unrelated events

- Lumping the child into a general category (kids like her are "all the same")

- Making an assumption—any assumption—without factual backup, i.e., you may have given him an instruction, but that doesn't mean he was able to understand it.

Peer power and the two-minute warning

Giving the child a two-minute warning when an activity is about to change is a good behavior practice. If he is resistant or reluctant, enlist a peer to help him. Peers often have more suggestive power than adults do.

Flexibility required

Congratulations! By learning to consult his visual schedule, your child or student has achieved a measure of independence in getting through his day. You're now ready for the next step: teaching him to accept change and overcome rigidity in thought and behavior. Begin this lesson while the child is young and behavior patterns are less ingrained.

- Alert him to blips in the usual routine with a red frame placed around the visual of the new event—school assembly, after-school doctor appointment. He has a better chance of integrating it smoothly into his day when it is not a surprise.

- Apprise him of changes in routine from two standpoints: he needs to know what will be different and new that day, and what usual event isn't going to happen.

- Insert a question mark (?) on her daily schedule from time to time. At first, it should represent something enjoyable to the child: a new way to play a game, a surprise snack, a special outing or activity. Gradually introduce less desirable events or conditions as the child becomes more able to tolerate changes. Building mystery into the routine helps kids become more adaptable when real surprises and changes occur in daily life.

Fun tips to encourage flexible thinking

Rigid and rule-bound thinking: it's pervasive among the autism population, and is a common source of behavior outbursts. While this type of thinking does have its positive side, being inflexible in thoughts and actions won't serve our children well in the long run. Start introducing blips in the routine in a fun way while kids are young. As children become more acclimated to accepting changes in routine, behavior issues will fade. One perfect arena for practicing flexible thinking is during family games.

Create a stack of cards you use during a board or card game. Julie Wilson, author of the *Doing Your BEST Social Tips* online newsletter (*SocialPerspectives.com*), and from whom this idea was adapted, suggests calling them "Brain Cards" and using clip art of brain images for the card deck. We like "Let's Be Flexible" or "The Silly Game" as alternatives.

On the back side of each card, write an instruction to do something that's unusual for the game. Suggestions include:

- Stand up during your turn.
- Give a whoop or other favorite silly sound before rolling the dice.

- Switch places with the person to your left.
- Keep your eyes closed until it's your turn again.
- Take five deep breaths before playing your turn.

Before each turn, the player picks a card, reads and follows the directions to show they can think in a flexible way. The idea is to introduce unexpected directions to the game in a fun way.

The idea can also be adapted for the classroom. Pass out similar cards to each student prior to a selected activity. When called upon, each student reads and follows the directions on the card before answering a question, spelling a word, reciting a passage, etc.

Tip

Precede the game with an introduction to the concept of flexible thinking, why it's important, what benefits it can bring, etc. Children with more impaired social thinking abilities will not automatically understand.

Beyond the mirror: Memory books and photo travelogues

If your child has a fascination with looking at himself, make it work for you. Take a camera with you, or use your camera phone to take pictures of your child wherever you go. Arrange them in a colorful scrapbook or digital album (such as Google's Picasa or Facebook album), so he can see himself at these places. Helping your child recall pleasant times can decrease anxiety about returning to these environments, or going to new places.

Helping a self-biter

The child who bites himself is surely one of the more alarming classroom challenges. Conducting a Functional Behavior Analysis to determine the trigger of the behavior will help you take steps to prevent it. In the school setting, have staff observe the child throughout the day and record the times he bites himself. Is it circle time, one-on-one work time with his assistant, transition times? Does it occur when a certain person is present, when the noise levels are elevated, just after lunch, or always during art? Or is the child hypo-sensitive and needing such deep sensory input that he resorts to biting to get tactile feedback from his skin?

We'll say it again: many negative behaviors are rooted in sensory dysfunction. In the case of a self-biter, the child may be receiving needed sensory input from the biting beyond just the expression of frustration or anger. Merely interrupting the behavior when it occurs without addressing the root cause will ultimately be ineffective. If the child is seeking the sensory feedback he gets from biting, he may simply shift to a similar self-destructive behavior (hair-pulling, nail biting, even cutting). In the interim, put something over the portion of his body that he is biting: glove, long sleeve shirt, ace bandage. Then consult an occupational therapist for safe, socially appropriate tactics for meeting this troublesome sensory need.

Note: Collar- and cuff-chewers are a subset of self-biters. You can use the same tactics.

Please remain seated

Children who have trouble remaining seated on the floor or in their chairs may be coping with several things ranging from poor postural control to vestibular or motor-planning problems. Defining their seating area in clear-cut ways may help.

- The raised edge provided by placing a strip of foam pipe insulation (pre-slit to slip over the pipe) to the edge of his chair may do the trick.
- A chair cushion or camp pillow
- A carpet square
- Tape applied to the floor around his spot

The gentle way to criticize

Let's be honest, who likes to listen to criticism, however "constructive?" Accepting criticism is a life skill demanding maturity and self-confidence that may be light years beyond your child's abilities right now. Should you never correct a hyper-sensitive child? Of course not. But it's all in the delivery.

- Never, ever try to impose discipline, correction, or disapproval when the child is in the middle of a meltdown, shutdown, anxiety episode, or any other emotional state rendering her unable to interact with you.

- Before you even speak, remember that your sensory-challenged, language-impaired child will react as much, if not more, to the qualities of your voice than to the actual words. She will hear the yelling, the derision, the rhetorical sarcasm, the hysterical pitch, but she will not understand the words and therefore will not be able to figure out what she did wrong. Speak in calm, low tones, and if possible, lower your body as well, so you are communicating on her level, not towering over her.

- Adopt a "social autopsy" approach:

  - Identify the behavior and handle it in a supportive, problem-solving manner as opposed to invoking punishment or other negative consequences.

    Note: Your child may need help in identifying the feelings that triggered the behavior. He may say he was angry when in fact he may have been afraid, frustrated, sad, overexcited, or jealous. Probe beyond his first response.

  - Practice or role-play a better way to handle the situation next time it occurs, actively involving the child in the solution.

  - Conduct the "autopsy" as soon after the incident as possible.

  - Expect to drill or role-play over time. There are no one-time fixes.

  - Tell her immediately when she gets it right—every time.

- Present the information visually through a storyboard, comic strip, photo essay, or social story.

- Ensure that you yourself are modeling proper behavior for responding to criticism.

This argument is over

Dealing with an argumentative child is surely one of your greatest challenges. While we would never suggest tuning out or ending a conversation in which your child is attempting to communicate a legitimate need, there will come times when you need to put an end to an argument, demands, or resistance.

Developing an arsenal of one-liners can be useful. One-liners should always be as short as possible and delivered respectfully and without sarcasm, name-calling, or anger (as you would want from him). Some suggestions we gathered from parents:

- Thank you for telling me how you feel.

- I'm sorry you feel that way.

- I won't change my mind.

- This discussion is over.

- I'm changing the subject now. (Then do, cheerfully.)

> **QUICK IDEA**
>
> The Behavior Equation: you + me + environment. Behaviors never occur in a vacuum. In the words of author Alice Walker (The Color Purple): "The most important question in the world is, 'Why is the child crying?'"

Humor can often interrupt anger and break tension. Sense of humor is a very individual thing (what's hilarious to one child may feel humiliating to another) so finding the humorous one-liners that work with your child may take some experimentation. But it's worth a try. Or, put a non-verbal end to the discussion with a small dinner gong, whistle, kazoo, or desk bell.

Take a different approach: if your child is adept at arguing from a factual, logical perspective, use emotion-based responses that connect his actions to your feelings and reactions to stop his arguing. "I asked you to pick up your room and you argued with me instead of doing it. That argument took time and now it's bedtime." Or simply, "Arguing is exhausting for me. When you argue, the answer will always be 'no.'"

I hear ya—and this argument is over

Here's a strategy from the baseball field that transfers beautifully to home. Ellen's son Connor is an umpire, a venue in which coaches often elevate arguing to a science. Connor circumvents lengthy disputes by establishing a twenty-second rule at the pre-game meeting. Connor explains:

> "If you have a legitimate concern, I will listen for as long as it takes to resolve it. But if you merely disagree with my decision and want to vent, you get twenty seconds. After twenty seconds, I will say 'I hear you, Coach' and I will expect you to return to the dugout."

Ellen wishes she had known this technique all those years before Connor became an umpire!

A token system

Many parents and teachers have found token systems to be a popular and effective technique for increasing preferred behaviors and decreasing negative behaviors. Your child or student earns a token each time he exhibits a targeted behavior. Once he earns a previously agreed upon number of tokens, he can trade them for a preferred activity or item.

Token systems are flexible and easy to use. They can be specific and short-lived, or require a child to work for days or weeks before attaining a reward. Token systems bring many benefits to the child, family, and teacher:

- Helps the child build his ability to wait for reinforcement (delayed gratification)
- Increases the child's sense of time and how long it takes to achieve a reward
- Promotes more fluid teaching; a parent or educator can quickly deliver a token without having to stop to reinforce (which can take time to execute) with each action
- More natural reinforcement: material, social, and situational rewards can be earned.

Guidelines for implementing a token system

- Agree on a specific behavior to target and describe the appropriate behavior to the child using words, pictures, or modeling. Check for comprehension. A child who isn't 100% clear about what to do will not find this system rewarding.

- Select a tangible token that is durable and easy to manipulate. Common tokens include stickers, coins, points, and tickets.

- Decide how to chart progress visually. A sturdy, appropriate token board that allows the child to Velcro the earned tokens can be motivating. Or decide on an alternative way to chart progress. Put coins into a cup or pouch, put tickets into a plastic sleeve. Use a punch card instead of a board—portable, easy to create and use, inexpensive. The progress chart must be available at all times to the student while he's working on the behavior, a visual representation of how much he has accomplished and how much more he needs to accomplish before reward is earned. Also helpful: including a picture of the reinforcement.

- Determine the criteria and rules for successful task completion and confirm that the child understands what is required. State rules clearly and model appropriate behaviors if needed.

- Structure the environment for success.

- Select rewards that are highly desirable and motivating to the child. If possible, incorporate choices into the token system. With a simple system, the child can choose his reward for each day from a basket of available options. A more complex system, such as a class store, might require a child to work toward specified numbers of tokens, depending on the menu of options available. Fifteen minutes on the computer might cost 20 tokens; a trip to get ice cream, 50 tokens; highly desirable DVD, 100 tokens.

- Photo-reinforcer. Cut up a photo of a favorite reinforcer to use with a token system, e.g., a photo of a computer for computer time, or the cover of a favorite video. He earns pieces of the image as tokens.

- Include verbal praise when giving the token. "Great turn-taking" adds an additional reminder about the behavior being worked on, and can eventually transform into social praise as primary reinforcement.

Deals and contracts

Contracts and deals can be effective behavior management tools, both at home or in the classroom environment. You already use them informally: "Pick up your room and you can go to the movies." "Finish your math and you can have computer time." More formal systems include point systems and token earning systems.

When used effectively, deals and contracts can reduce behavioral problems, keep attention focused, and help teach one of life's critical lessons: work = reward. However, pitfalls and traps abound in setting up contracts and deals, especially with individuals with autism or Asperger's, who often lack important social skills that contribute to a shared understanding of the contract's parameters. Adhere to these guidelines when setting up contracts and deals:

- Make the contract visual. It can be simple pictures or symbols or a formal, written document. Use a "Working for _____" card (e.g., a meaningful reward like a favorite toy or activity). The card can be as simple as a picture of the reward with a space to write in steps to achieve it.

- State contract rules in clear and concise language at the child's vocabulary level. Individuals with autism think in a literal manner. Use straightforward terms that can be clearly evaluated by both parties involved. Beware of sloppy and imprecise language. "If you're good, you'll get_____." "Good" is subjective; it can change from day to day and person to person. Spell out the required behavior.

- Start small and expand gradually: one piece of work equals one payoff or reward. Don't get anxious and raise the stakes too quickly. Each time the child is successful you have reinforced work and the child has had an opportunity to practice effective social interaction. That's progress!

- Be thorough. Think about the many contracts and deals in your life. Most include description of the work to be done, what behaviors or actions are expected of all parties to the deal, when the work is to commence and when it is to be completed, what reward the worker will receive and when he or she will get paid. We need to include all of these elements in our contracts with kids, too.

- Check for comprehension. Don't institute the contract until you are 100% certain the student understands what you expect of him, the timelines of the contract, and the reward. Go back and simplify or adjust the terms of the contract where needed.

- Honor the deal. Not doing so is one of the biggest mistakes well-meaning parents and professionals regularly make. Contracts involve at least two people, each with a defined part in the deal. I do this; you do that. If one party disregards any component of the agreement, trust is broken and often a behavior problem develops. An example: A teacher and student made a contract, but when the teacher changed the rules in midstream, the student revolted. "He finished the work before the period was over, so I asked him to do some more work. He became upset." Note the key word: finished. The student fulfilled his end of the contract. The teacher then broke the deal. The fact that the student finished ahead of time was a teacher-planning problem, not a student behavior problem. Next time the teacher might make the contract tighter or include more work for the reward. It's much easier to revamp a subsequent contract than to rebuild trust in a relationship after it is broken. Once you've set up a deal, stick to it!

> **QUICK IDEA**
>
> Negative attention is still attention, and can be rewarding. If your child craves your attention, accentuate the positive things he does throughout the day.

- Avoid setting yourself and the child up for failure. The result or actions specified in the contract must be attainable by the child, and the timeline for the contract must be within the student's ability right from the start. If the payoff is too far in the future, motivation will slip. Even worse, you may find that behavioral problems develop.

- Have alternate reinforcers available if the contract isn't fulfilled, remembering that we often have bad days at work and still get paid. Above all, refrain from using rewards that are so big or important to the person that losing them (or the anxiety caused by thinking they might not be attained) will be too stressful for the child to handle.

- Watch out for blackmail. Do you ever find yourself saying, "If you stop screaming you'll get _____?" Doing so teaches the child he can get paid to stop behaving in a certain way. What happens after that? The child makes you raise the ante before he stops misbehaving and the time interval between payoffs gets shorter and shorter.

Watch what you reinforce

Reinforcement is a powerful teaching tool at school or at home. When used correctly, great things can happen. However, it's easy to inadvertently reinforce the very behavior you're trying to extinguish. An example: Jacob doesn't enjoy circle time at his preschool and often runs out of the circle over to the art easel to draw. Knowing that Jacob loves goldfish crackers, the teacher uses them as the ending snack. As she starts sharing them with the other students, back comes Jacob, plopping himself down as the crackers make their way to his spot. The teacher responds to him "Nice sitting in group, Jacob," thinking she is reinforcing the appropriate behavior he is now exhibiting, and gives him some crackers. But Jacob didn't sit nicely in group; he ran out of the circle and only returned when something interested him. Yet he still got the reward. What the teacher wanted to teach him was to stay with the group during circle time. What she actually reinforced was that he could get up, run away, and still get crackers.

Avoid this common error by making sure that reinforcers follow performance and are specific to the performance desired. If the teacher had asked Jacob to do something when he got back to the circle or required him to wait for the next cracker delivery he might have learned the lesson she was trying to teach.

Proximity praise

Proximity praise teaches behavior via peer example—we compliment, thank or praise a student or child near our misbehaving child for modeling appropriate behavior. "Erica, I like how you waited until your mouth wasn't full to ask for the butter." This form of praise requires some advanced social thinking in the child, since it requires the student to understand that the peer's behavior may also apply to him. This level of social thinking may be absent from a child with autism, if it has not been formally taught. When your student complies as a result of proximity praise, recognize and reward it.

Seasonal interests all year long

If your child's object of intense interest is seasonal, and if playing off that interest is going to be key in motivating behavior and/or routine, make it a point to think ahead and stock up on related items at the appropriate time. Does he love Halloween? Stock up on stickers for his visual chart, paper napkins for his lunchbox, fake cobwebs for his room, etc. Is she a water baby? Snorkels, goggles, and float toys are fun in the bathtub, hot tub, and indoor pool all year; buy them in the summer for best selection. If your young paleontologist is going to want a dinosaur egg hunt at his birthday party in September, buy the plastic Easter eggs in the spring.

Sibling secret knock

Barging into a sibling's room or bathroom without knocking can be infuriating to the sibling; it is equally unacceptable in other people's homes or in a business setting. Have the two siblings develop a secret knock they must use to enter each other's rooms. (Emphasize "secret knock, then wait for Julie to say, 'Come in.'") Tell the siblings to practice it at odd times, even if it's only to check in and say hello. Give the autism sibling positive reinforcement each time he uses the secret knock.

"I can't" time capsule

His challenges are many. If "I can't do this" is a common refrain with your child, it's time to stage a burial for an "I can't" time capsule, to be unearthed later. This can be a solo activity or a whole-family or whole-class project. Participants write or dictate on slips of paper things they can't do that cause them frustration. The slips go into a jar that gets buried or stashed for a length of time you decide upon. By the time the jar is unearthed, much of the can't-do will have turned into can-do, a powerful chart of your child's progress. Note: keep copies of the can'ts that go into the jar so you can judge whether they've been met or whether you might need to extend the time on the burial. Reviewing too many unachieved goals defeats the purpose.

Proaction versus reaction

The difference between handling your child's thorny behavior proactively or reactively is whether you are controlling the situation or allowing your child to direct it. A proactive response is one that anticipates the behavior, sets the boundaries of acceptable behavior, and lets your child know ahead of time how you will handle it: "We know you like going to Aunt Sherry and Uncle Ron's house. But it's not okay to bang or throw Cousin Kenny's toys like you sometimes do. If you do, you will not be allowed to play in Kenny's room and will have to play only where we can see you."

Learn to recognize your own reactive behaviors and why they are unhealthy for you and your child.

- Giving in out of fear that something worse will follow. This is the equivalent of rewarding the behavior.
- Giving in out of guilt. You may feel your child's misbehavior is a result of our own faulty behavior, and you may be right. But the time to examine and change your own behavior is before you hand down the consequence.
- Repeated warnings. In the absence of follow-through, your child will quickly learn that repeated warnings are empty threats. Issue one clearly understood warning, with swift follow-through.

- Begging for compliance. Bribery, to which we've all succumbed when time, energy, or ideas are exhausted, falls into this category. But in doing so, you've shifted control of the situation to your child.

More about reviewing behavior

Mistakes happen. Despite our best intentions and most careful efforts, we realize we've been sabotaging our child or student's success in one way … or many. We're all human. Be forgiving and use it as a learning experience for next time.

- Don't focus blame on yourself, a teacher, therapist, or grandparent. Remind yourself that no one is perfect and move on.

- Do focus on finding solutions. Get additional training, ask for help, read up on alternative strategies, offer additional information that may help those working with your child. Don't assume a level of knowledge or understanding that may not be there.

- Do strive for consistency at all times. Giving in to the child's unacceptable behaviors when it is convenient for you sends the mixed message to the child that behaviors are unacceptable only sometimes, or only in certain situations or settings. You help your child best when you set the boundaries and hold to them. He is not able to interpret on his own what is unacceptable and where. Assuming he can just sets him up for failure.

  Note: It is much easier to be consistent about addressing unacceptable behaviors when you limit your efforts to one or two at a time. Trying to address everything at once spreads your emotional resources too thin and fosters an environment where the child is under constant criticism. Focus on the most troublesome problem or two first, and when they fade—as they will—move on to the next ones.

- Do plan behavior strategies in advance. "Winging it" during a behavior episode will only result in instances of enabling the child's inappropriate behaviors.

More about enabling behaviors ·····························

The reasons are varied and personal. They often reflect our own upbringing and basic attitudes toward parenting and behavior management. The common thread is that, without being aware of it, most adults do things that hold back their child's chances for success. This includes parents, teachers, and therapists, too. David Freschi, founder of Simply Good Ideas (*SimplyGoodIdeas.com*), a consultation and training company that works primarily with educators, offers food for thought about why these enabling behaviors occur and what to do about them.

Most reasons can be grouped into five broad categories:

1. Lack of knowledge of autism spectrum disorders and ways to help these children

2. Low expectations of the child and his ability

3. Inconsistent use of behavior management, language/communication, social skills, and sensory therapies between home and school

4. The search for the miracle or the one thing that will "fix" the child

5. Unrealistic expectations of self, others, programs

Some common examples of ways adults sabotage children's success:

Thoughts and perceptions

- They work so hard at school, they should be able to get a break at home.
- Look at those tears! She's been screaming for thirty minutes! It breaks my heart to see her in such pain!
- He has autism … it's part of his disability.
- I've done this lesson ten (twenty/fifty) times now. If he hasn't learned it by now, he never will. I give up!
- I tried that once and it didn't work … let's try something else this time.
- The teacher is being too hard on him; she's demanding too much.

Inadequate knowledge

- Of the basic principles of behavior management
- Of the difference between "bad behavior" typical of a child at a certain developmental level and autism
- Of the thinking patterns, perspectives, and social/emotional challenges inherent in autism or Asperger's
- Of programs/options that can be effective with children with autism or Asperger's
- Of your own feelings of guilt, inadequacy, fear

Other reasons

- Inconsistent application of program between school and home
- Focusing more on the child's weaknesses than working with his/her strengths
- Disagreement between parents on methods; lack of a unified plan
- Overwhelming grief, sense of loss as a result of the diagnosis that impedes a parent from moving forward

If any of these sound familiar, be gentle with yourself, but vow to start catching these behaviors and substituting new, more productive, positive strategies. Freschi offers these real-life solutions:

- Promote age appropriate habits. A 14-year-old boy still playing with preschool toys, or a 22-year-old girl who still carries her Barbie™ doll everywhere has an enabling adult in their lives. Age-inappropriate habits in other than private settings will prevent peer acceptance and inclusion. Gradually substitute the favorite object with a related one. Each time reduce the size and make it more

QUICK IDEA

Ask once—just once. If you're not getting the desired response, stop using language and step in with a nonverbal prompt.

appropriate. Thomas the Tank Engine can become a train book, which in turn can become a train charm on a key chain.

- Support your child's highest skill level. Kids with autism or Asperger's can make remarkable gains in functioning skills with the right program, but parents need to believe—really believe—they can do it and reinforce their independence, not their dependence. It can be a scary road for parents, but it's a necessary one to travel. For instance, Ralph learned at school to independently eat with a spoon, take small bites and swallow before he takes another bite. At a pre-school party with parents attending, Mom pulls Ralph up into her lap, as she does at home, then proceeds to break up his food and feed him little bites. For the next three days Ralph has meltdowns at school during lunch and snack. Always support the highest level of skill your child has learned and reinforce his efforts toward independence. Avoid the temptation to go backwards, even during those times when doing it for him is easier/faster/less trouble for you.

- Keep things in perspective. Skills don't develop overnight or after a handful of repetitions. A new therapy may cause disruption before it results in improvement. Let past mistakes remain in the past; focus on the future. Don't sweat the small stuff.

Saul has been doing wonderfully in school. He hasn't had a meltdown in three weeks and hasn't needed the time-away area for over a month. Staff members are very excited about Saul's progress and the ability to move forward with new goals. Dad insists on a staff team meeting to discuss the fact that Saul's aide used the time-away procedure incorrectly the first day the plan was tried—now six weeks ago.

Renee's dad, George, insists that data be collected on his daughter's progress in her ABA program. The staff agrees on the value of this practice; however, George insists that data should be taken every minute of every hour of every day Renee is in the program. He also insists the data should be analyzed, graphed, and discussed with him on a monthly basis. He believes that only data will give him an unbiased, accurate picture of how his child is progressing.

Avoid these types of parent behavior by knowing your goals and keeping your eye focused on overall progress toward those goals. Realize that progress is not linear, but a series of steps forward and backward. Accept that we all make mistakes, and know when to let them go, and when they warrant closer examination.

- Give up the idea that autism is an excuse. Shawna engages in severe behavior that often results in someone, usually a teacher or an aide, getting hurt. Part of Shawna's behavior is a result of her autism and part is related to the fact that she has developed the unpleasant habit of using this behavior to control, avoid, and intimidate. The IEP team has developed a sound behavior, sensory, and social intervention plan. Each time it is used Mom scans the school-to-home communication log, calls the principal, pumps the aide for information, and eventually finds something someone did "wrong" that she then insists is the reason Shawna acted inappropriately. This not only takes time (for both mom and teachers), but even more important, promotes an adversarial relationship. What to do? Agree on an intervention plan and then be supportive. Give it time to work. Realize that not all of Shawna's behavior is a result of her autism; her personality and temperament also affect how she acts. Autism is not an excuse for unacceptable behavior, for laziness, or for lack of trying.

- Be part of the plan. The road to success—becoming successful, happy, functioning adults—requires a coordinated, concerted effort between school and home. Kids with autism need repeated opportunities to practice emerging skills, to learn the social skills and language that come to their peers seemingly without effort. School can only do so much. Parents must take the lead in learning to be their child's most devoted teacher and advocate, 24/7. That means supporting teaching methods at home, being consistent with behavior principles and reinforcement, being ever vigilant for spotting "teaching moments" for the child at home or in the community.

Just the facts, please!

The complex nature of personal interaction can blind us to the actual facts of a situation. We view behavior through our veil of emotions and make assumptions about the motives and thoughts of others, and we are often wrong. It's not uncommon to do this when describing the behaviors of our children, and attributing reasons to these behaviors.

Next time you're reviewing behavior—your child's, your student's, or your own—step back and play the role of the observer. Look at the situation with as little emotion as possible and instead, report only the facts. Julian did this, I responded with that, then he did this, and I said that. Using this simple technique can often help you identify clues as to why the situation unfolded as it did, and when your behavior might be confusing to the child, or enable the problem behavior.

It was a good day

Our kids' black and white thinking patterns result in a lot of negative thoughts about themselves and their abilities, which turn into negative behaviors of minor and major consequence. Even the smallest mistake can be monumental in their eyes, the smallest rule infraction seems to them an indication of utter failure. And if, like many children who have behavior issues, he hears more criticism than praise, it only exacerbates the negativity.

- Reverse your child's tendency to dwell on the negatives by accentuating the positive, in him, in you, and in others.

- Have your child write (or dictate to you) one good thing about her day. Keep the thoughts in a journal and teach her to look back through it from time to time and recall positive moments in her life.

- Echo that idea during dinner: everyone mentions one good thing that happened that day.

- Carry it even further: ask the child's teacher to write in the school-to-home communication book one or more good things the child did at school that day. Parents: do the same when sending the book back to school.

- Point out the ebb and flow of times to your child, so she becomes aware that we all make mistakes and life goes on, that forgetting your homework doesn't need to ruin the entire day, that getting a spot on her blouse can be ignored.

- Feed language to your child by voicing your own feelings and giving repeated examples of looking for the positives in life.

- Volunteer as a family at a community service organization. The act of helping others illuminates the positive in our own lives.

Daily Living

I hear and I forget.
I see and I remember.
I do and I understand.

CONFUCIUS

YOU MAY NOT HAVE THOUGHT ABOUT IT consciously at the moment it happened, but in becoming a parent, yours became a goal every parent shares: to nurture and guide your child to productive, independent adulthood. The many objectives (the measurable means to the end) you set and achieve throughout your son or daughter's childhood and adolescence are all oriented to this goal.

Autism does not preclude a child from learning the skills that will equip him for an independent life. It just changes the way and pace at which we teach these skills.

For parents, it is critical that we disabuse ourselves of the notion that the schools will teach our child everything he needs to know to become that productive, independent adult. Many's the high school graduate who has learned how to pass a test or play a sport, but hasn't the foggiest idea how to prepare meals, do minor home or car repairs, or handle money responsibly. Teaching our children functional life skills requires long, patient, *hands-on* repetition, and reinforcement. There are no shortcuts; you have to invest the time and effort in being a can-do, will-do parent. It's troubling how easily and unknowingly we thwart this teaching: "I can't fix anything," or "I don't have time," or "I hate cooking/cleaning/yardwork." Every task we farm out to restaurants, maid services, and contractors is a lost opportunity to teach our kids the skills they will need to succeed on their own.

Teachers and others in the field of education: by choosing your profession, you've also accepted the goal of guiding children to productive, independent adulthood. Great teachers know how to make the curriculum relevant to students, and nothing is more relevant than functional life skills. Ergo, nothing is more important than tying curriculum to real life. Can your child or student read a map, a recipe, a grocery ad, a ballot, a weather report, and comprehend how they apply to the geography, health, history, sociology, and science of his own life?

Functional life skills can and should be taught from early childhood, in incremental activities and responsibilities that grow along with a child's cognitive and physical abilities. This goes for *all* children with autism, not just those who are "high functioning." Start small, build slowly, according to your child's abilities, and watch your child blossom as he or she achieves self-sufficiency and independence.

Matters of choice

Most of us take for granted the amazing number of choices we have on a daily basis. Minute by minute, we choose one option over others, and know that by virtue of both having and making those choices, we exercise a measure of control over our lives. For children with autism, choices are much more limited, which can contribute to lack of self-esteem, behavior problems, and a reluctance to interface with the people and situations around them.

Building your child or student's decision-making skills is essential to building his sense of responsibility, to himself and to his family, classroom, and beyond. Providing frequent choices gives him control over his life, and that control makes him more likely to interact successfully with people and his environment.

Your single most useful tactic is phrasing choices in the positive. What do your want your child to do? So often we think in negative terms or in imperatives—squelching behavior problems, forcing compliance, issuing directives. Instead, offer choices within have-to's, multiple options all of which you find acceptable. In a typical day, there are many opportunities to offer choices framed in the positive.

Choices, not threats. A my-way-or-the-highway choice isn't really a choice, is it? If your child has an obstinate or oppositional streak, he may push back, choose the punishment, almost like a dare, to see if you will follow through. That's not productive for either of you.

> Instead of: "Eat your breakfast or you'll be sorry."
> Offer: "Would you like toast or applesauce first?"

Concrete choices. Not only are open-ended questions often too difficult for your child to answer, they confront the child with the possibility of a "no" response. In the following examples, possible negative answers abound: we are out of that, you wore that yesterday, not that again!, etc. Notice how the concrete choices reduce wear and tear on both of you.

> Instead of: "What would you like in your lunch?"
> Offer: "Would you like a cheese or peanut butter sandwich today?"

> Instead of: "Go get dressed. Anything that's clean is fine."
> Offer: "You may choose the Nemo T-shirt or the green sweater."

Choices that have natural consequences. "You may pet Kritter gently behind the ears. If you poke her face, she may bite or scratch you."

Choices that have parent-imposed consequences. "You may play with your Hot Wheels upstairs in your room or downstairs in the family room. If you throw them down the stairs, I will take them away."

Humorous choices. This can soften a non-negotiable.

> Instead of: "You have to wear a seat belt, no arguments!"
> Offer: "Who do you want to be today, Captain Seatbelt or Darth Ultrabelt?"

No choice. "You may not stick your fork into anything whatsoever except the food on your plate." Children (yes, even children with autism) can be clever at trying to bend or challenge rules or choices they don't like. There will be times when offering a choice isn't realistic or safe. Avoid meltdowns by being clear and unapologetic:

- "I can't give you a choice in this situation because it is dangerous. You might get hurt."

- "I can't give you that choice because it would be bad for Danny" (have negative consequences for another child).
- "I give you lots of choices but this time it needs to be an adult choice."

Remember always that learning to make choices and decisions is a process. It's not enough to offer choices; you must also

- Allow your child time to think through the options you've given. Particularly when there will be consequences, tell him to pause and to picture in his head the outcome he'd like to have.
- Communicate a can-do attitude toward your child—let her know you have faith in her ability to make good choices.
- Acknowledge and thank him for making good choices, whether it's getting in the car without an argument, hanging his jacket up instead of dropping it on the floor, or sharing a toy.
- Offer only as many choices as your child is able to handle, which at first may only be two specific options. As his decision-making ability grows, add more choices, or broader, less specific choices.
- Offer choices that are motivating to the child, not reflections of your preferences. If you want him to eat breakfast but he hates Wheaties and Grapenuts (your favorites) offering a choice between those two items is no choice at all.
- Offer only real choices. Misuse of various forms of the "Do you want—?" question is a common teaching mistake. "Do you want to go to lunch?" "Do you want to do your homework now?" If we pose a question to a child when we're not really offering a choice, we teach him that we are untrustworthy in our actions, or that choices only happen sometimes or not at all. Don't offer a choice or ask that "Do you want—?" question unless you mean it and are willing to accept no for an answer. "No" is one of the acceptable answers to "Do you want—?"

Always remember that your goal in offering meaningful choices is to foster decision-making skills, not force compliance or transform negative behavior. We repeat this thought because it's key to using a choice-making strategy effectively. You want your child to be successful. As the adult in the interaction, set up conditions that enable him to feel positive about making decisions in his life. Don't sabotage his efforts by offering poorly planned choices.

Winning isn't everything

Should you let your child win at games you play together? Let the debate begin! In this corner, the naysayers: letting kids win sets them up for failure and humiliation when they play with peers, it sends the message that winning is more important than fun, it deprives them of the opportunity to learn to lose gracefully. And in the opposite corner, the advocates: adults have an unfair advantage, so letting the kids win evens the field, a child who loses every time will become discouraged and give up playing. And in yet another corner—the gray area: isn't there a difference between games of luck, like Candyland, and games of skill, like checkers or basketball? What if you only let them win sometimes? How often? What if you catch them cheating?

Make the whole debate moot for your child. If he is losing all the time, you are not playing the right games.

- Choose only games appropriate to your child's developmental age, which may not be the same as his chronological age. When he has the skill set necessary for the game, he will win some of the time without you having to decide whether to throw the game.

- Choose games of luck, which statistically give your child as much chance to win as any other player.

- You can give your child a handicap or head start, and be upfront in your explanation of why you are doing it. "I've played this game a lot and you haven't, so you should go first and take two turns to start."

- Choose games that are fun regardless of who wins.

- Play games in teams of two. Your child gets the benefit of discussing strategy and decision-making with a peer model or adult, which is not only a valuable learning experience, but it automatically softens a game loss. This is also a low-key way to introduce your child to games that are the next step up the developmental ladder for him.

- Play cooperative games, where all players work together for a common goal emphasizing participation and fun over competition and winning. Plug the phrase "cooperative games" into your internet search engine to find games with subject matter that will appeal to your child.

- You don't feel obliged to finish reading a boring book; don't feel obligated to finish a game just because you started it. If your child is tired, bored, getting too frustrated, or otherwise not getting anything beneficial out of the game, fold it up. Many's the Scrabble game Ellen's family started where they ended up having more fun complaining about their terrible letters, making up funky nonsense words, thumb-flipping the tiles back into the box, and heading to the kitchen for ice cream.

Just a minute?

Most kids will do it at some point: you make a request of your child or student and get the reply, "Just a minute!" It's easy to assume this is the response of a child trying to postpone something he doesn't feel like doing. But within autism, we never assume anything, and we look for the communication behind the behavior. "Just a minute" may indeed be a stall—or it may be a legitimate request for extra processing time. He may need those additional moments to decode your language and motor plan how he will fulfill your request.

You may be able to distinguish between procrastination and processing by asking, in a neutral tone of voice, "Why do you need a minute?" If the issue is procrastination, this prompt may be enough to get the child back to task. If the issue is processing, he may be able to tell you: "I can't find my shoes." "I don't get what you're asking." Kids who struggle with language may not be able to verbalize anything at all. Observe behavior, read between the lines, probe for more information: "Are you having trouble finding your shoes? Let's try to remember the last time you had them on. Where were you?"

Skill development through child's play ························

Play is the medium by which most children learn best, so games are more than just for fun. The right game can help you zero in on your child's particular skill development needs. In this book, we don't want to get into the business of recommending branded toys and games, so the following list is generic—but intended to give you an idea of how many skills are embodied in a whole child. Mastering many of these skills is challenging for the child with autism, but luckily, there are many fun ways to go about it.

Fine motor skills are needed for writing, dressing, grooming, and eating. Games and activities that promote fine motor skills are:

- Peg boards
- Bean bags
- Puzzles
- Stencils
- Geometric drawing toys with templates
- Dominoes—either playing the dot-matching game, or setting up the 300-piece (or more) domino rally
- Marbles
- Jacks
- Pick-up sticks
- Clay or play dough—especially activities using just the fingertips, such as rolling peas
- Paper dolls or other paper-cutting activities

Visual focus and movement. Like our muscles, the eyes tire with overuse and strain. And like our muscles, the eye can be trained to increase its stamina. Fluid eye movement is necessary for reading and other focused activities. Activities that enhance eye movement and control include:

- Punch-card lacing
- Table tennis

- Jacks
- Puzzles
- Musical keyboard activities
- Typing on a computer or typewriter
- Dot-to-dot drawings

Spatial Relationships. Children with autism tend to be less aware of their surroundings than the typical child. Games and activities that build spatial orientation can help them understand both the concepts and the vocabulary of distance, size, direction (up/down, left/right) and position (over/under, front/behind) in our three-dimensional world.

> **QUICK IDEA**
>
> Adapt some play games for a child with motor skill coordination challenges by using a half-dead battery to slow down the motion.

- Building models
- Blocks (multi-shape sets are particularly good)
- Lego's other building sets
- Martial arts (tae kwon do, karate, kickboxing)
- Topographic maps or dioramas
- Puzzles, both jigsaw and three-dimensional
- Wood or metal shop tool-work
- Origami, paper airplanes, pop-up cards, or other folding activities
- Reading maps, mazes, labyrinths, blueprints

Go ahead—scribble on the wall

She's going to do it anyway, so why not give her a legitimate canvas? Paint one (untextured) wall of her room, playroom, kitchen or other suitable location with chalkboard paint, available at most places that sell paint. If you don't have a whole wall to spare, use the spray paint version to cover a tabletop, floor area or other flat surface.

Ideas for easing separation anxiety

Shakespeare called parting "such sweet sorrow," but for fearful children and tearful parents, it can be the worst part of the day. Help the school or daycare drop-off go more smoothly for both of you:

- If you will be leaving your child with a new babysitter or preschool, set up a meeting or visit prior to his first day there. If you will be leaving him for the first time ever, do short practice sessions with a safe person— leave him for ten minutes with a trusted adult. Come back exactly at the promised time. Extend the period away by short increments, at his transition pace, not yours.

- Utilize your child's super-sensitive sense of smell to help. Place a drop of your perfume, shampoo, or other familiar-scented item inside the collar of her shirt. She can take a sniff any time during the day to feel connected to you. Or let her wear a T-shirt or sweater you have worn, which will also have a personal scent clinging to it.

- Create a small photo album depicting your child's day: waking up, eating breakfast, getting on the bus, engaging in the activities of her school day, coming home to Mom, dinner, bedtime. She can keep the photo album in her cubby or backpack and refer to it when she feels anxious.

- If your child has a favorite story character, talk about how he or she might handle being away at school. What would Dora do? Maybe she would make a list of all the fun things she does at school. Maybe she would think about other brave things she's done, like jumping off the diving board, or riding the bus, or sleeping in the bunk bed.

- A locket or other photo necklace around her neck is something she can pull out during the day for visual reassurance.

- Make breakfast a have-to each morning. Anxiety is more pronounced in children who are hungry, tired, sick, or otherwise stressed.

Tip

Anything nutritious is a breakfast food. Pizza, pork chops, spaghetti, and peanut butter are just as suitable at 7:00 a.m. as they are at 7:00 p.m. His stomach doesn't know the difference.

- Don't admonish, scold, berate, ridicule. (Does that work for you when you are feeling anxious?) And don't use adult logic with a child.

- As gut-wrenching as it can be for both you and your child, it can help to know that most families come through this transition just fine. However, if your child's separation anxiety seems unduly severe, lasts far longer than you thought it would, or disrupts daily activities, eating, or sleeping, it may be time to take a closer look. Confer with caregivers or teachers to pinpoint possible problems. If your child has symptoms such as panic attacks, hyperventilation, nausea and vomiting, or nightmares about being lost or abandoned, consult your doctor.

Tips for happier haircuts

Many aspects of a hair salon or barber shop are similar to a doctor's or dentist's office: strange furniture, scary tools of the trade, unfamiliar chemical smells, and potentially long, anxious waits. If getting a haircut causes your child an afternoon of anguish, consider these ideas and accommodations:

- Don't use the word "cut." Children know that cuts hurt. A cut finger hurts, a cut knee hurts; it follows that a haircut will hurt. Talk instead about getting her hair shortened, trimmed, tidied up, styled, or out of her eyes.

- Mom or Dad: visit the salon ahead of time and talk with the stylist about ways to make the experience as pleasant as possible for everyone. Can she use a chair at a quieter end of the salon, or away from the sinks, with their constant traffic going back and forth? Share tidbits of information about the child with the stylist (his favorite topics, DVDs, toys, etc.), and snap a photo of the stylist to show to the child prior to the visit. Prep the stylist too, telling him/her ahead of time about what might happen, how she should/should not respond, and when to let Mom or Dad step in.

- The typical salon chair that goes up and down and all around may not only be a vestibular problem—his feet don't touch the footrest—but also resembles the chair at the dentist's office. Ask the stylist to offer a stationary stool or chair with a solid footrest at the child's height. If the chair is much larger than he is, downsize the seating area by tucking a pillow on either side of him and/or in his lap.

- Ask your stylist to stash away curling irons, scissors, hair dryers, and other gear she will not be using for your child. Shiny metal implements may evoke doctor or dentist office associations. Skip the cape and the neck tape if the smell or texture bothers him. A soft towel (from home, if needed) works just as well.

- Ask that your child face away from the mirror during the haircut. Seeing sharp scissors or clippers flying about or near his eyes and ears may be terrifying.

- Plastic-handled or covered-handle scissors and plastic combs can reduce the amount of glare that can bounce off metal cutting/grooming utensils.

- Ask for an appointment at the slowest time of day and ask that overhead music be turned down or off. Ask for extra time so the child does not feel rushed or forced, and ask that your child not be scheduled when a person in a nearby salon chair is getting any type of strong smelling treatment (like a permanent).

- Don't schedule an appointment for a time when your child is likely to be tired (end of day or right before nap), hungry (right before lunch), or unhappy (he's missing his favorite show).

- Call ahead to confirm that the stylist is running on time. Ask that everything be ready to go when you walk in so there is no anxiety-building wait.

- Offer a hand-held game or a board book as a distraction.

- Ask the stylist to explain, briefly and in simple words, what she's going to do before doing it. "I'm going to spray water on your hair first, then comb it, then start shaping it." Many children with autism can't stand having their hair sprayed; if this is true of your child, ask the stylist to dampen his hair by spraying the water on her hands or comb, then running it through his hair. She can also ask him if she can spray his arm first, to demonstrate. (Honor whatever he says.) Our favorite stylist has a lot of luck with fearful kids by letting them spray her first. They love it.

- Many children with autism can't tolerate buzzing clippers. Anything that makes them jump, cringe, or twist in the chair is a safety hazard, with potential for injury to tender ears, eyes, and necks. Opt for a scissor or razor-cut style.

- If your child shows interest, the stylist can demonstrate the equipment before using it on the child. For instance, she could run the electric clippers (with the guard on) across her arm so the child sees it won't cut his skin. Or bring a stuffed toy or a doll and have the stylist first demonstrate on the toy. Parents can also use the animal or doll as a visual cue to pantomime instructions from the stylist, such as "turn your head to the right," or "chin down."

- Have the stylist shape up the front, sides and nape of the neck first. That way if the experience goes sour before the cut is complete, he won't look lopsided. Our stylist calls this her "fireman's cut." When she's cutting hair at the fire station, the bell may ring at any time and firefighters must be ready to go that instant. Your otherwise reluctant youngster just might agree to sit like a fireman.

- Ask ahead of time if the salon offers treats or rewards. If it's something your child is not allowed to have (sugar, allergy trigger, non-kosher), ask that it not be offered, or that a substitute item be offered (such as a sticker).

- Take a fresh shirt to the salon with you. Those tiny leftovers hairs around the collar could drive him crazy.

- Buy an inexpensive doll at a garage sale or thrift shop and let your child give the doll a haircut. If he doesn't handle scissors yet, he can still pantomime the haircut. Repeat the haircut simulations from time to time between actual haircuts.

- Finally, if your child isn't able to tolerate salon visits yet, inquire about having the stylist make a house visit instead. Many do. Or, seek out a stylist who works out of her home. In most cases, you and your child will be the only clients there, and it allows you and the stylist to better control the environment to suit the child.

Tips for reluctant shampooers

Even the happiest and most willing of bath babies may balk at shampoo time. This very invasive but necessary grooming routine can seem like a battlefield, but there are things you can do to ease the discomfort.

- Water coming toward the face area can feel aggressive. Offer earplugs, goggles, swim mask (covering his eyes not only keeps the water out but allows him to keep his eyes open if he's the type who fears surprises).

- Have your child lie down in the tub with just a few inches of water and wash from the back, bringing nothing into her field of vision.

- Let him wear his clothes, swimsuit, pajamas, whatever he chooses. The weight of the wet clothes may help proprioceptively. Or offer a wet towel or blanket.

- Use small amounts of shampoo to reduce rinse time.

- If rinsing with a cup, tell your child how many cupfuls you'll need to get her rinsed, then count. Knowing exactly when the torture will end may help her get through it.

- When rinsing with a cup, hold the cup lightly but directly to the scalp so the water is flowing but not striking the head. A measuring cup with a pour spout can help you better direct the flow of water.

- Commercial shampoos are heavily scented and even kid fragrances like bubble gum may be offensive. Many unscented, hypoallergenic shampoos are available now.

- Don't insist on washing his hair with every bath or shower. Once or twice a week is sufficient for most children; knowing the interval is infrequent may decrease resistance.

- Test the water temperature, adjusting so that it is not too cool or too hot (for her—not you). Warm the shampoo in your hands before applying; it may feel cold straight from the bottle, or the oozing sensation on her head may be disturbing.

- If the rubbing/massaging motion of shampooing bothers him, ask if he'd like to do it himself.

- Try a car wash sponge for wetting and rinsing. Let her play with the sponge when you are done washing her hair.

- If you use a hand-held sprayer or squirt bottle, let him spray you back. It's just water, right? A little silliness goes a long way.

- Have everything you need ready before you start. A small checklist may help: shampoo, towel, washcloth to hold over face, goggles or bath visor, etc. A fumbling parent only adds to the child's anxiety.

- If your child tends to dump or ingest substances, remove shampoo from flip-top or screw-open bottles and place in a locking pump bottle. Keep out of sight between washings.

- An alternative shampooing product may be the ticket: dry-shampoo products that spray on and brush out, or one of the no-rinse shampoo products available: apply shampoo, lather up, and towel out. Find products like these through internet shopping outlets.

Nail trimming

As with the haircut, avoid using the word "cut." Explain that the nails need to be shortened, trimmed, or tidied. Other ideas:

- Always clip after bath or shower when nails are soft.

- If doing all ten fingers or toes at once is intolerable, do one a day in constant rotation as part of the general bedtime routine. Work up to two per day, etc.

- As early as possible, teach the child to do it herself.

- Stabilizing the finger over the edge of a hard surface such as a counter, table, book, or knee may help.

- Have Dad or a sibling trim their nails at the same time. They can take turns.

- Recite a rhyme, poem, or story. Customize a favorite song to suit him.

- Trim while he is engrossed in a favorite TV show.

- The fine-paper side of an emery board may be more tolerable and has the added benefit of eliminating sharp snags that may result from conventional clipping. Keep up with it on an every-few-days basis. Children's nails grow fast!

- Search the internet for adaptive devices. Comfort Care Baby Nail Clippers by The First Years comes with an attached magnifying glass (decreases the chance of nipping tender skin) and large grippers for better control. Lil Nipper Clippers are plastic-encased clippers with a slot in the faceplate that the child slides his finger into, never actually seeing the clipping mechanism. Munchkin Safety Nail Clipper has a plastic safety guard and a safety-grip ring underneath to slip your finger through, steadying the clipper.

- When all else fails, do it while she is asleep.

Just take a bite

This plaintive title of Lori Ernsperger's 2004 book is one to which many parents will instantly relate. Dr. Ernsperger, an autism and behavioral consultant, and co-author Tania Stegen-Hanson, a pediatric occupational therapist, offer solutions to clashes over food aversions and eating challenges, including these tactics:

- Develop a written mealtime schedule that includes snack times. The child can eat only during these times.

- Offer one preferred food at each meal/snack.

- Restrict milk and juice between meals.

- Parents and siblings eat together.

- Do not force the child to eat.

- Use measuring cups and spoons at each meal, and offer only portion sizes that are age appropriate.

- Involve the child with mealtime preparation.

- Offer opportunities throughout the day to learn about new foods. The education extends beyond eating to creating a food-rich environment.

- To combat gravitational insecurity, arrange the child's seating to allow his feet to touch the floor or footrest.

Did you know? Many kids experience "neophobia"—a fear of anything new—between the ages of two and six, which may partly explain an aversion to trying new types of foods during those years.

Helpful eating adaptations

Poor oral-motor or fine motor control can also make meal-times difficult. Adaptive utensils can help.

- Websites like *ElderStore.net* carry weighted utensils, as well as utensils with swivel heads, twisty handles, and other accommodations. Also available: weighted cups, spout cups (a grown-up version of the sippy cup), double handled thumbs-up insulated cups.

- Homemade adaptations to help with grip: poking the handle of the utensil through a foam or rubber ball, or covering the handle with some rubber tubing or pipe insulation foam.

- To keep her plate or bowl from sliding away, place it on a foam-backed vinyl placemat, a wet washcloth or textured shelf liner paper.

- Or, attach no-slip devices (cork, bathtub appliqués or small suction cups) to the bottom of a few special plates just for her.

- Decrease the distance from plate to mouth by placing the plate on a box or phone book.

> **QUICK IDEA**
>
> If your child is not getting the recommended levels of fruit and vegetables into his daily diet, try adding cooked and pureed fruits and vegetables to other foods: cauliflower to pasta sauce, sweet potato or applesauce to pancakes, zucchini to chocolate cake (ask Ellen for her recipe), ground veggies to meatloaf or soups.

- Sitting in a straddle position across a bench or bolster may allow more upper body control. Because feet or knees must be firmly planted on the floor, this will work best at a child-sized table.

Note: If you find yourself resisting this idea because it means the family does not eat all together at the table, think a moment about separating issues and goals. Is the goal helping your child achieve independence in feeding himself or is the goal to have family together time at the table? Either is legitimate. But one is likely a temporary accommodation that can, with patience, lead to the other.

Narrow food preferences

Many kids with autism are picky eaters, and the usual tactics frequently don't work. Ellen says she could have offered her son a "broccoli forest" or a cheese sandwich with a raisin face 8,000 times and he would still be looking at it saying: "It's broccoli. Why are you playing with food?"

If your child is nutritionally at risk because of limited food choices, there's likely a strong underlying sensory factor or a biomedical issue that needs addressing. However, if your child is a finicky eater because of preference, or his sensory issues can be improved with regular occupational therapist desensitizing exercises, here are a few ideas to try:

- As with academic or other new areas, approach the subject of eating or new foods through your child's area of interest. Choose a flavor, taste, or color she likes and ask her to help you plan a whole meal around that flavor. Some examples:

  - All lemon menu: Fish, chicken, or pasta with a lemon marinade or sauce, lemon-poppy seed muffins or quick bread, lemon pie or sorbet, lemonade

  - All orange menu: Salmon, yams, carrots, peaches, and cantaloupe, pumpkin pie, orange sherbet, orange juice (yeah, we know, it's really yellow)

- Whether or not your child eats a single bite of her special meal is not important. Contributing to the food preparation process is, as is her broadening awareness of the vast variety of food possibilities available to her. For some kids, just being in the same room with the unfamiliar foods may be success at first.

- Some children will try new foods if allowed to explore them tactilely, at their own pace. We know a kiddo who began eating eggs only after several weeks of tactile experiences—handling hard boiled eggs warm and cold, coloring (and smashing) Easter eggs, separating the eggs from the shell, the white from the yolk, rolling the yolk into little balls. Be sure to clearly define when food exploration is allowed or not allowed (e.g., outside only, never at the table, etc.).

- Use a favorite food as an introduction to a wider variety of foods around it. If he just loves hamburgers:

  - Pick up menus from restaurants offering multiple burger choices. Talk about the kinds of burgers offered—mushroom, cheese, gardenburger.

  - Ask friends or family members what kinds of condiments they like on their burgers and record the answers, maybe even make a graph.

  - Go on the internet and find facts about burgers: Who invented the hamburger? Is there a Guinness record for hamburger eating? How many hamburgers are eaten in the United States each year? Where is the Hamburger Hall of Fame (and yes, there is one)?

  - Plan a week of menus: Hamburgers are the main dish every night, but your child has to think up the side dishes. (He doesn't have to eat them—just think them up.) You can make suggestions to help him along—French fries, green salad, baked beans—but then let him take over. His responses may surprise you. And yes, cook whatever he suggests, however bizarre the combination may be to you.

  - Spark interest in kitchen activities through recipes for nonfood items. She may respond more quickly knowing she won't be asked to eat it. These might include bubble solutions, facials, potpourri, doggie treats, play clay or dough, soap, or bath salts.

Cooking co-ops for special diets

If your child is following a GFCF (gluten free, casein free) diet, you know only too well how time-intensive and expensive a special diet can be. A special-needs take on the basic idea of a family cooking co-op could save you and other families like yours many hours and dollars.

A cooking co-op is a group of several families that batch-produce meals or food items for all participants. In the typical model, there may be four families with each cooking one night of the week and delivering meals to the other three families, so each family cooks once but eats four times. Your cooking co-op can make its own rules. Here are some suggestions for a successful co-op.

- You needn't swap full meals. Perhaps one family bakes gluten-free bread and another produces cookies. A third does soups and a fourth produces fruit- and vegetable-based side dishes.

- If weekly is too often, make it bi-weekly, monthly, or quarterly.

- Establish a list or menu of items everyone agrees upon. This may be challenging, so come to the table with enough suggestions to accommodate varying tastes and preferences.

- Agree upon amounts of food to be prepared.

- Set up a delivery schedule.

- Agree upon a system for trying new foods and discontinuing those that most didn't enjoy. Agree to administer the "no thanks" votes gently and to accept them graciously.

- Contribute some of your grocery savings to a kitty to buy new cookbooks for the group.

- When it's your day to cook, involve your child. It's a natural opening to talk about his diet and the reasons for it. Learning to make wise food choices and prepare healthy food is one of the most valuable life skills of all.

- Meals and items that can be frozen are cool. (Pun intended!) Some co-ops swap only freezer items.

● In a typical co-op, member families generally don't eat together, but your group may enjoy an occasional gathering where no one has to worry about watching every crumb that goes into your little ones' mouths.

Help for resistant tooth-brushers

You don't have to brush all your teeth, our dentist tells us—only the ones you want to keep. Oral defensiveness can make it hard for a child to tolerate foreign objects, or invasive tactile or gustatory (taste) sensations in his mouth. Tooth brushing can be an ordeal for such children, but it is essential to good health.

● Remember that the purpose of brushing is to remove bacteria, and a toothbrush is just a tool for doing that. It's not the only tool, and there is no one right toothbrush. You can try:

- Shaped and angled toothbrushes

- Heads of various shapes

- Soft, medium or firm bristles (most kids—and most dentists—prefer soft)

- No brush at all. Use a piece of gauze or washcloth wrapped around a finger. Dip it in toothpaste, fluoride wash, or just plain water if that's all your child will tolerate. You'll still be removing a large amount of bacteria.

- A battery-operated toothbrush. Many children find the vibration soothing, although some find it irritating.

- Adaptive toothbrushes such as the Nuk toothbrush trainer (rubber latex brush) or Nuk massage brush, or the Collis-Curve™ Toothbrush, which brushes on all three sides at once (*Colliscurve.com*). Another is the sixty-second TimeMachine Toothbrush, a timer toothbrush that brushes front, back, and chewing surfaces of both upper and lower teeth at the same time. Available from *MagicalToysAndProducts.com, BestBabyStore.com*, and other websites.

● Brush with warm water to reduce sensitivity.

- Experiment with consistencies and flavors of toothpaste. Paste may be too gritty but gel may be just right. And remember that proper brushing technique is much more important than whatever toothpaste you choose. As one hygienist put it: "It's the brushing that does the work, not the paste. Don't fight toothpaste battles. The flavor and foaminess are often more about your adult preferences than your child's."

- If your child is sensitive to food dyes, artificial sweeteners, and other substances, be aware that many common-brand toothpastes contain such ingredients. The FDA does not require toothpaste be labeled as such, but if the paste has stripes, blue speckles, or a pink glow, you can bet it contains dye. Visit health food stores for natural herbal toothpaste options. Many, such as Auromère, contain ingredients from the "tooth-brush trees"—neem and peelu.

- If brushing all the teeth at the same time is too overwhelming, break it up. Brush just the bottoms, take a two-minute break (or five or ten), then come back and brush the tops. Break down further as needed.

- Sing a short song with each section as a way of letting your child know how long it will take. Suggestions: "Bingo"; "Farmer in the Dell"; "Old McDonald"; "Down by the Bay"; "Five Little Ducks"; "Row, Row, Row Your Boat"; or "Twinkle, Twinkle Little Star."

- Post a visual chart illustrating each step of the tooth brushing process to help build independence and self-esteem.

- Most young children will need your assistance to achieve the proper angle and motion for effective cleaning. Stand behind your child to help, as the dentist does. Let him rest his head against you. Letting him sit may make it easier. Teach him to hold the brush along the gum line at a 45° angle and move the brush in small circles, not up and down. Understand that you may be assisting your child with this up to as late as age ten. Many children will not have the necessary manual dexterity until that age.

- Follow up tooth brushing with a pleasant, anticipated activity (such as reading together or listening to music).

Your friend, the dentist ·

Old stereotypes are hard to kill, but one that richly deserves to die is the notion that dental visits are torture, something to be feared, dreaded, and avoided. While the ideal of "painless dentistry" may not be 100% realistic in every instance, twenty-first-century methods and practices are making dental visits tolerable and comfortable, even for a child with autism. There's no denying that a dental office is fraught with innumerable sensory confrontations, but by your wise choice of a dentist who meets your child's individual needs, those check-ups can become just another day in the life of your family.

So put away the thought that you can postpone dental care until your child is older, that those baby teeth don't matter. They matter a great deal, and not just as place-holders for permanent teeth. Baby teeth figure into language development, and the ability to chew is necessary to developing good eating habits. Oral health is critical at all ages. In a heartbreaking and well-publicized case in 2007, a twelve-year-old boy died when infection from a tooth abscess traveled to his brain.

In writing this section, we asked parents of children with autism and the dental professionals who treat them to share stories and thoughts. The responses came from around the world, and they were overwhelmingly positive, even in public health settings (where parents cannot choose the dentist their child will see). Sometimes it took more than one try to find the right dentist, and what worked for one family did not work for another. The following thoughts and suggestions represent the experiences of a variety of families.

- Look for a pediatric dentist. The chances are greater that a pediatric dentist will have taken coursework and been exposed to a larger number of special needs children than a general dentist. Their offices are equipped for children, and some even offer designated days when they see only special needs children.

- If you like your general dentist, ask if he is comfortable seeing your child with autism. If the answer is hesitant or qualified, ask if he can recommend someone.

- Ask other families with children. "Even in small towns," a hygienist told us, "there will be at least one or two dentists who have all the special kids. It's because they're good, and because other dentists and parents refer to them."

Parents reported a variety of accommodations made by the dentist and staff:

- Dentist operates on time, with no long sits in the waiting room.

- Dentist and team of assistants are fast, gentle, and calm, and never force a child to do anything.

- Fear of the dental chair was a widely reported issue. Some dentists will let your child lie in your lap or an assistant's. One mom reported that her dentist gets down on the floor for a child who will tolerate a cleaning only if they are lying flat. Ellen's dentist treated her son in his office chair.

- Dentist will end the visit before the child becomes overwhelmed and schedule another appointment on short notice if more time is needed to finish the work.

- Dentist allows families to drop in anytime just so the child can practice being in the chair.

- Dentist offers videos, either handheld, or mounted on the ceiling (some children love this, others find it too distracting) and/or offers headphones with music or audio books.

- Dentist offers lead blanket as a weighted calming device.

- Assistant will hold x-ray film in place rather than making child bite down, taking separate pictures of top and bottom.

- Dentist offers a mild sedative if needed.

- Dentist lets child know when and how she is going to touch him.

Other ideas:

- *Hiyah.net* offers free educational software made for children struggling with language delays. Download "Going to the Dentist."

- Choose a dentist who will let your child acclimate to the office slowly over time before the actual cleaning or checkup. First visit—look inside the door. Second visit—say hello to the dentist. Third visit—dentist looks in child's mouth. Fourth visit—child brushes his own teeth then leaves. Fifth visit—child watches dentist work on sibling or other child. And so on.

- Deep pressure input before the visit may help: use a vibrating toothbrush, have your child wear a snug hat, leggings, or a weighted vest, do some quick push-ups against the car or a wall before entering the building.

- Put together a story with photos of the dentist, the assistants, the waiting room (and toy room if there is one), the chair, the sparkling smiles at the end of the appointment.

- If your child will be seeing your dentist, schedule your appointments together.

- Don't schedule the appointment at an hour or day when your child is likely to be tired, hungry, or otherwise out of sorts.

- Don't tell your child a week ahead of the appointment, allowing anxiety to build and classmates to weigh in with their own stories. Tell him the day of the appointment that you're going for a check-up, that's all.

- And this from a pediatric hygienist with thirty-two years of experience *and* a son with autism: "The worst thing you can say to your child is, 'don't worry, honey, he won't hurt you,' or 'If you're good/brave....' Chances are your child wasn't worried about pain until you brought it up. And what's 'good?' We do our best to ensure your child experiences as little pain as possible, but if he does, we want him to tell us, and not try to be 'good.'"

The biggest difference of opinion between parents and professionals is the issue of whether the parent should accompany their child to the treatment room. Some parents will not consider a dentist who doesn't allow them to "come back" with their child, while many dentists discourage it. This attitude is different from what most parents experience in a doctor's office, where the parent is expected to accompany the child to the examination room and control his behavior. Our hygienist offers food for thought on the subject: "Please understand this is a 100% safety issue. When we are inside a child's mouth with high-speed drills and sharp instruments, it is imperative that the child be focused on and listening to one individual only—the dentist. Any distraction, however momentary, carries the potential of severe soft tissue damage—think tongues, cheeks, gums. The best thing you can do for your child is tell him to listen to the dentist, and then you wait outside." The exception, she points out, is if your child is truly in need of your comfort during the procedure. Any dentist will accommodate legitimate need.

Cuts, scrapes, and bruises

Kids' boo-boos are inevitable. Scraped knees or elbows, cuts, falls, and bug bites can be particularly distressing for the child with tactile sensitivities. In addition to the healing power of your love, use these extra hints for dispensing minor medical attention at home or at school.

- Stay calm at all times. Keep your voice steady and offer assurance that you know what to do.

- Keep your language simple and brief. Use picture cards if needed. At times like these your child's language processing fades.

- Explain each step of what you need to do. Show the child the materials you will use. "I have to wash the cut to remove any dirt or germs." "I need to press down on the cut with my fingers to stop the blood."

- If there is blood, use a dark washcloth or towel to clean up. The sight of their own blood sparks panic in many children.

- If something might hurt (many children with autism have a high threshold to pain—don't assume discomfort that may not occur), let the child know ahead of time. If it's temporary, say so. "I'm going to put ointment on the cut with this cotton swab. It might sting for a few seconds and then it will be over. One, two, three—done."

- If bandaging is needed, explain its use to the child and tell him to let you know if it is or becomes too tight, too sticky, wet, smelly, or otherwise uncomfortable. "This dressing must stay on your arm for two days or until I replace it. Leave it on, but tell me if it's bothering you."

Managing the hospital visit

Sometimes accidents happen that require a trip to the hospital or the emergency room. Hospital visits may never be easy for a child with autism, but with planning, you can make it go more smoothly for everyone. Before this situation happens with your child, prepare a one-page summary sheet you can give to hospital staff to quickly acquaint them with your child and help him through the experience. Keep a copy in the car at all times. Include:

- A general description of how your child's autism affects his behavior and communication
- Your child's specific strengths and weaknesses
- How your child processes instructions, e.g., visually as opposed to auditorally
- Your child's need for extra time in processing verbal instructions
- Sensory sensitivities: noise, shiny objects, the hum of testing equipment, how touch affects him and which kind is best (e.g., light or firm), taste, smell, or texture, etc.
- Your child's literal interpretation of expressions (e.g., "Jump right up here")
- Your child's lack of eye contact and difficulty understanding social cues
- Any stims or echolalia, especially in stressful situations
- Distress over changes in routine
- Motor skills challenges
- Signs of a meltdown and how to handle one if it occurs, including use of restraints

Help for a runny nose

Some kids seem to have a perpetually runny nose throughout the winter, and difficulty with hygiene opens the door to ridicule from classmates. The child may not even be aware of the mess, and if he is, may have trouble using water for facial cleanup. Keep a box of hypoallergenic wipes handy to the child so he can clean up independently, and have a mirror at his eye level in the classroom or at home to help him see what needs to be done.

Potty training

Two little words, but such an enormous subject. And because it is such a complicated and emotional subject, and because whole books have been written about it, we are not going to address it substantively in this one. We won't leave you without resources, though.

Find two idea-packed articles about potty training on the *Autism Asperger's Digest* website (*AutismDigest.com*): "Toilet Training the Older Child" by Maureen Bennie, and "Toilet Training Your Child with Autism: Ready, Set, Go!"

We also recommend Maria Wheeler's book *Toilet Training for Individuals with Autism or other Developmental Issues*, a bestseller for over 25 years.

Using public restrooms

Congratulations, your child is potty trained! Now you face the next challenge: making it work in a public setting, where most restrooms are designed for adult users. Sinks, toilets, soap and towel dispensers are too high or too far away to reach, automatic flushers and hand dryers shriek and scream at unpredictable intervals, the bathroom itself is cold, clammy, and smelly, or overheated, fetid, and smelly. Diapers starting to sound good again? Don't retreat; you can outwit the most thoughtless architect.

- Automatic-flush toilets operate by using an electronic eye to detect when the user has moved away. Such toilets can be terrifying for children, especially if they are too small to prevent the electronic eye from tripping and the toilet flushes while they are on it. To prevent this, simply cover the electronic eye while your child uses the toilet. If you are not accompanying your child into the stall, carry a suction cup that fits over the eye, and show your child how to attach it. Practice at home.

- The Potty Poncho™ is a portable toilet seat protector with a rubberized vinyl backing that resists slipping on the toilet seat. It can be cleaned after each use with an anti-bacterial wipe or machine washed, and folds to fit into a small carrying case. Start your child on it at home and then transition to public bathrooms. (*PottyTrainingConcepts.com.*)

- Carry extra wipes for hand washing (individually packaged towelettes or a travel package of baby wipes), since many public restrooms do not have kid-accessible sinks or hand dryers. If your child is noise-sensitive, beware of electric hand dryers. Show them to your child immediately upon entering the restroom so she will not be spooked by the unexpected howling sound of someone using one while she is still in the stall. If necessary, put your hands over her ears.

- If your child has gravitational insecurities (doesn't like her feet off the ground), a public toilet where feet must dangle in mid-air may be an insurmountable challenge. Go into the stall with your child, kneel on one knee, and let her use your raised leg for a footrest.

- If your child is confused by restrooms that have multiple stalls (as in schools and public buildings) teach him or her to access the first open stall door. During the years when you are accompanying him into the restroom, familiarize him with the different types of stall latches.

- Upon reaching your destination, locate the nearest restroom and point it out to your child. Knowing where the restroom is before it's needed will ease your child's anxiety about accidents.

- Take practice trips to destinations you know to have kid-friendly facilities such as family bathrooms, private handicapped or single-user restrooms. Your child may feel more secure in a single locking room (more like home) than in a partitioned stall in an echo-y tiled room with a dozen other stalls.

  Note: Dads out in public with daughters face the most challenges. Think the situation through before you leave home.

Adaptive clothing fasteners

Common clothing fasteners can be uncommonly challenging for children (of all ages) with fine motor difficulties. Scratchy zippers and tags, cold snaps, and bumpy buttons may be tactilely irritating as well. More important than fashion is the independence your child gains by being able to dress herself, so opt for clothes that don't require fasteners: pull-on pants, T-shirts, skirts/dresses, cardigan jackets, and sweaters that she can wear open. Then ease her into the world of fasteners.

- Have her dress in front of a mirror so she can see what she is doing from a face-on angle, not looking down.
- Start with Velcro® closures.
  - Look for starter clothes with large zippers or buttons.

Tip If you are handy with a sewing machine, you can enlarge the buttonholes on ready-made clothes and change out the buttons for larger ones.

- Focusing on the task may be easier from a sitting position, possibly with back stabilized against the wall or a chair.
- Start the process for her: thread the zipper, then let her pull it up. Attach a large zipper pull for better grip.
- Other clothing adaptations:
  - Tube socks, which don't require placing the heel
  - Seamless socks for ultra-sensitive feet, available on websites for diabetic or orthopedic care (made for children who wear leg braces)
  - Open-ended sleeves, wide, no cuffs

Stepping out ··

It's natural that there will be times when you feel apprehensive about taking your child into public settings. But with care and planning, outings with your child can be successful for both of you. The key, as always, is to build competency and tolerance in increments that are manageable for him.

1. Keep the trip short, especially at first. When starting out, there is no such thing as too short. If you only get to the end of the driveway, know that you'll eventually make it to the corner—and beyond.

2. If you are going on errands, decide beforehand the number of stops you will make. Depending on the day, your child's mood, and the destinations, one or two stops may be all that's manageable.

> **QUICK IDEA**
>
> Next time you're planning a vacation, consider renting a house, cabin, RV, houseboat, or camper. You can prepare your own meals, keep to regular schedules more easily, and have spaces for extras like visual schedules, can't-live-without toys, etc.

3. Keep your word. If you tell him you will be making two stops, make only those two stops. Even when things are going well, resist the temptation to squeeze in "just one more … " That may be the tipping point between success and disaster. It also teaches him that he can't trust what you tell him.

4. Plan stops in order of importance. Be prepared to abort the trip calmly if it veers toward unsuccessful. Praise and/or thank him for the part of the trip that was successful.

5. Schedule outings based on your child's needs and ability levels first. It may mean you go out only once a week, or never two days in a row. It may mean outings are limited to mornings and never more than thirty minutes away from home. Honor your child's needs while you teach and build his skills, knowing that he will grow and progress in his own time. Let him know he can always trust you to protect his safety: physical, mental, and emotional.

Snappy comeback

No matter how carefully you manage your child's daily routine and activities, there will inevitably come the moment when he melts down in front of the disapproving eyes of your mother-in-law, neighbor, or strangers in public. While we'd love to think you have a hide of steel and are able to ignore the misplaced judgment of people who have never walked a meter in your shoes (let alone a mile), we also know you may feel compelled to say something in your own defense. If so, having an arsenal of comebacks means you will never be left fumbling for words during those difficult moments.

While profanity or sarcasm may appeal, humor is better. We also favor the remark that reminds the listener that your child is not the first or last to lose his cool in such a manner. Some suggestions:

"Yep, it's the Theatrical Threes (Ferocious Fours, Friggin' Fives), all right."

"She's really having a Monday, isn't she?"

"There he is, the next Richard Burton."

Remarks like these, delivered confidently, let the onlooker know that you have the situation in hand.

Some parents who prefer the silent treatment or are uncomfortable making verbal comments (too tempting?), yet still want to impart a measure of social awareness on autism spectrum disorders, calmly give out an "Autism Awareness" card that briefly explains that their child has autism, what it is and the behavioral manifestations of the disorder. These cards are available through a number of chapters of the Autism Society of America, *Autism-Society.org*.

In recent years, a number of websites have sprung up, touting acid comebacks and supplying lists thereof. "You're right, if I spank him, he'll just stop being autistic. And if I holler loudly enough at you in Spanish, you'll just become fluent!" While this type of comeback can be momentarily satisfying, there's a good chance it does more harm than good in the long run. Out there on the horizon, but still very far off, is the day when the general public has a deep enough understanding of autism to recognize it and respond to it with the empathy and support it so desperately needs and deserves. Until that day arrives—and even long after—we are the ambassadors of autism and, as we do with our children, must model the attitude we hope to foster.

Most of the time.

Restaurant dining, autism-style

Eating in restaurants is an unremarkable part of life for many families, but for your child with autism it may not be a five-star experience. We cannot urge you strongly enough: *keep expectations reasonable.* Included in that advice is emphasis on acknowledging that restaurant dining is an optional part of daily life, not a right or a necessity. It may be that your child at his present level of development isn't ready for it. That doesn't mean he never will be. Ellen went through years of not taking her son into restaurants—it wasn't so bad, really, and even had some distinct advantages—but when he was ready, it was worth the wait to be able to enjoy the experiences with a pleasant and composed child.

Enjoyable restaurant-going with your child with autism begins with choosing the right restaurant—for him.

Keep expectations reasonable. Timing is everything. If your child has difficulty waiting, choose a restaurant that accepts reservations. Don't sabotage the experience by choosing a popular restaurant at a popular time requiring a long wait in a cramped, crowded, raucous waiting area complete with blaring music and flashing lights. Echoing the wisdom of Ellen's pediatrician, if you take your sensory-challenged child into such an environment, "you deserve what you get."

Aside from the waiting area, take the general noise level of the restaurant into account if your child is either a noise-maker or noise-sensitive. You don't want the noise level to be overwhelming, but some level of noise may be desirable if you want your Boisterous Bobby or Bobbi to blend in.

And it's worth an ask: even restaurants that normally do not accept reservations may do so if you explain you have a special needs member of the family.

Keep expectations reasonable. Holding your child to a higher standard of etiquette for restaurant dining than is required of him at home is flat-out unrealistic. If your child is accustomed to eating only with fingers at home, he will not magically pick up a fork and knife just because you are in a restaurant.

With time and patience, he will learn, so begin this training long before he sees the inside of a restaurant, or choose a restaurant when his level of capability is acceptable.

Keep expectations reasonable. If he is not an adventurous sampler of new foods at home, the restaurant outing is not the time to expect him to try new foods or even new aromas. The new Indian cafe may tantalize your taste buds but if the smell of curry is going to make him retch, you'll have a more pleasant dining experience with your pot roast at the American diner next door.

Tip

If he's willing and able to sit with you in a restaurant whose food he doesn't like, call ahead and ask if you can bring in food for a child on a special diet. Some restaurants allow this but some do not, citing state health laws. Many restaurants will offer to make a special meal to your specifications, especially if your child prefers plain food. Above all, don't leave him sitting there with nothing to do while everyone else is eating.

Keep expectations reasonable. Simulating the restaurant experience at home will help your child feel more familiar with it when it's time for the real thing. Every so often, have the family gather at the dinner table and hand everyone a menu. Try to offer at least one choice—the entree is the same for everyone but your child can choose between two drinks or two side dishes. Serve the drinks and then insert a short wait. Two minutes may be all your child can handle at first, but gradually you'll be able to extend to five or ten minutes. Repeat the routine for dessert. And don't forget—no one leaves the table until the bill is paid. Hugs, high-fives and thank-yous are accepted currency.

Designate a particular food, beverage or privilege he likes as a dine-out-only treat. We deplore the pervasiveness of soda in contemporary society and would love to see it relegated to occasional-treat status. The motivator doesn't have to be junk food, though; it could be a certain restaurant's pizza or burgers, or it could be the Italian place you like that has the video games in the back. He gets four quarters if he makes it through the meal in reasonable fashion.

Buffet restaurants are great starter experiences. The child can get his food without waiting and choose exactly what he wants and how much. He can put it on the plate the way he wants it—you won't have to worry about the meal being ruined because there's pickle touching the French fries!

Moving to a new environment

New house or apartment, new school and/or a new town—such enormous changes can present a towering challenge to the child with autism. But there are many things you can do to ease the transition.

- First and most important: take your child's needs into consideration when choosing the home. If he is noise sensitive, don't locate near a subway, stadium, concert venue, raceway, factory, etc. Stand in all parts of the home and the yard and listen carefully. Noise can carry for several miles under certain weather conditions, and what may not be immediately noticeable to you may be unbearable for him. Does your child's behavior erupt frequently? Choose that apartment carefully—ground floor, end unit.

- Be sensitive as to how you phrase your descriptions of the move. If the term "new house" seems to trouble him, call it another house, a blue house, our next house. Same goes for all the other "new" things that will happen.

- Assure him, in a manner he understands, that all family members, not just him, are making the move and that all of his stuff is going with him—unlike vacation, where he leaves some things behind. Also, be clear that neighbors and friends will not be coming along.

- Knowledge is power. The more he knows about his next home or school, the more familiar it will seem to him. Reporters think in terms of the five "W" questions: what, when, where, who, and why (with "how" thrown in for good measure). News stories are constructed in pyramid fashion, with the broadest and most important information coming first. More and more detail is added as the reader or listener's attention allows. This is a good way to think of presenting information about the move to your child. He can then acclimate to the information at his own pace and not become overwhelmed by new facts, ideas, rules, and decisions.

- As your child gains more facts, help him make up or write a story comparing and contrasting the differences between the environment you are leaving and the one to which you are going: these things about my family will be the same, and these things will be different. Emphasize what's in it for him at the new location. Does the new town have an aquarium, a state-of-the-art movie theatre or library, a public swimming pool nearby? Does the new house have a bigger yard, a sidewalk for riding his scooter, an eating bar in the kitchen, a cool fireplace for roasting marshmallows?

- Take photographs of the house from as many angles as possible, and do drive-bys, if possible. After the previous owners have moved, include photos of the interior and the back yard. (Photos depicting previous owners' belongings may be confusing or set up false expectations.)

- Will your child have his own room, and will you allow him to choose new accoutrements such as carpet or paint? Providing carpet square samples and paint chips from which to choose gives him some control over his new environment. (Give him only samples and colors that are within your budget and your willingness to execute. Don't give him a palette of paint chips in the orange category if you are not going to be able to tolerate looking at orange every day. Or, if you can tolerate the lighter shades but not the darker ones, cut the darker end of the chip strip off before giving it to him.)

- If the new school is in a distant town, ask the school secretary, resource teacher, or other willing staff member to take digital photos that can be emailed to you or posted on a site you can access. If you do not have computer access, request that printouts of the digital images be mailed to you. Ask that the staff member envision your child's day and take pictures of the following things: the classroom and teacher, the hallway, the cafeteria and head cook, the gym and PE teacher, the library and librarian, the playground (preferably during recess with kids on the equipment), the music room and music teacher, the principal and office staff, and the resource room. Include photos of items of special interest to him: art supplies, science books, medicine balls.

- Upon arriving at the new house, set up his bedroom before anything else so he can see that his bed, his books, his computer, and his toys are all there. If your move is local, try to accomplish this while he is away at school so he comes home to a fully functional, comfortable room, even if the rest of the house is still in chaos.

- Follow up with a visit to the old house in its empty-shell condition, so he can see that all his stuff is at the new house.

- Be clear about any household rules that follow you to the new house (no shoes in the living room, no food outside the kitchen) as well as any new rules (no jumping off the stairs when moving from a one-story to a two-story house). A visual chart helps.

- Maintain as much consistency as possible. Can you shop at the same supermarket, or one that looks just like it? Can he continue with the same karate teacher? Will the family pet be making the move too? Can the old winter coat last one more year? Breakfast should look the same and so should bedtime.

- When you find yourself expressing the inevitable anger or frustration at the foibles of moving, take a minute to clarify for him that it's not his fault. Children internalize a great deal more than we realize.

- Allow him to acclimate to the new house in his own time and in his own way. It not only looks different to him, it smells different, it sounds different, and it requires different navigation skills. He may stick to his room for the first few days or even weeks, but eventually you will be able to help him explore. Giving him a specific job that requires him to come out of his room each day may help: feeding Snowball, putting his clothes in the laundry room, or watering the houseplants (break into groups so he does a few each day).

Off-gassing: A word of warning

If your child is chemically sensitive, be aware that new carpeting, flooring, window coverings, paneling, and even shower curtains may off-gas dozens of chemicals that may make your child ill, at least temporarily. Formaldehyde, ethylbenzene, toluene, xylene, styrene, benzene, and a host of other substances are used to manufacture synthetic carpets and flooring, their backings, the glues that attach them to sub-floors, and the stain-proofing/moth-proofing applied to them. Indications of sensitivity include eye, nose, and throat irritation, cough, flu-like symptoms, headache, dizziness or disorientation, overall malaise. If possible, install new carpeting, paint, and window coverings in your new home several weeks before moving, and keep windows open as much as possible in the interim.

Green options are increasingly available. Look through books and catalogs for green products, low-chemical paints, stains, and floor sealants. And remember, the more energy-efficient the home, the harder it is for trapped gasses to escape.

Consider installing natural-material hard surface flooring such as bamboo, tile, cork, or wood (with minimal chemical stain), accented with natural-fiber area rugs for warmth, texture, color, and comfort.

Green houseplants can also help, assuming spore and mold allergies are not an issue.

When mom or dad is away

Mom or Dad being away on business or family-related travel can severely disrupt your routine-dependent child, affecting the rest of his world enormously. Here are a few ways to help him through it:

- Respect his anxieties and don't spring the trip on him as a surprise. Show him pictures of where you are going to be. If he has a favorite story character, role-play a parental business trip. What might Elmo think or do when his parent is away?

- Leave voice and/or video recordings as touchstones. Read several of his favorite stories. Record a message for each morning or evening: "Good morning, Parker! It's Tuesday and today is the day you go to the library. Remember to return your book. Thanks for feeding Rover last night. Good job!"

- Set up prearranged times you will call home, and then do it at that time. A nebulous "I'll call sometime" can create never-ending anxiety. Choose a time you know you can stick to, taking into account any time differences and your child's state of mind at the time you plan to call. If hearing your voice right before bedtime sets off tears, call right after breakfast, after school, or after dinner.

- If one or both parents are going away, be doubly sure the caregiver who will be in charge is apprised of all details of the child's daily schedule. (A visual chart is good for caregivers too!) Keep everything as familiar as possible; this is not the time to try new foods or institute new teaching strategies, even when one parent is still at home.

- If your child has a familiar or favorite food that only you know how to make, make it ahead and freeze it so he can still have it while you are gone.

- Let your child know that while he is out of sight, he is not out of mind. Leave small notes around the house in unexpected places he will find over the course of your time away—under his pillow, in his sock drawer, in the cookie jar, folded into his towel. Keep the notes simple: "thinking of you," "you make me proud," "have a great day."

- Make your child a special photo item of yourself that he uses only when you are away. Print a digital photo of yourself onto iron-on transfer paper to create a pillowcase or sleep shirt she can use while you are gone.

- Ask a colleague to snap a few pictures of you in the course of your trip, using your digital camera or camera phone. Take photos of your hotel, the room, the view from the window or balcony, the bathroom. Include the airport or taxi. Use photos to put together a picture book for the next trip. Email a few home during your trip if you can, or post to your social network or web page.

- If your child likes miniatures, bring him the items from your hotel room: tiny bottles of shampoo, bars of soap, little bottles of ketchup, or small jars of jam from room service. Cocktail napkins, tiny straws, or swizzle sticks from the bar may also fascinate.

- Don't overlook unusual items like the shoe-polishing cloth, shower cap, or barf bag from the airplane.

- Is your child a collector? If you travel more than occasionally, you can spur an interest in new places by bringing him a small souvenir from each place—spoons, thimbles, snow globes, and "greetings from" postcards are common, inexpensive items found virtually everywhere.

- You being away is not only hard on your child but may be hard on the substitute caregiver as well. Don't extend your trip unnecessarily.

- Let your child know exactly when your absence will end. Crossing off the days on a calendar is one way. Or, relate it to his daily routine by telling him, "Mom will be back after three sleeps." (If naps are still part of the routine, specify "night sleeps.")

Dress rehearsal for special occasions

A full-blown dress rehearsal at home for important events such as weddings, parties, or formal dinners is worth the effort. An hour before Cousin Emma walks down the aisle is a bad time to find out your son's suit pants ride up his bottom when he sits, the clip-on tie bothers his throat, the dress socks are too tight, and the shirt cuffs are too short. Think comfort first for your child. "Real" ties that slip under the collar will lie smoothly and allow him to leave the top button of the shirt open. Short-sleeved shirts are fine for your child and so is any style of sock that keeps him comfortable—who's going to be looking at his feet anyway? With planning, your child can enjoy a special event alongside everyone else.

- First, be honest about whether your child is ready to attend such an event. If he truly can't keep all four legs of his chair on the floor, gets easily overloaded in a room full of people and noise, still thinks a fork is for combing hair, and eats applesauce with his fingers, it may be kinder to all to leave him with a sitter this time.

- Visit the venue—restaurant, house of worship—with your child beforehand to give her a visual image.

- Explain what the event is (wedding, bar mitzvah, grandparent's birthday, family reunion) and what will happen at the event. What will she be expected to do? Sit quietly during the service, sign a guest book, get food from a buffet?

- If possible, arrange seating where she will be able to see the event. However, if you think she may not make it through the entire event, sit where you can take her out unobtrusively.

- Preview the menu and, if it is not appropriate for your child, ask the hotel or restaurant for a special meal. Most are glad to do it. Offer to pay separately. If special arrangements are not possible, bring something for your child as inconspicuously as possible, or feed her beforehand so she is not sitting around ravenously watching everyone else eat. When you've done what you can, don't sweat it further. Holidays and events are so exciting for many children they don't eat much anyway.

> **QUICK IDEA**
>
> A few months before a holiday, ask your child's speech language pathologist to begin teaching holiday vocabulary, and incorporate topic boards and conversation related to the event.

- Teach him a simple introduction and, if he can tolerate it, a handshake.

- Let him know there will be lots of people there, but he doesn't have to hug or kiss anyone he doesn't want to, especially strangers. Then stay close to support him in this. "Josh prefers not to hug," delivered in a pleasant, unapologetic tone of voice is perfectly acceptable.

- Give appropriate fifteen-, ten- and five-minute warnings, then leave while he's still having fun and the memories will be good. In other words, before the too-much-party meltdown.

- Having him tell the host "thank you for inviting me" before leaving puts nice closure on the event.

Never forget that autism has given your child the gifts of rote memory, imitative speech and literal interpretation. Refrain from wondering aloud in the car on the way to the party if Uncle Joe will over-imbibe as usual, unless you want to hear little Hannah check in later with "I want to sit with Uncle Joe so I can see if he really does drink like a fish!"

To hug or not to hug

Nowadays we teach all children, under the banner of "stranger danger" and child-abuse prevention, to protest any touch that makes them uncomfortable. Children with autism experience this tenfold. Many have an aversion to hugs and kisses, even from well-meaning relatives whom they may or may not know well. The reasons are many: the contact comes without warning, the person hugging him smells funny, the touch is too light or too harsh, it disturbs his vestibular or proprioceptive equilibrium.

- Inform and enforce. Let family members and those in daily contact know that hugging and other touching must be at his discretion only. Be prepared to be firm with Aunt Rose who insists it's "dust a wittle hug-hug!!"

- Always give him the choice, then validate that choice. Ask, "Is it okay if I give you a hug?" If the answer is no, respond with a pleasant, "That's okay!" (Because it is.) If he does agree to the hug, a simple "thank you" is appropriate.

- Give a warning before touching: "I'm going to boost you up to the car seat now, okay?"

- Use firm pressure when touching. In this regard, sometimes Dad will have more luck with getting cooperation than Mom, whose touch may be lighter. Many children prefer Dad's help in the bathtub or swimming pool for just this reason.

For example, Davis loved his grandma and was willing to accept hugs, but at first it was only if he "backed into it." That is, instead of the usual chest-to-chest hug, he backed into the embrace. Grandma accepted this as normal and wonderful, and in time he was able to transition to typical hugging.

Shared sibling activities

Inevitably, there will be times when it seems to your neuro-typical child that his sibling with autism receives a disproportionate amount of Mom's attention. Quell sibling rivalry and resentment by creating opportunities for them to build a shared history of good times to fall back on during the stormy times.

Planning shared activities that are fun for both of them can seem daunting when there is a wide spread between their ages and abilities. Ellen's two sons are almost five years apart in age (the younger son is the one with autism), and although many family outings were "divide and conquer," the boys had no trouble coming up with a long list of fun stuff to do together.

- Visiting local rock-clad river beaches and skipping stones, throwing rocks in the river, or using their sling shots
- Visiting amusement parks with carnival rides and game arcades
- Doing jigsaw puzzles
- Making forts out of large appliance boxes
- Older brother was pitcher/assistant coach for younger brother's baseball team
- Local farm experiences: picking blueberries and apples, although sometimes throwing and splatting the rotten apples on the tree trunks was more fun than picking, and sometimes sticking their heads in the sprinklers was a better time than picking
- Cooking a spaghetti dinner or baking brownies
- Sleeping over in each other's rooms or at Grandma's
- Making a film with the camcorder

Reinforce all the good memories with a small photo album they can keep in their nightstand. Update as needed.

Equal sibling time

Siblings are important members of the family team, frequently offering remarkable support and advocacy for their brother or sister with autism. But they are also children with needs and uncertainties. Set aside dates for them—regularly scheduled special times when they get your undivided attention to do something of their choosing. It could be dinner out on Wednesdays, a bike ride on Saturday mornings, a once- or twice-a-month movie or browsing the used bookstore. Being secure in their individual importance to you helps them weather the tough times with their sibling, and strengthens their motivation to advocate.

The newspaper: Window on the world

It is undeniable that much of what appears in the newspaper—be it a print or online edition—is disturbing to children, above their reading comprehension level, or not of interest. But there is still much that is relevant to a child. Your long-range goal is helping your child build a habit of staying connected to world events through reading daily news. However, the process of acclimating your child to the newspaper may be a long one, so start 'em young and take it slowly. Start with print editions with younger children. Getting them used to referencing a daily or weekly publication may start with pictures.

- Comics and cartoons for children are easy introductions and their visual orientation will naturally draw some children with autism. Choose a child-oriented strip and follow it every day or every Sunday. After a while, you can follow up with a suggestion that your child draw his own cartoon or comic strip. (Note: some children will not be able to relate to the fanciful characters and beings in comic strips. You can tell them what your favorites strips are, and why. But don't force it. Many children with autism or Asperger's relate more to photographs than artwork.)

- Look for kid-appropriate photos to discuss. What do you think is happening here? Oh, look—it's the park near our house! And here is an interesting flower show/boat show/sand castle contest going on; shall we visit it? This baseball player has your favorite number on his jersey. What do you think this policeman is trying to do?

- The weather report is always relevant and is pictorially represented in many papers. Have your child try to predict from the pictures whether it is going to be sunny, cloudy, rainy, hot or cold. How hot/cold was it yesterday or last night? What will the weather be in Grandma's city? Why is the temperature 85° in Australia when it is 20° here?

- Articles or weekly columns about pet care, kid-friendly websites or new children's books by a favorite author may be of interest.

- Read movie reviews of the latest family-appropriate movies, plus any "making-of" features or stories about the actors in a favorite film.

- Scan the sports section for stories about kids. Or follow a favorite team, checking their stats each day.

    Note: If your child does show an interest in a sports team, take the opportunity to point out how sports phraseology (idioms) find their way into our everyday language. For instance, when someone says they are "way off-base," they mean they are wrong about something. If someone makes a "ballpark estimate," it means they're making a guess.

Happy birthdays start here

The contemporary culture of holding birthday parties outside the home is one that may be out of the question for your child. Arcades, play zones, movie theatres, and bowling alleys are inherently crowded and may be unendurably noisy. Partying at home allows you to control all the factors that influence your child's behavior, which goes a long way toward ensuring a happy and memorable occasion that will be just right for him. It won't cost any more than a go-somewhere party and it needn't involve grotesque effort, either.

Before the party starts. Sit down with your child and calmly talk through the coming event so he knows what to expect. Practice any social skills he'll need as guests arrive, and remind him of any house rules that apply. Do familiar calming and deep pressure movements or activities before guests arrive. If needed, let him wear earplugs, a thick headband or a weighted vest or compression garment; some newer fashions are cute enough to wear to a party. Be sure your child understands when it's okay, and how to remove himself from the commotion and take a short break to calm or regroup if he's feeling agitated.

The activity. Keep the party at your child's developmental, not chronological age, and always attuned to his sensory sensitivities. He may be more comfortable with parallel play than interactive play. Open-ended play may be more fun than structured games that require a lot of language. If so, forego competitive games with rules and scorekeeping. Opt for active, sensory-filled activities such as a bounce house (rent from a party company), bubble machine (chase 'em! poke 'em! tackle 'em!), sand table or box, water gun fight and/or slip 'n' slide, homemade ball pit (inflatable pool filled with plastic balls), tug-o-war. If you have a large wall, cover it with butcher paper and put out crayons and markers for the guests to make the biggest-ever birthday card. Or cover a table with plain fabric and have the guests doodle and sign the tablecloth with fabric pens or paints (handprints are always fun). At an indoor party, quiet kids down or get their attention by dimming the lights rather than raising your voice.

Make traditional party elements part of the action.

- Cupcakes have advantages over the traditional frosting-encased cake. They are just the right portion size for kids, and decorating them is a party activity in itself most kids love. Cupcakes freeze well, so you can make them ahead of time. If your child follows a special diet, his cupcake can look just the same as all the others. Put out small bowls of frosting, sprinkles, chopped nuts or candies as appropriate, and of course, a candle for the birthday child. Would he or she enjoy those trick candles that keep relighting themselves? Talk about prolonging the moment! Available at party stores.

- The forgettable junk in those ubiquitous "goody bags" may hold a child's interest in the short term, but doesn't it more often end up in a raucous tussle with your vacuum cleaner? Here are two alternatives that make kids work for their loot: the piñata and the treasure chest. Making a piñata or plotting the hunt are enjoyable lead-up events that include your child in the big picture of party planning.

  - Make your own piñata from a grocery bag with handles, involving your child at any level at which he is able to participate. You don't have to be an artist, and it doesn't take long. An octopus face with crepe paper tentacles couldn't be simpler. Use clip art enlarged on the copier a couple of times, or spray paint the bag and add stickers. Whether the artwork is pristine—or even recognizable—is not important. It's going to get smashed in a matter of minutes, right?

- A treasure hunt has similar allure. Siblings or other family members can create the clues (at the birthday child's level of representation: photos, drawings, single words, simple rhymes) and set up the hunt. Any sturdy container will do for the chest; go with a plastic storage container, or shop thrift stores or yard sales for a suitably battered box or trunk.

The guest list. You know best how much commotion your child can handle. If a small celebration is best for him, be ruthless about limiting the guest list to an appropriate number (the old rule is age plus one). Be clear on the invitation that you are including the guest and one parent only. And be considerate—if you aren't inviting his whole class, do not send the invitations to school. Mail, email, or use social networking or e-vite services.

The party's o-o-over. Put a clear end time on the invitation and if parents are dropping their child off, remind them. Have a quiet closing activity (sorting or swapping toys and candy from the piñata) before cheerily announcing "That's all, folks!" If parents accompanying children linger past the end time, it's okay to make a point of telling everyone "thanks so much for coming; Drew was such a fun guest; Kyra can't wait to read the Arthur book," and begin cleaning up.

The gifting. Some guests will ask what the birthday child likes. Steer them toward your child's interests, even if limited. There's nothing to be gained by being coy; gifts that have no meaning for him may confuse and upset him, and if he likes airplanes or she likes hats, getting six of them will be sheer delight. At the same time, be prepared to handle his or her reaction to a gift that may have no meaning.

- Giving your party a theme is an easy way of suggesting gifts that will appeal. A theme can be as simple as having the invitations, paper plates and napkins, piñata/treasure hunt carry a common motif: pirates, horses, fire trucks, flowers, dinosaurs, etc.

- At a minimum, your child needs to be able to say thank you to each guest for the gift. It may be difficult for her to understand why she must acknowledge a gift she doesn't like. It's never too early to start telling her that part of the gift is the effort the guest went to in trying to choose something thoughtful. Rehearse the scenario and the thank-you beforehand. Round up items from around the house and role-play opening a variety of gifts. (See **Gift-getting etiquette** later in this chapter.)

Ending on the right note. In addition to saying thank you for the gift, saying "thank you for coming" puts an end bracket on the event for both the guest and the host.

A cake by any other name

And speaking of cake, it may be traditional but whose party is it? If your little one is indifferent to cake, substitute something else. Anything edible accompanied by "Happy Birthday" and a candle to blow out is acceptable. Over the years, we've seen birthday pie, birthday watermelon, birthday cookies, brownies, ice cream sundaes, popsicles, a giant Three Musketeers bar with candles on it, and a log cabin made out of Tootsie Rolls with a candle in the chimney. Now really, what could be sillier than worrying about whether guests will be "disappointed" if they don't get cake? Mom and Dad, check your own attitude on this too. We've encountered too many parents who make themselves miserable because their child doesn't want cake, and a birthday without cake "just isn't right."

And your child's idea of fun with a cake might be something other than eating it. In their younger years, Ellen's two sons had other ideas. Son #1 wanted to eat his cake without benefit of fork or hands—in other words, face first into the frosting. Yes, it was allowed—once, and at a family-only celebration, not a party. The photos were priceless. Son #2 disliked cake but loved construction equipment. He wanted a thickly frosted cake with a construction motif, so he could plow the frosting and excavate the cake using Hot Wheels vehicles as cake toppers. Rock candy embellishments added to the realism. The video was priceless. Always let the good times roll and everyone will have a better time—including you!

Uncommon gifts for uncommon kids ························

Birthdays and holidays can be gift-giving challenges if you have a child whose interests don't fall neatly into the typical toy store catalog. Think outside the traditional gift-box and in the direction of your child's real interests; ordinary items unusually presented can inspire true glee. The following ideas were hits within Ellen's family and might appeal to your child too.

- Everyday items that reinforce sensory experiences make for intriguing gifts, and almost anything in a surprisingly generous quantity is fun. For instance, our son's most beloved gift for several years running was a basket of many cans of shaving cream, to dispense in any quantity desired in bathtub, driveway, or kitchen sink. Other comers in this category were balloons (blow up a hundred and he gets to pop them all at once) and marshmallows (he never actually ate one; his shtick was melting them in the campfire. Incinerating an entire package without hearing "you're wasting them!" delighted him.).

> **QUICK IDEA**
>
> Holiday decorations may be overwhelming to your child. Decorate the house and tree slowly, in stages. Day 1: the tree goes up. Day 3: the lights are added. Day 5: the garland goes on, etc.

- Flashlights are cool, another ordinary sensory item that can become extraordinary. Can you ever actually find one when you need it? Give a whole basket full of flashlights. Even modern kids can succumb to the simple diversion of lights-off flashlight tag, and "light shows" on the ceilings and walls, with or without music. Enhance the experience with a book like Frank Jacobs' *Fun with Hand Shadows* or Bill Mayer's *Shadow Games.*

- Pirate Treasure. The year my costume jewelry kept disappearing was the year I discovered my kids were borrowing it for pirate booty. I got my stuff back via a garage sale, where I found an old treasure chest-style jewelry box and the loot to fill it. Old thrift store jewelry is perfect too, or just ask each of your friends for one piece they never wear. Or fill the chest with whatever else your child enjoys most. Then go all the way—

bury or hide the chest. Devise a treasure map or series of clues the child/children must decode to get to the loot. The process is a gift in itself. If your child/children are young or non-readers, the clues can be photographs or drawings. As they learn to read and become more proficient, the clues increase in complexity.

- The most ordinary item in an unexpected container can spark amusement—a toolbox filled with homemade cookies, a six-pack cooler filled with socks. A hollowed out pumpkin with—what else?—a Cinderella doll inside, or a child's rain boot, lined with tissue and filled with candy and a fistful of favorite-character or favorite-color toothbrushes (which she gets to open all at the same time if she wants to).

Remember too that an equally important piece of the gifting process is the giving part. Children with autism or Asperger's already struggle to understand and interpret the feelings of others. "What do you think Dad would like?" may be a question whose answer is beyond their reach. But it is not a reason to leave them out of the gifting process "for now." "Later" may not come without long, loving, and gentle repetition and reinforcement. Start now by having them participate in the creation of gifts that are guaranteed to please. Seeing expressions of pleasure and receiving profuse thanks directed specifically at them will eventually imprint.

Guaranteed-pleaser gifts are those that contain a piece of the giver, such as a photo snow globe. Kids can help select the photos and cut them to shape. The globes are usually double-sided, so the child can decide what goes on each side. Maybe one side is a current photo and the other side is a baby photo. Maybe one side is a miniature piece of their artwork or thumbprint heart. Variations: photo bobbleheads, photo or artwork Christmas tree ornaments, calendars, or lockets.

Gift-getting etiquette

Often overlooked in carefully laid plans to teach your child party or holiday gift-etiquette is the art of opening a gift. Here's how the gracious giftee does it:

1. Open and read the card first, then open the gift.

2. Keep scissors nearby for the bow or ribbon that just won't come undone.

3. Find the seam in the paper to start tearing.

4. Once it's fully opened, thank the giver. Be sure your child understands 100% honesty is not always appropriate at times like this. Rehearse beforehand with your child a single, universal phrase, like "thank you so much" or "this is so thoughtful" that will work in all situations.

5. Set the gift aside gently, whether you like it or not. Flinging or throwing an undesirable gift hurts the giver's feelings.

6. Open all his gifts before dashing away to play with a favorite.

7. Post-party written thank you notes are a must. As long as they are personal, they can be dictated to you and signed by the child, handwritten or drawn by the child himself, or e-mailed. This further reinforces how much we appreciate the effort, thought and expense to which the giver went, and gives you and your child a chance to explore social thinking, handwriting, and composition skills.

> **QUICK IDEA**
>
> Help a child weave plaid, satin or any novelty ribbon through the upper holes of pretzels twists for a charming garland for the mantle, door or holiday tree. After the holiday, drape it around an outdoor tree for the birds.

Frame it

Take that artwork off the refrigerator or out of the pile in the corner of the classroom. Having the child's work professionally framed says, "You are mighty special" and the constant stream of visitors' attention—especially at home—validates their efforts over and over. Or, transfer drawings into digital images, and use one of the photo book software programs to create unique art books, perfect for birthday or holiday gift-giving. Have the child add a simple inscription, or even a lipstick kiss or miniature handprint.

Autism safety

A stunning 92% of respondents in an online survey conducted by the National Autism Association said their child was at risk of wandering. If your child or student has the tendency to bolt, you need to implement a safety plan immediately. The advice and tips that follow come from parents across the nation. Many are adapted from the Autism Safety Toolkit available online at NAA: *NationalAutismAssociation.org*.

Prepare an informational handout about your child that includes a current photo. Share this handout with first responders in your area. Keep copies with you at all times at home, in your car, and in your purse or wallet, in the event you become injured or incapacitated while with your child. Circulate the handout to family, friends, neighbors, and co-workers. Include information such as:

- Name of child or adult
- Current photograph and physical description including height, weight, eye and hair color, any scars or other identifying marks
- Your child's favorite song, toy, or character
- Names, home, cell and pager phone numbers and addresses of parents, other caregivers, and emergency contact persons
- Sensory, medical, or dietary issues and requirements
- Inclination to wander off and any atypical behaviors or characteristics that may attract attention
- Favorite attractions and locations where child may be likely to go
- Likes, dislikes; approach and de-escalation techniques
- A list of things that frighten the child
- Method of communication, if non-verbal: sign language, picture boards, written word

- ID wear: jewelry, tags on clothes, printed handout card
- Map and address guide to nearby properties with water sources and dangerous locations highlighted

Get an ID bracelet for your child that includes your name, telephone number, and states that your child has autism and is nonverbal, if applicable.

A temporary tattoo with your contact information is another option if your child will not wear a bracelet or necklace.

Personal tracking devices are now available in a wide range of prices and in many forms, including tracking units that work with your computer or mobile phone, tracking wristbands, and city-wide first responder systems such as Project Lifesaver Tracking Systems.

Safe in the yard

Set up visual boundaries defining the area in which your child may safely play.

- Walk around the perimeter of the safe play area with your child; do it every day or every few days until it is imprinted.
- Paint or make a large red STOP sign at the end of the driveway.
- Use a line of orange traffic or sports cones to define boundaries.
- Spray-paint a bright orange or yellow line around the boundaries of the yard. If on the lawn, yes, it will have to be reapplied every couple of mowings.

Home safety for escape artists and acrobats

If your home feels like an obstacle course in the face of your perpetual-motion, master-of-disaster child, heed these safety suggestions from parents like you:

- Replace plate glass windows with unbreakable glass, Plexiglas®, or glass blocks.
- Cover holes in the wall with laminated artwork bolted to the wall with molding.

- Bolt your entertainment center to the wall and install a Plexiglas® door on it to prevent breakage or damage to television, stereo, etc.

- Install Tot Locks on cabinets. They install on the inside of the cabinet and are invisible on the outside. They open by magnetic device.

- Yes, there is kid-proof fencing. One family's story: "We have a fence in our front yard so my daughter cannot escape. It is made of PVC material. She squeezed through that by bending the material, so we put metal rods down inside them. The locks (there are three) to the gate are on the outside. Now she is safe."

- Keep your little Houdini safely strapped into the car with a "bus vest," which zips in the back and is then hooked into the seat belt system. See this and other related items at the E-Z-On® Products, Inc. website, *www.ezonpro.com/products/schoolBus/vestClosure.shtml.*

- Thwart furniture-flippers with built-in beds, built-in shelving and built-in storage. Sink the bed and enclose the corners to further prevent mattress removal.

When your child isn't sleeping

Sleep disturbances among children with autism are extremely common. It's important for parents to define their child's sleep problem in order to best address it.

- Going to sleep: chronic problems can occur in the absence of a consistent bedtime routine, including a specific bedtime and clearly defined sleep location, both a bedroom and a bed. Intermittent problems with going to sleep can arise from a long daytime nap, fears such as a monster in the dark, too much stimulation just before bedtime, or a medication side effect.

- Staying asleep: problems can arise if the child is allowed to fall asleep in one location and is then transferred to another, or if a caregiver remains in the room until after the child falls asleep. In either of these scenarios, the child awakes to an environment other than that in which he went to sleep, which can be disorienting or disconcerting, and make it difficult for him to fall back to sleep. Hunger or thirst during the night, medication side effects, illness, daytime stressors that cause bad dreams, or unexpected external noises can all contribute to wee-hours wakefulness.

- Sleep phase (the hours the child is asleep): problems can result from excessive stimulation, letting a child decide when to go to bed (inconsistent bedtime), or changes in the Circadian rhythm (a person's individual biochemical 24-hour cycle). Disruptions during sleep can be caused by sleepwalking, bed-wetting, teeth-grinding, head-banging, and night terrors.

Ten tips to help restore sleep: (See also **Sleep on It** in Chapter 1.)

1. Start a Sleep Diary and document exactly when and how often the problems occur.

2. Look for physical problems that can impair sleep.

3. Look for behavior problems that can impair sleep.

4. Set up a regular bedtime routine and stick to it; use visual cues or a visual schedule if needed.

5. Avoid excessive stimulation before bed. This includes rough or energetic play (you think it will wear him out, but it often has the opposite effect), stimulating foods such as chocolate or high-sugar drinks or snacks. The last hour before bed should be free of electronics—no TV, computer, games, DVD players.

6. Allow your child to fall asleep in one location only, the location that is meant only for sleep—his bed. Discourage use of his bed as a daytime play space.

7. Create a sleep environment—quiet, dark, controlled temperature (not too warm), and a comfortable bed and linens.

8. If the child often wanders out of his room, gate the doorway or install a Dutch door with the top open and the bottom locked.

9. Survey the room for sensory-disturbing items: clicking clocks, tree limbs that scratch against the window or side of the house, the on/off hum of the heating or cooling unit outside or next door, the feel of the sheets or the pattern.

10. Maintain the same sleep environment when the child is falling asleep as will exist when the child stays asleep or wakes in the middle of the night. That means parents should resist staying in the room until the child falls asleep.

Relax through breathing

Pranayama, or the yogic practice of deep breathing, is used to still the mind, calm the senses and relax the body. When anxiety soars in your child or yourself, follow yoga wisdom and breathe. Incorporate breathing exercises into your daily routine; benefits include a greater sense of overall peace and calm, the ability to reduce tension more quickly, and more restful sleep at night.

Watching the breath

Start by having the child quiet down and observe his breath going in and out, in and out. Nothing forced, nothing the child has to "do." Simply breathe and observe his breath. Once the child is comfortable with doing this type of breathing, introduce one of the deeper breathing techniques that follow.

Belly breathing

Have the child stand, sit or lie on her back and rest her hands lightly on her stomach. As she breathes in, tell her to expand her belly as if blowing up a balloon inside her tummy. As she exhales, let the belly/balloon deflate. Instruct children to notice how their belly rises and falls in a natural rhythm. Do this three to five times to start, working up to ten belly breaths in one sitting.

Three-part breath, or elevator breathing

In this technique, the child breathes into three areas of his body: his belly, his chest, and his head. Introducing the idea of an elevator ride can be a helpful visualization. This exercise can be done standing, sitting, or lying down, although children often find it easier to feel their body parts if it's done while lying down.

- Start by having the child breathe in and out a few times to settle down.

- Start the elevator ride by breathing in through the nose and exhaling the breath, sending the elevator down to the "basement" level, the child's toes.

- Breathe in and the elevator starts to rise to the first floor, the abdomen. Have the child hold the breath for a few seconds (while the elevator stops at that floor) and then exhale completely.

- Breathe in and the elevator continues up to the second floor, the chest. Have the child feel his ribs expanding and his back press into the floor. Hold the breath again for a few seconds and exhale completely.

- Breathe in a third time, sending the elevator to the top floor, the head. Have the child feel his head fill with air. Hold for a few seconds and then exhale completely, sending the elevator back to the basement level.

- This exercise should be done slowly. As children practice deep breathing, their lung capacity will increase and their breaths will be larger and fuller.

With any deep breathing exercises, let the child rest a minute or so before standing up and moving on to another activity. Deep breathing is calming and can be done while a child is in bed, right before he goes to sleep. Make it part of his regular bedtime routine.

Yogic breathing can also rev up a tired, lethargic child (or parent). One such breathing exercise is called Shining Skull—just a minute or two of this exercise can bring a noticeable lift to your day!

- Sit in a comfortable position, on the floor or in a straight-backed chair. Sit tall and close your eyes.

- With the mouth closed, take a big, deep breath in and then "snort" the air out through the nose in short, repeated bursts. When the breath has been depleted, breathe in and repeat.

- Start slowly at first, just thirty seconds, as the child can get dizzy until it's practiced a few times. Work up to one to two minutes of this exercise. Shining Skull brings rich oxygenated blood quickly to the brain. Enjoy the afterglow it produces!

Explaining death to the child with autism

The loss of a relative, friend or pet can leave parents pondering how to explain the disappearance of a loved one without unduly frightening their concrete-thinking child. Spiritual concepts of God, heaven, angels and souls may fall flat and add to the child's bewilderment. *Lifetimes: The Beautiful Way to Explain Death to Children* by Bryan Mellonie (San Val, 1983) will be imminently useful for such children: "There is a beginning and an ending for everything that is alive. In between there is living," it explains.

The book is a beautiful and sensitive but concrete discussion of the framing of a life between birth and death, how life spans differ among plants, animals and people, about the markers and touchstones in those lives between birth and death, and about how beginnings and endings are going on around us at all times. It passes no judgments as to what may or may not be "fair" and does not discuss grief, or the feeling of loss associated with bereavement, or with spiritual concepts of afterlife.

Understanding Death and Illness and What They Teach About Life: An Interactive Guide for Individuals with Autism or Asperger's and their Loved Ones (Future Horizons, 2008) is a guidebook for the difficult but necessary conversations parents will someday need to have with their children. Author Catherine Faherty presents the subjects of illness and injury, recuperation and healing, death (including pets), rituals, and traditions in clear, straightforward, autism-friendly language. She delves beyond factual discussion of death and illness to explore feelings, emotions, and personal reactions in a way that is both comforting yet instructive for the child or young adult with autism or Asperger's. Chapters such as "What People May Learn When Facing Death" and "Be Inspired: Role Models and Mentors" put death into perspective in terms of life, and stir us all to live fully.

Change only one thing at a time

Parents are often so anxious to see changes, improvements or other progress in their child that they attempt several therapies or interventions at the same time. It then becomes impossible to determine which intervention is producing a positive change in the child. Is it the new diet, the change in medication, the new sensory therapy, or the modified educational program?

Start one thing at a time. In most cases, a 30-day trial period is sufficient to observe emerging changes or effects of a new treatment.

Help the medicine go down

As your child gets older, medications will appear less often in liquid form and more often in pill form. Don't wait until illness is upon your child to see whether he can choke a pill down. Practicing under calm, non-emergency conditions will yield better results. Our pediatrician recommends practicing with a bottle and a non-medicinal item such as M&M's® or mini-M&M's®. Glugging the water out of a bottle forces the head back and helps the pill go down.

A little more help

Medication costs are skyrocketing. Contact the pharmaceutical company that manufactures the medication(s) your child uses. Many companies have programs to help patients with the cost of prescriptions.

Spray vitamins

Spray vitamins can be an easy way to make sure your child is getting essential vitamins and nutrients, even if he is on a limited diet. No pills for kids to wrestle with swallowing or to spit back out, no added fillers, no need for Mom to crush up the vitamin and or hide it in food. Another benefit: spray vitamins enter the child's circulatory system in less than thirty seconds, bypassing the GI tract, so more of the good stuff gets utilized by the body. Find manufacturers of spray vitamins via any major internet search engine.

Reduce allergens, prevent ear infections

According to Dr. Stephen M. Edelson, Ph.D., formerly of the Center for the Study of Autism in Salem, Oregon and now Director of the Autism Research Institute in San Diego, "several large-scale surveys have shown that ear infections are more frequent in children with developmental delays, autism, and fetal alcohol syndrome." Recurring ear infections can lead to speech and language problems in later years.

"There is mounting evidence," says Dr. Edelson, "that many ear infections, possibly the majority, are primarily a reaction to an allergen. These allergens may be airborne (e.g., pollen, mold, second-hand smoke, dust, animal dander) and/or certain food items. The common food items are: dairy products, wheat, eggs, chocolate, nuts, and sugar."

If you suspect airborne allergens are contributing to your child's chronic ear infections, restrict smoking and pets to areas outside your home. (Smoking should be restricted to outside the home even if your child appears healthy.) Think about installing a freestanding or furnace filter to kill airborne microorganisms. If you suspect a food item, such as cow's milk, eliminate it from his diet for a period of several weeks to see if there is any change.

- Eliminate only one food at a time so you can isolate the offending substance.

- If the culprit is a food allergy, it is most likely something he likes and is eating regularly. Taking it away cold turkey may be needlessly upsetting. Weaning your child away from the food item over a period of a week or two is just as effective but much less traumatic. For instance, if it's milk, first swap the cheese in his sandwich for a non-dairy filling. Then substitute a dairy-free frozen dessert for his usual ice cream. Then go from three glasses of milk per day to two. A few days later drop to one, then none. Or switch to any of the non-dairy milk alternatives now available: soy milk, rice milk, almond milk, hemp milk. If calcium is the concern, there are now many calcium-fortified juices.

Medications: Be thorough

You should never dispense medications to your child just because a doctor says so; you need complete information when a psychotherapeutic medication is recommended as part of your child's treatment plan. Some physicians may not disclose all the information they should without your prompting, and some prescribe medications "off label"—meaning they have been tested with adults but not with children, or have been shown to be effective in treating a similar, but not the same, condition. Only by asking questions can you better understand the possible benefits and side effects of recommended medications, and thereby make an informed decision as to whether you wish to pursue the treatment.

1. What is the name of the medication? Is it known by other names? Is a generic equivalent available?

2. How do body systems absorb and eliminate the medication?

3. What do researchers know about the medication's effectiveness in patients with autism or Asperger's?

4. Has this medication been tested with children?

5. In what way do you expect the medication to help my particular child (not just children in general)?

6. How long does it take before we see improvement?

7. What are the common side effects? What are the less common and/or possible serious side effects?

8. Under what conditions should we immediately stop its use? Is it dangerous to stop use immediately (drug withdrawal; needs to be tapered)?

9. Is this medication addictive? Can the child abuse it?

10. What is the recommended dosage? How often will the medication be taken and at what time of day? Does "three times a day" mean around the clock or three times over the waking hours?

11. Are laboratory or other tests needed before taking the medication? Will any tests be required while using the medication? Where will the tests be administered? Will anesthesia be required?

12. Will a physician monitor my child's response to the medication, making dosage changes if necessary? Who will assess my child's progress and how often?

13. How long will my child need the medication? What factors will lead to a decision to stop this medication?

14. Should my child avoid any other medications or foods while taking the medication? Should he take the medication on an empty or full stomach?

15. Should my child stop participating in any particular activity while taking the medication?

16. What do we do if a problem develops? For example, what if my child becomes ill, he misses doses, or we see signs of side effects?

17. What is the cost of the medication (and its generic, if available)? Does my health insurance cover it? Is financial assistance is available?

18. Do we need to tell the school staff about this medication?

19. Where can we get written information about the medication? Where can we read objective evaluations of the medication written by sources other than the manufacturer?

20. Are there other medications for this condition? Why do you recommend this one over the others?

Start an autism book circle

To paraphrase the old adage, many eyes make light work.

A book circle can be a powerful tool for getting a broad sweep of information from multiple books when time is precious. The usual book club format has everyone reading the same book and then discussing it in a monthly meeting. If that format appeals to you, great. But if it sounds like only more time pressure, create an alternative that better suits your lifestyle. Your reading circle, comprised of you, family members, and other parents or teachers of kids on the spectrum, can be a more efficient variation on that popular format.

- Instead of everyone reading the same book, each reads a different book and shares the information and his/her personal impressions with the rest of the group.

- Sharing of information can be through conventional face-to-face meetings, or virtual, through group emails, round-robin emails or postings on a website or social networking page.

- Members may decide to loan each other books based on information shared during meetings.

- Members may decide to pay annual or semi-annual money (say, $20) into a kitty used to purchase agreed-upon books for a group library. Members can agree to replenish the kitty as needed.

So many books, so little time

Thank you for reading our book! As the airlines like to say, "We know you had a choice." In fact, as of the time we are writing this, *Amazon.com* offers over 23,000 choices for the keyword autism and over 6,000 for the keyword Asperger's. How do you choose the book that makes the most of your limited time and dollars? Here are some guidelines.

- How much and what type of information do you need right now?

  - Do you need an encyclopedic overview of all issues within autism? If you are new to autism, you might choose a comprehensive book offering a little about everything. You can use this book as a reference tool, returning to segments as needed and as new issues crop up.

  - If you are past the initial diagnosis, you may want to narrow your focus to a specific issue such as social skills, eating problems, or fine motor difficulties, addressed by a more specialized author.

  - Are you seeking education or inspiration? Sometimes knowing others have gone before (and survived!) is as important as learning a new behavior strategy.

- Reject books that

  - Offer one-size-fits-all solutions or the "only solution you will ever need."

- Don't take into account the fact that each child, parent, and family is unique.

- Prescribe parameters that are too narrow, offer too little choice or flexibility within the formula for success, aren't adaptable to the multiple settings in which we live our lives.

- Test-drive the book

  - Before buying the book, do some internet research on the basics of that special diet or therapy. The intervention may be successful, but may require large amounts of time, patience, and tenacity. If your initial reaction to the approach is a flicker of "hey, that could work!" proceed past Go. If your initial reaction is exhaustion at the thought of administering such a program, move on to something better suited to your lifestyle and temperament.

  - Borrow the book from a library, school or social service agency to see if you truly will use it or enjoy it. If you can't borrow the book, apply this test in the bookstore: open the book in three random places. If you don't see anything that strikes a chord with you in three random spots, chances are the book is not for you.

  - Use internet options such as Google Book Search or *Amazon.com*'s Search Inside feature to explore the book. You can read an excerpt, review the Table of Contents, flip through the index and read the back cover. You'll have a good grasp of the format, tone, and content of the book without laying down a dime.

- Know your own reading style

  - Do you want to explore alternative methodologies, or are you more comfortable going down a tested path already well trod by others? What type of author draws you in? The parent writing from personal experience, the professional who has worked with thousands of kids, or the person with autism or Asperger's writing from the "insider's perspective"? All are valuable, but you may prefer one voice over others.

- Be realistic about how much time you have to read. If it's only an hour a week, select a shorter book that gives you broad information on a topic. That way, you'll know what to home in on next. If you have more time, go for something with more depth.

Still having trouble choosing? Look to reliable authors whose books have stood the test of time. The autism category does have its core of popular, knowledgeable authors to whom readers return again and again. Tony Attwood, Temple Grandin, Brenda Smith-Myles, Linda Hodgdon, Carol Gray, Michelle Garcia Winner, Jed Baker, Carol Kranowitz, and Stanley Greenspan gain that national attention and recognition for a reason—their books are worth reading.

> **QUICK IDEA**
>
> Reinforce your child's efforts to follow directions by placing little surprises at midpoints. For example, when setting the table: "Get the forks and knives, then put them on the table." In the silverware drawer, have a smiley face picture or "good job" symbol.

I can do it myself— the preschool years

Foster independence skills starting at a young age. Keep it fun and rewarding for the child while embedding the concepts that will develop into functional life skills.

- Give the child a title; "Mommy's little helper" is too generic; try something specific instead that describes the job: Dining Room Manager or Pet Supervisor.

- Assign only jobs your child can be successful in performing, introducing new skills as he masters existing ones. Choose duties according to your child's interest and abilities. He may love feeding the dog or the fish; she may enjoy helping you match socks or rake leaves.

- Use a visual schedule to help your child chart his working progress. Have a spot where you can check off "job completed" and "okay to pay" so the child can visually see his progress toward pay day.

- Yes, pay day! Create a payment structure for the job. How often does the job pay? Hourly? Daily? Weekly? Match this to your child's need for reinforcement: immediate or delayed.

- Be generous with praise while the child is "on the job." Address the child often using his title: "Excuse me, Mail Manager, can I send a letter today?"

- Use the job as a means of getting your child attuned to concepts such as making a mistake, trying harder, being on time, gentle correction, etc. As his skills develop, introduce more complex job duties and responsibilities, such as using appropriate social language, or sequencing job duties to be more efficient.

I can do more myself—as children grow

As children's skills develop, continue to promote independence in everyday life activities by setting up an environment that encourages him to try to succeed.

In the kitchen, making a snack (with your permission):

- Designate a shelf in a lower cabinet for items he may need: unbreakable plates, bowls, and glasses, eating utensils. If needed, label the door with words or a picture symbol so he can easily find the items.

- Repackage difficult to open and close snack items into easy access zip lock baggies or plastic containers. Place these on his shelf in the cupboard.

- Do the same in the refrigerator: put favorite items on a lower shelf he can reach himself. Repackage as needed into unbreakable and easy access containers.

- Locate a step stool close by the kitchen or bathroom sink so he can clean up hands or put plates in the sink.

In the laundry room, washing, drying, putting away clothes:

- Put his clothes in a hamper or sorting basket or bag: whites, colors, dark

- Take the clothes from the washer and put in the dryer

- Put his clean clothes away, folded clothes in drawers, hanging clothes on hangers in the closet. Some parents find it most expedient to install a low rod and hang all clothes.

Then teach your child how to successfully complete the steps of the activity. It might be making himself a peanut butter sandwich or packing his backpack for school. Post written directions for multi-step activities and/or a visual strip or a story sequence if needed.

I can do a lot of stuff myself—the older child

By age ten or twelve, most children have the manual dexterity, sequencing and sorting ability, and basic arithmetic skills to handle quite a few household chores. Reflecting again on our own behavior, sometimes we deprive them of the opportunity to learn; we become impatient or irritated when they don't do it "right," don't do it fast enough to suit us, or don't do it at the exact moment we deem it should be done. How conveniently we forget that we did not learn these skills overnight either. Ellen, the mother of a teen with autism who was largely self-sufficient by age fifteen, suggests that children ten and up:

- Learn to sort laundry, operate the washing machine and dryer, and fold clothes
- Begin accompanying Mom or Dad on the weekly grocery shopping trip, learn to locate favorite items, choose favorite produce, read shelf labels, exchange money with the checker, or operate the debit card machine.
- Learn to clean a bathtub, sink, toilet, and bathroom floor (can use Swiffer or other commercial wet mop product).
- Help with dishes, empty and/or load dishwasher
- Learn to use and become responsible for a house key.
- Learn to cook or prepare simple foods he likes (see below)

We emphasize: all of these life skills are developed only through teaching, practice, patience, and reinforcement. Never assume he understands how to do things he hasn't been explicitly taught.

You can do it yourself—the reluctant child ·

Teaching life skills is the exception to our rule of never assuming anything. You must teach life skills, starting while children are young, based on the assumption that your child will want to be independent in his adulthood. But believing that your child's interest in becoming an independent adult will spark on its own, and waiting until that point to take on this enormous task, will leave you floundering to catch up. It's an area in which, again, we have to be attuned to whether—or to what degree—our child's behavior and attitude are reflective of our own. If your child doesn't want to, or refuses to do, anything for herself, could it be because you or someone else has always done everything for her?

Confront this reluctance by thinking about ways to reframe one of your child's challenges into a vehicle for teaching independence. For instance, many children with autism have very rigid preferences. Channel this desire for strict control of environment into self-sufficiency. If your child wants his food, clothing, and routine just so, empower him to achieve it himself.

- If the Star Trek T-shirt and the black jeans are the ONLY option for each and every Thursday, teach him to use the washing machine and dryer.

- If he stresses about being late or worries about transitions, get him a watch and teach him to tell time in both analog and digital formats. (Many public buildings still have analog clocks.) Learning to pace himself in class, during the morning routine, and during evening homework will relieve much stress and boost feelings of self-reliance.

- Teach him to cook or prepare his favorite things. Hot dogs, pasta, grilled or plain sandwiches, and chicken breasts are easy places to start. This can be a win-win, freeing you from the drudgery of being a short-order cook, and freeing him from having to eat what everyone else is eating when it's something he dislikes.

Let your child know that the more he can manage his own self-care, the more you'll be able to introduce increased responsibility, privileges, and flexibility.

Modeling the behavior you are trying to instill is always essential. One of Ellen's early childhood education team members put it best: "I never ask a student to do anything I am not willing to do myself. Whatever 'it' is, we do it together. And I never tell a child he has to do anything. I show him what wonderful things can happen for him if he does." The old what's-in-it-for-me school of thought can be both effective and appropriate.

Guiding your child with autism to adulthood

Seeing our children through childhood to productive, independent adulthood is the mission we accept when we become parents. When your child is young facing the myriad issues within autism, that "independence day" can seem very far away. And that's good news!

Preparing your child for adulthood begins long before job skills training or learning to balance a checkbook. The seeds of preparation lie in the uniqueness of your child—his special abilities, strengths, interests, and motivations. The most important brick in your child's road to adulthood is recognizing those special components and using them to develop your parent-child relationship in a way that gives him both roots and wings. Roots—knowing that he belongs, is connected to others, is valued and capable, and needed. Wings—knowing he has the inner resources to learn and do and, with practice and patience, succeed.

- Recognize that your child's relationship with you and all members of your family will be the single strongest determinant of his success as an adult. Emphasize his strengths, and use them to build his self-confidence.

- Don't let his autism drive a wedge between him and the rest of the family. See your child as a full-fledged member of your family—with needs, yes, but also with responsibilities to others. Don't focus 100% of your attention on him in a manner that suggests other members of the family are not equally important, sacrificing all of yourself for the needs of your child and neglecting siblings, grandparents, cousins, and friends. This sends a message to the child that he is the hub of the wheel around which everyone else turns. It's a message that will not serve him well in adulthood.

- Take time to nurture yourself. Letting your child see you as a multi-dimensional adult who enjoys life, is involved in community, takes good care of her own health, allows herself fun, respite, and recreation—sets the best possible example for your child.

- Praise your child's efforts, not the outcome or the result. Keep the focus on what she can do, not what she can't. Know that every child has the capacity to achieve more than what he is currently able to do, but that for him, learning a skill requires more repetition and practice than it might for a typically-developing child. Your responsibility is to create not only the opportunities for practice, but also to maintain patience throughout the learning process. Impatience, exasperation, or "letting him learn the hard way," through humiliation or embarrassment, will not help your child learn anything other than mistrust in you and your word.

- Don't "therapize" your child, filling his days with rounds of adults who are all trying to fix something about him or in him. Again, think about the message this sends to the child. Engage your child with both yourself and your family in every creative way you can. Do what your child loves and do it with him—practice motor skills, social skills, language skills, by getting in the pool or the ball pit with him. Go to the zoo and the library and the park, play in the snow and the sandbox and the puddles.

- Throw out standard measurement assessments such as growth charts or speech-cognitive-motor milestones aimed at the general population. Don't use "normal" as a measure of where he should be. Encourage him to explore, interact with people, laugh and be curious, and do it with the understanding that regardless of ability or disability, he is going to grow and develop and flourish if his way of learning and pace of learning is celebrated.

- Trust your instincts. Talk to and listen to other parents, but don't accept their experiences as have-to's for your child. Regardless of whether every single family you encounter is using this diet or that therapy, if your gut and your experiences tell you it isn't right for your child, listen to that little voice and keep looking for the best fit for your child and family.

- Think of your therapists and professionals as guides, not bosses, on your child's journey to adulthood. Be willing to listen to the information they give you, even if you are not quite ready to hear some of it. Don't feel obligated to react to everything you hear at the moment you hear it. Remember this autism experience is a process. You can take time to acclimate to new information before acting upon it—or choosing not to.

- The most important thing parents can do to help their child is laugh, play, and build relationships with all of the people in their lives. When a child feels connected, he has the internal motivation he needs to do all those other things.

- Remember that you have time. You have today, and tomorrow. You have next week, next month, next year, and many years to come.

Never forget that a parent's attitude toward the child is going to be that child's attitude toward himself. Creating a sound social-emotional sense of self must be the focus of what you provide your child; without it, no amount of therapy or education is going to matter. See him and celebrate him as the capable, interesting, productive, and valuable adult you have every reason to believe he can be. And hold that vision, because through your eyes, he sees it too. Seeing is believing, and believing makes it happen.

Thinking Social, Being Social

A man has as many social selves as there
are individuals who recognize him.

WILLIAM JAMES

ONVERSATIONS WITH PARENTS, professionals, and adults with autism and Asperger's have been a daily component of Veronica's ten years as Managing Editor of the *Autism Asperger's Digest*, a national magazine on autism spectrum disorders. Her personal involvement with these individuals has shaped her ideas and perceptions about people who have autism and Asperger's and people who don't. More than a thousand of their voices have been heard by the autism community through collaborative articles published in the magazine. Ten times that many selections have crossed her desk.

"No one way; no one voice" is what fascinates Veronica most about this community. The diversity of thought, despite the common thread they all share, stirs her inquisitive spirit. In describing her own thinking toward autism and Asperger's, Veronica paraphrases a 1970s Martin Mull song, "I'm elastic, not plastic, I'm flexible!"

Perspective-taking. Flexible thinking. These are the keys that unlock the door to your child's social functioning and give him access to the social customs that connect us all. Ours is a world of tangible and intangible social structures. Most of us don't wake up each morning having to consciously process how to be social, think social, act social. (Although Veronica says more people should give it some regular thought!) We awake with our social awareness present and operational.

But our children with autism and Asperger's arrive in this world without a social navigation system, without the neural network of social understanding that allows them to notice where they're going in the social world, or course-correct when they take a wrong turn. Every day we ask our kids and students to maneuver within a world built upon an undercurrent of instinctive social abilities, taught by adults who acquired many of their social abilities instinctively, within a teaching environment that assumes that the social instinct exists in every child.

What might the world be like for a child who doesn't feel social connection? What would life be like if she experienced every feeling and event—joy or pain or anything in between—in social-emotional isolation? The idea that a child can turn to Mom or Dad or a sibling for information about herself and her surroundings is fundamental to most of us. But in many children with autism and Asperger's, this hard-wiring is missing from the brain's social processing network. Really let this idea sink in: Her only arsenal of knowledge comes from situations she herself has experienced. A good experience imprints as a good experience, hopefully one that will be repeated. A bad experience imprints negatively: Red alert!—avoid in the future at all costs!

It's up to us to adopt a perspective that acknowledges and accepts the different social thinking that is at the core of autism spectrum disorders, and teach our children to take the perspectives of others. By doing so we move them out of "mind-blindness" and into flexible social thinking, giving them skills that will allow them to be successful in making friends, doing well at school, finding a job, falling in love.

We've come a long way from just a few decades back when it was thought that "most" children with autism were also "retarded." Indeed, nowadays many of us know children on the autism spectrum whose cognitive intelligence approaches genius level IQ. But IQ scores, by themselves, are never a true indication of a child's abilities. In the journey of life, social relationship skills are a stronger precursor to success than are a high IQ or academic honors. Lack of social relationship skills is far more likely to get you fired from a job or leave you sitting home alone on a Saturday night. Now is the time to advocate that social and emotional skill development become as much a priority as cognitive learning in all our teaching arenas.

No one book, workshop, or study group will ever be enough when it comes to understanding and teaching social skills. Social skills are life skills, and this is an ongoing journey that requires patience, repetition, and above all, adaptability—a comfort and ease with not having answers in any given moment, and exploring together the thoughts, feelings, motives, and desires that collectively contribute to being social and connecting on a social level. Veronica compares this journey toward social skills to the autism community's history of understanding behavior. To teach our child or student to be social requires that we first look at ourselves and understand our own social nature and the preconceptions and assumptions we hold inside. Such intense and constant scrutiny can be challenging and intimidating. It requires courage and self-acceptance, by both adult and child.

Teaching our children and students what it means to be social, think social, and act social is one aspect of autism spectrum disorders to which few hard rules apply. The questions outnumber solutions a million to one. Those who can confront uncertainty, be motivated by curiosity, and forge solutions through honest exploration of what it means to be social will find it a fascinating journey.

Social referencing skills

The foundation for social relationships is laid very early in life. One of the first relationship skills infants develop is social referencing. Think back to when your child was young and he encountered something startling and new. What was his reaction? Typically-developing children will immediately look at Mom or Dad as an information source: Is it safe? Am I in danger? Should I be fearful? Am I okay? At only six months old, they already seek out their parents for valuable clues about the social world around them. In children with autism, social referencing is absent, leaving the child unattached and alone in how he experiences people and events in his earliest, formative years (and beyond, if this social skill is never taught). Parents and preschool teachers must teach social referencing, as it is a foundation skill upon which many other social skills are built.

- Any type of game or activity that teaches the child to reference you as an information source is ideal for teaching social referencing. Try Peek-a-Boo or Hide and Seek, with exaggerated gestures and exclamations.

- Change play routines mid-stream so the child needs you to show or tell him what to do next.

- Have the child crawl on his belly or hands and knees through a long fabric tunnel or a couple of pup tents aligned end to end. The parent or adult remains at the end, with her face either just inside the end of the tunnel, as a reference point, or playing Peek-a-Boo with the child as he crawls through.

- Back and forth activities, such as rolling a ball along the floor or batting a balloon, require the child to pay attention to his partner's actions.

Joint referencing

Simultaneous, shared attention to an object or event, with the child understanding, is called joint referencing. This pivotal social skill emerges in the typically-developing child around nine to twelve months of age.

Pointing is one of the earliest indications of joint referencing. Witness the exuberant child, who upon seeing a balloon floating in the sky, points to it and looks at Mom to make sure she sees it too. The meaning behind shared experience—the feeling of connecting to another human being—is already developing in the child. He is eager to share his joy and excitement with a parent and feels the social connection that shared experiences bring.

As with many other foundation social skills, joint referencing is absent in many children with autism. Parents and early educators can and should teach a child to feel social connection through shared activities and games.

- Timed, synchronized movements the child and adult perform together, especially those that elicit laughter and fun, give the child a sense of shared experience. Try running together holding hands, falling together, carrying objects together, or racing cars side by side. String a variety of movements together to keep interest levels high.

- Start-stop activities, with each person taking turns as the leader are also effective. Paddle drums and drumsticks, hand clapping, or Simon Says variations work well.

- As skills develop, incorporate more variation and fewer routine actions into the game. Introduce minor, planned disruptions so the child can practice self-regulation of speed, action, voice, etc.

Social stories

Throughout this book, you will see references to social stories as a means of facilitating behavior modification, transitions, and social understanding. The term is both generic and specific, depending on how it's being used and the type of story it references. Used in a generic way, social stories represent verbal or written scenarios that offer important information about the environment, the people in it, social behaviors, and social thinking. A generic social story might be a handful of lines written on the spot to deal with a specific situation, or a longer story created in reference to an event yet to come, or to help a child better understand an event that has passed.

Michigan teacher Carol Gray pioneered the idea of using a story format to teach social skills in the early 1990s and created a specific formula for writing such stories. Gray's Social Story™ describes a social situation, skill, or concept according to ten defining criteria. The goal of a Social Story is to share accurate information meaningfully and safely, in an overall patient and reassuring tone. Carol went on to form The Gray Center for Social Learning and Understanding (TheGrayCenter.org). Their website is excellent and offers sample Social Stories and meticulous guidelines for conceiving and writing them.

The range of topics about which a social story (generic or one following Gray's format) can be employed is limitless, and anyone can write one. Your school's autism specialist, speech language pathologist, occupational therapist, special educator, or psychologist are probably familiar with Social Stories; consult with them about behavioral, communication, sensory, or social skills goals that might be successfully addressed through a social story format. Examples: eating at the cafeteria, taking turns on the playground, moving to a new school, riding the bus, visiting the doctor, buying something in a store, acknowledging a favor or gift.

Ask him to teach you

Everyone is good at something. Ask your child to teach you something at which he or she excels while you may not. Does she have a natural golf swing? Make up her own songs? Role-reversal that puts the child in charge is empowering.

Relating to the outside world

Many children with autism prefer to remain within a physical realm that feels safe, whether it be their bedroom, home, or classroom. Feeling comfortable in the big, big world beyond the home may not come easily. As a first step, you can heighten her awareness of the larger world by starting a Window on the World journal with her. At random times of the day and throughout the weeks, have her look through one same window and communicate what she sees and hears. She can dictate to you, write it herself, or express it in drawings. Over time she will familiarize herself with temporal concepts (light in the morning, dark at night), weather conditions (sunny in the summer, windy in the fall, grayer in winter), sounds (garbage trucks, sprinklers, mail carrier), animals (birds, squirrels, cats, insects). It's a safe way to become comfortable, and maybe even excited, about the fact that the world is an ever-changing place.

Friendships with younger children

If your child shows an inclination to befriend children younger than himself, encourage it. Developmentally, he may identify more with a younger child, giving him a sense of social competence he doesn't get from his same-age peers.

Guidelines for developing play skills

Kids in all countries and within all cultures play. While play skills may come naturally to the typically-developing child, many of the social/interpersonal facets of play need to be taught to the child with autism or Asperger's. Any strategies developed for your child or student should include these elements:

- Connect and engage: get their attention and make a personal connection
- Motivate: give them reason to want to be with their peers and participate
- Structure and practice: help them learn the conventional aspects of play through preparation, practice, and support
- Include: gradual, planned, and well-supported inclusion into groups and the community

Friend to friend

Enlist the help of your child's peers in teaching the social skills needed for making and keeping friends. Kids are generally eager to help a friend or classmate when they understand how best to do it. Start by sharing these basic friendship tips with the child's classmates:

- Get your friend's attention before saying anything else. Say your friend's name, stand or sit where you know she can see you.
- Use short sentences and small gestures.
- Give choices of activities you know interest him.
- Observe like a detective: Watch your friend to see what interests him, upsets him, or makes him nervous or stressed out.
- Ask your friend to talk, join in a game, come visit.
- Use friendly words and gestures. Tell your friend when she has done something you like.
- Accept differences. We're all good at something and not so good at other things.

Facilitate playground interaction

Recess time spent on the playground can be a less-than-desirable activity for many children with autism. Issues relating to noise, environment, teasing, or his uncertainty in handling spontaneous social interactions can be highly stressful. Some children harbor a deep need to be first in line to come in from recess (possibly a personal space issue). They spend the period filled with anxiety, not participating in playground activities, hovering at the edges of the play area.

> ### QUICK IDEA
> If your student enjoys word puzzles, create word searches or crossword puzzles using the vocabulary of emotions or etiquette.

Teachers and parents can be mindful of these challenges while still providing structure and opportunity for the child to become more comfortable on the playground.

- Bring another child over to interact, perhaps showing a ball or asking a question about a topic of interest. If the interaction continues, push it a little farther—throw the ball against the wall or into a hoop. Even if the child interacts only with the ball, it is progress.

- If he is used to spending recess in the library, have him come to the playground just once a week to start. Eventually increase to two days, and not two days in a row. Allow days when he can still opt for the library. Have him participate in choosing which days will be playground days and which will be library days.

- Pair him up with a peer buddy for recess—preferably one who shares some of his favorite interests. Peer model instruction can happen naturally, without calling attention to the child, as would a teacher's involvement. Peer buddies can be rotated. If you ask for volunteers (discreetly), you might be surprised how many classmates are willing to help.

- Set up group activities that capitalize on the child's special talents. He gets to share his vast knowledge base and his peers experience him in a positive light.

First in line—for a reason

A child who insists on being first in line may be telling you something about his poor motor planning skills or ability to process vestibular and/or proprioceptive input. He may have difficulty walking in the middle of the line. Does he kick, jab, or run into other children, or step on their feet? It is likely he needs more space around him when he walks, along with increased awareness of his immediate surroundings.

- Place him at the front or the back of the line so he can self-regulate the amount of space around him.
- Have his paraeducator walk in front of him so he has adequate personal space.
- Have him carry a heavy object (backpack/books) close to his chest with his hands holding the opposite arm.
- Have him think of a special song he hums to himself when he walks in line.
- Teach him appropriate protests to use if someone gets too close: "Please move back," or "Please don't touch me."
- Transfer that intense need to be first in line to a positive setting. Would he like to be first to choose a topic for the writing workshop, first to give a speech, first to share his drawing or science project? Initiate this in small groups—speaking to the whole class from the front of the room would give many children, not just the ones with autism or Asperger's, the frights.

Custom board game

Logical progression of thoughts, perspective-taking, and an appreciation of beginning/middle/end, are all thinking processes that impact social skill development. An interesting and fun way to teach these concepts is to create customized board games.

Start by drawing a blank board game with squares in a path, like Candyland. Have your child (with your help if he needs it) invent a game and write an instruction in each square. Roll dice to advance pieces. The path can be across a distance, across time or depict a process.

- Start in your hometown and end in a place you'd like to visit
- Start in kindergarten and end in high school
- Start in the wading pool and end up on the high dive
- Start in Little League and end up as Cal Ripken
- Start with flour, eggs and sugar and end up with a cake
- Start with lemons, water, cups and quarters and end up with a lemonade stand (or other small business)

Board game adaptations

Board games reinforce social skills such as turn-taking, and many are great vocabulary builders as well. Try some of these simple modifications to a few of the more common games to make your child's experience more enjoyable.

- *Pictionary.* Allow the child to bypass words he doesn't know, or remove them from the deck beforehand and add your own cards with words known to be in his vocabulary. He can't draw a silo if he doesn't know what it is but he could draw a barn or a farmhouse.
- *Outburst.* Make your own category cards based on her interests (animals we see at the zoo, flavors of ice cream, crayon colors), reduce category items from ten to five, extend or eliminate response time.
- *Scrabble.* Limit everyone to two-syllable common-usage words, allow the child to exchange letters at will, don't keep score.
- *Memory Game.* Make your own sets of matching cards using a camera and a color copier. Use family members, classmates, his Matchbox car collection, her Beanie Babies.
- *With other games:* Start the game with pieces halfway to the finish to help kids with short attention spans interact positively.

Toy story

Finding a toy that appeals to your literal-thinking child can be a challenge. Before hauling a rejected plaything off to Goodwill:

- Except for choking hazards, disregard the age range cited by the manufacturers. If it works for your child, it works.

- Put the toy away and try it again at a later date. The sing-along DVD that didn't even get a second look at age two may be well received at age four.

- Think your child is beyond a toy now? Try it again in a few years. There may be aspects of a toy that appeal at different developmental stages. The same goes for books.

- Try jigsaw puzzles made from foam letters with textured surfaces, or Spell-A-Puzzle™ that combines pictures, letters, and words. When you put together the word puzzle, you also create the corresponding picture of the object spelled.

- Remember the definition of "toy"—an object used for play or amusement. Commercially produced toys may amuse or appeal to you, but many children with autism or Asperger's are fascinated with play objects that don't come from toy stores or catalogs. Rocks, boxes, tools, kitchenware, rubber bands, clothespins, empty food containers, money, camping gear—anything that inspires creative play is a toy.

Mine! Mine! Mine!

The concept of sharing toys is difficult even for typically-developing children but can be nearly impossible for the child who identifies with only a few items. Your child needs patient coaching in the art of sharing. If the word "sharing" itself sets off firestorms, call it something else and place a tolerable but gradually increasing time parameter on it. Call it a trade, an exchange, a swap, a switch. Set a timer so the child knows when he can have his original item back. Make the initial time brief so he gains confidence in the process. Gradually increase swap time.

"Trading" as opposed to "sharing" also implies that the child gets something in return for giving up his item. It is reciprocal, and eliminates the open-ended quality of "sharing" that can be so distressing.

Meanwhile, teach sharing through modeling. Build opportunities to share throughout your day.

- Offer to split your apple or cupcake with him.

- Let him know when you lend your book, sweater, or lawn mower to a friend or neighbor.

- If you make cookies, bread, or applesauce together, have him pass the plate or bowl to each person at the dinner table.

Teach him that sharing is not an all-the-time, every-time thing. There are times when sharing is not required, and there are times when sharing may not seem fair.

- Sharing not required

  - Allow your child to have at least one special toy or possession that is too precious to share with others. He can either put this favorite away when others are around, or he can learn to say, "The dump truck is only for me, but you can

> ### QUICK IDEA
> Create a matching game or bingo game using photographs of facial expressions or body positions or gestures and emotion vocabulary cards.

    play with the cement mixer or the fire truck." This is a lot for him to learn and express—you will most likely be the one modeling this approach for him until he can master it.

  - When a friend, sibling, or classmate has a history of certain behaviors that don't translate well to sharing, it is okay to say no to sharing. If Chris loves to snap crayons in half, your child needn't share his crayons with Chris.

- When sharing doesn't seem fair. Turn-taking is a form of sharing, and it's impossible to keep turn-taking equitable at all times. To your concrete-thinking child, this doesn't seem fair. This can happen in the classroom setting, where supplies, books, and computers are shared among all classmates. It can happen in any group setting when time runs out for a given activity. Through conversation, picture strip, story, play-acting, or whatever works for your student or child, convey that:

When we share, everyone gets a turn but not at the same time.

Sometimes he gets a turn, then someone else gets a turn.

Sometimes someone else gets their turn first.

Sometimes everyone gets a turn, and sometimes there isn't enough time for everyone to get a turn.

He will get a turn next time. Whenever possible, give a concrete time for his next turn. Say "Tomorrow" or "Wednesday" as opposed to an undefined point in the future.

Teach him to think about sharing. Talk about how he feels when he wants to play with something that isn't his. How does he feel when the owner says yes? When the owner says no? When he does share, how does he feel about someone else playing with his toys? He wants them to be careful with his things, and that's also what he should do when playing with toys and possessions that belong to others. Children with autism love absolutes, and there is no better absolute than the Golden Rule: treating others as he would like to be treated himself.

Teach cooperation through play

Give several blocks, Legos, or Duplos to each child and post a picture of a structure. Children must look to find who has pieces they need or pictures that use their block, Lego, or Duplo. Vary the building material depending upon level and interest. Duplos or painted blocks are nice because of color cue.

Teach cooperation through food

Make a production line for the family lunch. Each child or family member has only one part of the makings (such as peanut butter or bread) and needs to move among all family members to get the rest of the items, using polite words.

Theory of mind skills

Many of the social nuances that seem to elude children on the spectrum can be attributed to challenges with a brain processing function called Theory of Mind (ToM). ToM involves attributing mental states to others, and more specifically, realizing that people have different ways of thinking and feeling about things, and that they have different interests, likes, and dislikes that impact their thoughts and feelings. ToM entails understanding that these different ways of thinking and feeling produce different behaviors from person to person, and that these behaviors are not always consistent. Sound intricate? It is, and that's why lack of social understanding can have such monumental impact on a child throughout his life span. Teaching ToM skills in a manner that makes sense to our children must be an ongoing, everyday endeavor, starting at home while children are young, joined by educators incorporating this into the daily school curriculum.

QUICK IDEA

Intense emotions can be negative or positive and either can be socially inappropriate at times. When using a scale to describe emotion intensity, call intense positive emotions "fireworks" or another word that is meaningful to your child.

- Foster the child's understanding of the mental states and emotions of others. When reading a book, discuss facial expressions of the characters as indications of their thoughts; do the same when watching videos or movies. Create games such as "What's He Thinking?" or "What's She Feeling?"—have fun and purposely be silly from time to time to illustrate our many mental states.

- Pretend play (such as playing house, school, truck driver) gives children practice in the social and emotional roles that comprise real life. Put together thematic boxes or bags of items that can prompt play scenarios: restaurant (cookware, utensils, play food, tableware, pad for taking orders), travel (suitcase or backpack, train or plane ticket, sunglasses, camera, foreign or play money), pet store or zoo (rubber or stuffed animals, dolls), and the perennial favorites—old blankets to make a fort and large empty boxes (See also **A Dozen Things to Do with a Refrigerator Box** in Chapter 1.)

- Talk about your thoughts and feelings aloud to your child on a regular basis. Set up a "Today I Feel _____" board at home or school and have each member actively participate. Incorporate Comic Strip Conversations (originated by Carol Gray)—simple drawings used to illustrate conversations between people.

Perspective taking

To be successful in any social situation, our children need to understand that people can share similar thoughts, impressions and ideas, and yet have dramatically different ideas about the world around them. Taking the perspective of others is not an easy concept for our kids to grasp and generalize to different situations. The time to start introducing these ideas is while a child is young, in simple, concrete ways. As the child's perspective-taking abilities widen, so will your teaching examples and the nuance of the lessons involved.

Michelle Garcia Winner, author of *Think Social!* and other popular social thinking books and curricula, has taken these complex, abstract concepts and whittled them down to four steps people use to regulate their behavior while maintaining constant social thought about others around them.

Level 1: I have thoughts.

Teach the child to be aware of his thoughts about other people. Who is behaving appropriately? Who is not? Who makes the child feel good; who makes him feel bad? Who is following the rules; who is breaking them?

The key to teaching the child with emerging perspective-taking ability is to make all lessons relevant to his experiences, his life, his world. His appreciation of "other minds" is non-existent or is just beginning.

Level 2: Other people have thoughts.

What might brother Sean be thinking about as he pets the dog? Daddy looks happy with his birthday gift; what might he be thinking? Explore with the child who is doing what is expected, and who is breaking the rules. Teach the child to make simple predictions about others: what do you think they like to think about?

Level 3: I can figure out what you are thinking about or what you know.

Our children are often unaware of the many nonverbal body signals and environmental clues available to figure out what other people may be thinking. Those children with more impaired perspective-taking skills do not intuitively understand that we use our eyes to convey information. Temple Grandin, one of the most noted adults with autism in the world today, did not learn this valuable social clue until she was fifty-one years old! Teach children to watch people's eyes to figure out what they are thinking about, based on what they are looking at. Help a child discern when someone is thinking about her versus another person.

Level 4: I can (and should) adjust my own behavior based on what I think the other person knows.

Who should I tell about my family's weekend at the beach? Mom, Dad, my teacher, my classmate? (Answer: The child should tell his teacher and classmate, since his mom and dad were already there.) Why should he tell his teacher or classmate? (Because they were not there.) Help children learn to think about what other people know or don't know before engaging in conversation. This level of awareness also helps develop narrative language. (Use comic strip characters and thought bubbles as visuals).

Social thinking—something that most of us learn without formal training—can be challenging to teach. Approach social-thinking training as you would physical training. At first each exercise is difficult; our muscles are not familiar with performing in a certain way, we are uncoordinated and clumsy. With repeated practice our muscle tone develops, our strength, stamina, and coordination improve. We begin feeling the positive benefits of using these muscles in new and better ways. It's the same with social thinking. Start slowly and build over time. Some of these concepts may take months or years of practice before they become second nature to our kids.

Understanding emotions

Tuning in to emotions—their own and those of others—is a towering challenge for children with autism. Even harder for them to understand is the relationship between emotions and behavior. Help your child understand the difference between the two. Emotions, or feelings, are something everyone experiences. They happen inside us. Many feelings are natural and understandable. We feel angry or hurt when someone teases us; we feel scared by sudden noises or unfamiliar places. We can't always choose how we feel, but we can choose how we act upon our feelings. Behaviors happen on the outside; they are the actions we take in response to our feelings.

Help your child express her feelings by starting sentences with "I," followed by asking for what she needs. Acknowledge how difficult this may be for her. Even though she is angry with Anthony for saying her shoes are ugly or continually stealing her eraser, conking him with her math book is not an acceptable response. Coach her with "I am angry at Anthony. I want him to sit somewhere else."

Identifying emotions

Recognizing, acknowledging, and understanding emotions, whether in oneself or others, is a core skill in interpersonal relationships and a challenge area in children with autism spectrum disorders. They often cannot identify the array of emotions that make up the human condition, nor do they appreciate that people have responses and emotions that are unlike their own.

Recognizing emotions and responding with empathy (or at minimum, socially appropriate behaviors) are social skills that will need to be taught. In addition to market-ready books and visual tools, try these suggestions.

- Start with the basic emotions first: happy, sad, angry, and scared.
- Take pictures of your child, and some classmates, siblings, cousins or friends if possible, play-acting a range of emotions. Let them really ham it up. If your child isn't expressive himself, use classmates or similar-aged family members.

- Use the photos to help your child or student "read" the facial expressions associated with the basic emotions. Mindy looks sad here, Nathan looks angry, Julia is feeling happy. Point out the physical facial characteristics that clue you to which emotion is being expressed. See the wide-open eyes, his crinkly nose, or how his mouth and cheeks are all scrunched together? Discuss in detail what appears obvious to you. If it were obvious to the child with autism or Asperger's, he'd be able to pick it up himself.

> ### QUICK IDEA
>
> If you are using a social story to establish a certain behavior or routine, setting it to music (or other mnemonic device) may help the child commit it to memory.

- If your child doesn't show an interest in other children's faces, start with just photos of his own face.

- Once the child can recognize the facial expressions himself, introduce the emotions associated with each expression. What does it mean to feel happy? What makes you feel happy? How is a person likely to act if he feels happy?

- Slowly introduce other, more subtle facial expressions and the words for their corresponding emotions.

- If your child enjoys looking at himself in a mirror, practice facial expressions using small hand mirror, or together in the bathroom mirror.

- Create collages or a small book with pictures of facial expressions found in magazines, picture books, even greeting cards.

- Model the vocabulary of emotion in your everyday conversation with your child or student. Are you nervous about a presentation you have to give at work today? Are you confused about whether or not your mother wants to go shopping? Are you feeling disappointed, skeptical, or confident? Use words for feelings as frequently as you can.

- Draw her attention to the emotions of other people you encounter within social settings: Play a game in guessing what another person is feeling by his facial expression. Do the same while watching movies at home.

Teach intensity of emotion

The black-and-white thinking patterns common to individuals with autism or Asperger's come into play with emotions too, and many children do not understand that emotions come in levels of intensity. In addition to naming, recognizing, and responding to emotions, help the child understand that feelings come in varying degrees. Learning to appropriately identify their own level of emotion can be challenging for our kids.

Help your child move beyond two-level thinking (sad or not sad; happy or not happy) with these strategies.

- Create a concrete scale to identify levels of emotion. *The Incredible 5-Point Scale* by Kari Dun Buron and Mitzi Curtis offers one model.. Creating an emotion thermometer is another way to visually depict levels of feelings. Google Images offers several examples of these.

- Assign descriptive words to each level of emotion. On a three-point scale for younger children, the levels might be a little happy, more happy and very happy. That same scale used with older children might use descriptors such as pleased, happy, and ecstatic.

- Explore levels of emotion starting with the child's own direct experiences. Once she can recognize different levels of emotion in herself, she can move on to observing emotions in others through real life examples, videos, conversation, etc.

Separate feelings from actions

Once your child has a grasp of basic emotions, move on to helping her identify the more complex ones. Label emotions in yourself, your child and others during the day so your child learns to recognize them. You and she may know what makes her happy, but do you know what makes her feel hopeless, or helpless? What or who inspires her? What might she try if she wasn't afraid of failing? Does she trust her parents, her teachers—or fear them? Or perhaps feel no connection at all? Ask about her deeper feelings, using whatever communication tools are appropriate: words, drawings, stories. Teach her that being able to recognize and understand our emotions is a continual life process.

Help your child to keep a feelings journal. One sentence a day or a few times a week is enough to start. If he isn't writing yet, he can dictate to you, talk into a recording device, or even just paste facial expression stickers on a blank calendar.

- Part of the journal might be a running list of people, places and activities that inspire positive emotions in him. He might also include a list of people, places, and activities that provoke negative emotions in him. This list can be a good starting point for a discussion of how to avoid or cope with troubling persons or situations. (When talking about it, be wary of idioms like "set us off" or "push our buttons" which the child may not understand.)
- Good idea gone one better: you keep an emotions journal or calendar too. You may be surprised what you learn about your relationship with your child or student, opening up new vistas for discovery, discussion, and understanding.

Understanding "polite"

Polite words sound better to our ears and make us feel better about things. Try comparing polite words to tone of voice. Ask your child if he can hear the difference between "Give me that" (using gruff rough voice) and "May I have it please?" (using cheery light voice).

Anger management

Anger is an emotion that develops in three stages. It begins with a build-up or escalation, which can take anywhere from months to moments. It then reaches its crest or boil-over point, and then there is the aftermath. Your child will be better able to manage anger as a normal part of life if he has an understanding of how it happens and how it is resolved. Ideally, he (and we) can recognize anger as it is building and take steps to mitigate it. But for all those times there is an explosion, be sure your child knows there is a plan in place to air, understand, and resolve the situation that caused it. Knowing there is always resolution can decrease the outbursts in the long run.

We can work it out

Kelso's Wheel of Choices (KelsosChoice.net) is a widely used conflict-management curriculum that can help your child deal with the minor disagreements that invariably arise in interpersonal communication. Included with the program is Kelso's Wheel, a concrete, easy-to-understand visual giving children nine options (arranged in a nonagon) to try to resolve the conflict.

- Go to another game
- Share and take turns
- Talk it out
- Walk away
- Ignore it
- Tell the person to stop
- Apologize
- Make a deal
- Wait and cool off

The choices end with instructions to tell a trusted adult if confronted with a big problem. A big problem is: 1) a situation where someone might get hurt, 2) a law or an important rule is being broken, or 3) something frightening is happening.

Print Kelso's Wheel on a card small enough for the student to keep in his desk for reference. Even better, ask your child's teacher or principal to adopt Kelso's Choices as a classroom- or school-wide guideline. The authors are available for staff trainings.

That's private

Let's be honest: all kids find certain body noises entertaining. Tooting, breaking wind, cutting the cheese, bottom burps, trouser trumpets, and barking spiders are all euphemisms for the same bodily function. Such endless euphemism, inference, and idiom will confuse your child greatly, so take a direct approach when teaching which body sounds are okay around other people and which need to be private. The easiest way is to distinguish between sounds that come from our respiratory system (lungs and breathing) and sounds that come from our digestive system (stomach and elimination). Respiratory functions like sneezing, coughing, nose-blowing, and hiccupping can be done in company, albeit politely and with proper etiquette—as quietly as possible, with tissue covering mouth and nose. Digestive functions like belching and tooting need to be done in private when at all possible. When teaching this distinction, remember that the bigger the reaction you give your child, the more likely he is to continue the behavior. Be consistent; when he belches or toots, respond only with a brief, matter-of-fact reminder along the lines of "excuse you" or "that's private." Over time, the behavior will diminish. Peer pressure will play a role in this when odor is involved.

Naturally, if there is a legitimate and ongoing physiological problem, you will want to consult medical professionals.

I need a break

Being able to indicate, in appropriate ways, when he needs a break from social interaction is an important self-regulation skill. It can be as simple as saying, "I need a break" or handing a "Break" card (teach him how and when to use it beforehand) to the appropriate person. A self-regulation break is just that— a break to regroup, regain a sense of calm, and then return to the activity or interaction. Don't call it a time-out, which may have punitive connotations. And help the child understand that expressing his need for a break is a tool he uses to stay calm and in control. Taking a break should not be a reward for appropriate behavior, nor a way for the child to avoid an undesirable activity.

A break can be as simple as going to the water foundation, even if he is not thirsty. A reading corner with a basket of hand fidgets helps many children regroup. Or create a sensory space—a dedicated room designed with sensory needs in mind, for children who need to regroup in more major ways. However self-regulation breaks are implemented, they should help further the child's ability to be successful in daily interactions with the people around him.

When "sorry" seems to be the hardest word

It seems like it should be such a simple thing, teaching your child or student to say "I'm sorry" when an apology is warranted. But far beyond repeating a conditioned response, truly understanding the nature of an apology and being able to act upon that knowledge in a sincere and meaningful way requires layer upon layer of social competence that many adults find difficult, let alone your child with autism. Parents write us saying, "my child steadfastly refuses to apologize." When a child exhibits resistant behavior—of any kind—it's our job as parents and teachers to try to pinpoint the source of the resistance. So let's break down a "simple" apology, and look at the steps we can take to help our child understand and apply this critical interpersonal skill.

First, does your child understand why an apology is needed? Learning to recite the words "I'm sorry" isn't enough—it doesn't help the child understand what he did and the consequences it had on another person. All children, not just children with autism spectrum disorders, have elements of selfishness, defensiveness, and impulsivity to their personalities. Empathy is a learned thinking and behavior. We must consistently and persistently teach the words and actions of empathy and apology.

- Label the behavior, not the child. Say "Name-calling hurts people's feelings" rather than "You're mean."

- Is he emotionally able to apologize? Don't insist that an apology come instantaneously. There is huge distinction between apologizing and actually feeling remorse. Remember that even while the heat of anger stills burns, a child (or any other person) may say "sorry" but true feelings of regret may not come until later. When anger is high, the child may need a cooling off period before he can apologize sincerely. (This happens to you too, doesn't it?) This requires striking a balance—you want the incident handled in a timely and relatively immediate way, but an insincere apology is not an adequate apology. The cooling-off period will vary from child to child and from incident to incident. It may be two minutes this time, twenty minutes next time. But attempting to teach anything when the child is still emotionally overwrought is wasted effort.

Teach the steps to an effective apology:

- In concrete language, explain to your child what he did that requires an apology. Do not assume he knows. Use an informative, not punitive, tone of voice. Taking a problem-solving rather than castigating approach preserves your child's fragile dignity and makes it much more likely he will learn.

> **QUICK IDEA**
>
> At home and at school, your only basis of comparison must be your child or student's previous performance, not that of his siblings or classmates.

- Ask the person who was wronged to tell your child how it felt. "Calling me a butthead hurts my feelings." Have your child repeat it back.

- Have your child issue a specific apology: "I'm sorry I broke your crayon/called you a butthead/ruined your computer game/ate your brownie." Give him a choice of ways in which he can apologize:
  - with spoken words, face-to-face, or over the phone
  - with a note: handwritten, typed, e-mailed. A pre-printed note can be used with young children, adapted with increasing complexity as the child gets older. At first, he may just fill in the name of the person to whom he is apologizing and then sign his name. Later, he can fill in "I'm sorry for _____." Eventually he works up to a fully original note.
  - with a drawing

- Have the child make restitution where possible and reasonable. "You can have my green crayon" or "I'll get you a Band-aid."

- Ask the wronged party for closure: "That's okay," or "Thank you for apologizing," or "I forgive you."

All's fair?

Grasping abstract concepts such as fairness is enormously difficult for our concrete-thinking children. Building a concept of "fair" requires instilling an understanding of his place as a member of a group, and that rules are made for the protection of all people in that group. Discuss with your child that at times rules may seem unfair to an individual, and that formal and informal ways of communicating these grievances helps us air our feelings and settle differences. Hearing both sides of a story is integral to the concept of fairness.

Give your child a way to communicate his feelings of unfairness in a concrete fashion. It could be a form that either you or the child fills out.

Who is the grievance against (classmate, sibling, teacher, parent, etc)?
What happened (_____ said this and/or _____ did this)?
When and where did this happen?
What rule did this break?
How did this make you feel?
What do you think should happen next?

The appropriate protest

You've seen it a thousand times—the pursed lips, the abject refusal, the running away and the head shaking, accompanied by shrieks of "no! no! NO!" Or it might take the form of a complete shut-down or physically aggressive behavior like hitting or biting. What's at issue here is the child who hasn't learned to say "no" in a socially appropriate manner.

Equip your child with more socially appropriate ways to protest than just overt behavior or the emphatic "NO!" Teach him to say "I don't know," "I don't want to," "I don't like that," or suggest walking away without verbalizing. Teach the limited-speaking or nonverbal child to use a simple hand gesture or communication card for "Stop."

I predict that . . .

Watching a movie or television program with the sound turned off is a great exercise in perception, prediction, and querying. What do you think is happening? Look at the characters' faces—are they happy with what's going on? Scared? Worried? Are they friends or do they not like each other? What do you think will happen next?

Stop the movie or program and have the child write or make up his own ending. Predicting an event or a sequence of events will be hard for a child whose thinking tends toward black and white. Once he becomes familiar with the concept, move on to noticing and taking advantage of the many opportunities for practice in daily life.

Asking others for help

This is such a big skill to learn that it may go unnoticed when the child has mastered the skill but taken it too far, becoming too dependent upon the teacher or paraeducator. When this happens, teach the child to generalize the skill to others. When he isn't sure what to do, instruct him to look around at others at his table or near his desk before asking the teacher. Teach him to ask a neighbor, "What page are we on?" or "What are we supposed to do?" If he still needs help, instruct him to raise his hand to ask the teacher.

This step is particularly important for the child who may seem oblivious to his environment. He's the one still at his desk after everyone else has lined up for recess. But he ultimately has as much to learn from his peers as he does from the teacher. Cooperative learning is critical, and a skill he'll use throughout his life.

Teaching honesty through example

For many children with autism, telling a lie is, like empathy, a learned behavior. White lies notwithstanding, your child's innate truthfulness is something you want to celebrate, not squash. Our concrete-thinking kids will call a situation exactly as they see it, unless over time, we 1) by our own behavior, give them examples of how to use dishonesty to avoid consequences and/or

2) give them reason to lie by administering consequences that are emotionally unbearable (humiliation, feelings of chronic failure, physical punishment). To help your child learn to embrace honesty:

- Model honesty about your own behavior. Become aware of how often we not only employ small dishonesties in our daily lives, but also make our children complicit. "Don't tell Dad I bought another pair of shoes," or "Tell (the unwanted caller) I'm not home." Better to say: "I'll skip lattes and lunches out this week so I can buy the shoes" or "Tell (the unwanted caller) that I cannot come to the phone right now."

- Let your child know that the lie they tell is worse than whatever the behavior they are lying about. Then stand by that thought. This does not mean there are no consequences for behavior. First, tell him you are proud of him for telling the truth even though it was difficult. Then decide whether you can ameliorate the consequences, or perhaps give a free pass (amnesty) for a first offense.

- Children with autism think in absolutes, and this is one area where it's appropriate. Let him know that in his relationship with you, you expect truthfulness at all times, not just when it's convenient or easy.

  Note: we'll repeat the operative phrase: "in his relationship with you." Teaching the nuanced landscape of so-called white lies is trickier business. In his relationships with others, lies can be acceptable when sparing someone's feelings. And teach him that there can be truth in silence. Remember *Bambi*? Thumper's mother is right: if you can't say something nice, don't say anything at all. "This dinner tastes just awful" may be truthful in his eyes, but it will surely hurt his host's feelings.

Everyone makes mistakes

Most children with autism or Asperger's love absolutes, and one of life's greatest absolutes is that everyone makes mistakes. But autism leaves your child without the ability to generalize, and each mistake or failing stands as his and his alone. Imagine the monumental anxiety this creates for him. We all make so many little mistakes and boo-boos throughout our day that we likely are not even conscious of them, correcting them without thinking, and moving on. On a typical morning, we may dribble coffee on the counter, let the shower curtain drip on the floor, smudge lipstick, misplace our keys, tear the sports page, and step on the cat's tail. Most of the time we take all this in stride and don't miss a beat—while our child is upstairs melting down because he squeezed the toothpaste too hard and it's all over his hand now.

Fear of failure can paralyze your child. Take a two-pronged approach to drawing him out: instill the understanding that everyone makes mistakes, and that everyone needs help. Modeling both of these behaviors makes it real for him.

- Everyone makes mistakes.
    - Most of our mistakes are small, correctable and have few lasting consequences. Point out small mistakes and label them as No Big Deal. We wipe the counter, we change our shirt, we move on.
    - At school, there's another word for mistake when we misspell a word or get the math problem wrong: practice. Missed spelling words and math problems are No Big Deal; they simply mean we are learning.
    - Sometimes another word for mistake is accident, and most accidents are No Big Deal. If we have an accident that affects someone else, it's usually easy to make amends. "I'm sorry I bumped you and spilled your juice. I will clean it up and pour you some more."
- Everyone needs help.
    - Ask your child for help throughout your daily life.
    - Ask other adults, siblings and peers to ask him for help.
    - Point out the many instances during his day where adults and kids ask each other for help. When did Dad need help? When did Joey or Katie or Henry need help? When did the teacher need help?
    - With your child, make a list (using names or photos) of people he trusts whom he can ask for help when he needs it—parent, teacher, sibling, friend.

- Brainstorm with your child to think of several ways to ask for help, either with his words, or with pictures or cue cards.

  – I need help, please
  – I didn't understand that (I don't get it)
  – Can you say that again, please?
  – What do I do next?

- Set up a classroom or home help exchange. Students or family members write down something (non-immediate) with which they need help. All the ideas go into a box. Either randomly or at set times, pull a slip from the box and read aloud. Class or family can then discuss ways in which they can help their classmate or family member. The help exchange can be anonymous or not, as appropriate.

- A classroom visual depicting ways to ask for and receive help benefits all students, not just the ones with autism.

- A peer buddy system in the classroom lets classmates ask each other for help in a relatively private way.

A word about "normal"

Now there's a word we'd like to see omitted from your social vocabulary entirely—in not just what you say, but how you think about your child and his autism or Asperger's. For many parents, emphasis on this two-syllable trip-off-the-tongue utterance can become a handicap of immeasurable dimension. Learning to think social and be social to whatever degree your child is able challenges him enough without our heaping on the additional burden of meeting the subjective measure of "normal." Here's another true story with a happy ending from a middle school in Some Place, USA.

"I just want him to have a lot of friends like I did," Mom frets to the speech language pathologist. "To have fun doing all the normal kid things and teen things that we all did together."

"When your son came to me last year," the SLP tells Mom, "his social thinking skills were pretty nonexistent. He didn't understand why

he should say hi to people in the halls, he didn't know how to ask a question to further a conversation, or how to engage with a peer during the lunch hour. Now he's working on those things. That's a huge amount of progress."

"But he's only made two friends."

"I would rephrase that: he's made two friends! One shares his interest in model trains and one shares his interest in running. He knows how you feel, though. So I am going to share with you what he told me the other day. He said, 'I don't want a lot of friends. I can't handle a lot of friends. More than one at a time stresses me out. I can talk to these two friends about things I'm interested in. They are great for me.'

"Walk through this or any other school," the SLP continues. "You'll see a huge range of 'normal' middle school behavior. You'll see nerdy normal, sporty normal, musical normal, artsy normal, techie normal. Kids tend to gravitate to groups that make them feel safe. For now, your son has found his group. You and I walk a fine line: honoring his choices while continuing to teach him the skills he needs to feel comfortable expanding his boundaries."

Your child has many social selves. To embrace all of them, and therefore him as a whole child, is to redefine how we view normal—one person at a time.

Teachers *and* Learners

You are all learners,
doers and teachers.
RICHARD BACH

HERE'S A STATEMENT THAT DEMONSTRATES our remarkable grasp of the obvious: autism is complex. Anyone who's ever spent time around a child with autism or Asperger's knows this to be true. So we continue to be amazed by the frequency with which we get questions (often from reporters) asking us to synthesize autism or some aspect of it down to "the single most important thing." As if there could ever be such a thing. Nevertheless, when such a reporter recently asked Ellen, "What is the single most important thing parents need to know about special education?" she had an answer ready.

In this thing called education, every person is a teacher and every person is a learner. The most important thing every parent and every teacher needs to know about their student with autism is that his success depends upon theirs—upon how successfully they collaborate as partners and team members with the common goal of enabling the child to meet his full potential. Autism imposes no inherent limits on a child, but we as adults often do—through our failure to adapt our teaching to the different manner in which our student with autism processes information, experiences his physical environment, and relates to others.

So that single most important thing parents and teachers can do for their student with autism is to create and sustain a productive partnership. A productive partnership is one in which all members accept and fulfill their responsibilities as team members, readily share information they've gained about their student with other team members and remain child-focused (leaving personalities and politics out of it). They embrace the idea that they must learn from their student in order to be able to teach him. They know that creativity, curiosity and patience, along with a willingness to let go of old ideas about how to teach (or parent), are indispensable to everyone's success.

And when our teaching isn't working, we take it upon ourselves as the adults in the situation to recognize that it is the teaching that needs to change, not the student.

A strong, productive team dynamic is the only way the formal education setting can truly work for your student with autism. Parents are the captains of this team as the ones who remain constant in the child's life. Through them, information passes from year to year, teacher to teacher. Each teacher who touches the child's life plays a critical role, one that stays with the child long after he's left that particular classroom. Will that legacy be one of endowing the student with a sense of can-do and achievement, or one of simply getting through to the end of the year? By virtue of the fact that you are reading this book, we suspect you are in the first camp. Thank you, thank you. The world needs more like you.

This chapter comes last in the book because it is only when all the obstacles autism throws at your child or student have been removed that he can succeed in meeting the academic and social requirements of the formal education environment. That success comes when we've accommodated his delicate sensory system and given him a functional means of communication. When we've identified the root causes of difficult behaviors and eliminated them at their source. When we've taught him the skills needed for self-managing the tasks of daily life, and when we've instilled in him the ability and the confidence to interact with others on every level life requires, from one-on-one to responsible community citizenship.

This learning is ongoing, for all of us. We wouldn't want it any other way, would we? The single most important thing we teachers can instill in the children who come to us is the joy to be found in seeing themselves, through our example, as lifelong learners.

Our friend David Freschi of Simply Good Ideas (whom you met in Chapters 2 and 3) leaves us with this thought: "End every day asking yourself these two questions: what did I teach today, and what did my student learn?"

It's good for all kids

The ideas in this chapter address the classroom challenges of children on the autism spectrum, but many of them will also be of great benefit to all kids. The more a child's accommodations can be integrated to the general classroom, the less the child stands out as different, the more socially accommodating other students are likely to be, and the more the child with autism or Asperger's is likely to feel a part of the classroom community.

Respect the child

Nearly every professional interviewed for this book emphasized the importance of not talking about the child in front of him. When you think he's not listening, he is. When you think he can't hear you, he can. Too often we discuss our child in front of her teacher or our spouse as if the child isn't in the room. We discuss their behavior, their academic or social difficulties, casually compare them to siblings or classmates, lament how tired we are, make deprecating remarks that we understand to be humorous … right? Put yourself in your child's shoes and imagine your bosses or parents doing the same to you. Uncomfortable, isn't it? This advice applies even when "catching" your child or student at something good. He may overhear you saying, "Jacob did a great job on his math sheet," but it's better interpersonal communication to tell him directly: "Jacob, you did a great job on your math sheet." Or, ask his permission to tell a third party: "Jacob, may I tell Mrs. Porter what a great job you did on your math sheet?"

Walk a mile in these shoes

In the course of the thirteen or so years of a child's school life, parents encounter teachers they love and teachers who fall short. (Teachers feel the same way about parents.) Some teachers seem to fit a child, his needs, and learning style, while others never achieve the reciprocal learning-from-each-other needed to be able to effectively teach this child who thinks so differently. Yet, child, teacher, and parent must contend with each other over the course of the year, sometimes longer.

"Walk a mile in my shoes." "Spend a couple of days at our house." Thousands of parents have shared such thoughts with us, sentiments they wish teachers would read and take to heart. The life lesson here is not one of taking sides, or finding fault, but recognizing that each person experiences the world in his or her own unique way. For parents and teachers to work productively as part of a team for the betterment of the child, it helps to imagine life through one another's eyes. Here are some of those parents' thoughts.

- Please make no assumptions about what it is like to parent this student. He may exhibit an entirely different display of behaviors at home—for better or for worse. An open, non-judgmental, and ongoing exchange of information between home and school is the only way for all concerned adults to get the complete picture they need to help the child.

- Whether you think you can or whether you think you can't, "fix" or "cure" are words better left out of thoughts and discussions about your student with autism. Autism is a spectrum disorder and kids with autism will be as different as snowflakes. Each one's learning path is unique, and that requires accommodation and adaptation, but not "fixing." Suggesting a fix means the child is being seen as less-than, and that attitude can only cause friction between parent and teacher.

- Autism is an open-ended disability; beware the expectation that is too low. The hopes and dreams parents hold for their child help them maintain the stamina they need to stay the course long after their child has left your classroom. Respect and honor their dreams, and dream large for this student while he is in your class. Mom and Dad need to know that you, like they, are encouraging their child to be everything he can be.

- Respect and make use of the time and effort to which your student's parent has gone in educating herself about the various aspects of her child's different ability. She has a need to know as much as she can about how her child sees the world, and much of what she has learned can make your job easier. It can also be comforting and sustaining for her to know that she is helping others, because …

- Parenting the child with autism can be a lonely, exhausting experience. Offer positive reinforcement, an ear, or a shoulder when needed. And—judiciously—let her know that you have days like that too, so you can support each other's efforts.

Probe beyond the obvious

When a first-grader frequently put his hands over his ears, his teacher assumed the problem was noise. Upon closer observation, an occupational therapist discovered the child would sometimes press deeply on his cheekbones and temples, indicating a sensory invasion other than noise. His teacher was then able to pinpoint other irritations—kids crowding in line around him or glare from the window that was affecting his sensory systems.

Avoid teaching compliance

Finding the source of behaviors can be tricky. Teachers who have marginal experience working with the autism or Asperger's population can easily misinterpret behaviors that occur as a result of one of autism's underlying challenges—sensory issues, social misunderstanding, communication difficulties—as unwillingness to comply with instructions. When faced with a behavior that remains unchanged despite best efforts, teachers may request that a behavior specialist step in and create a plan to extinguish the noncompliant behavior. It may work, but then what happens? Another behavior problem emerges.

Don't focus on compliance as the goal; look for the root causes of behavior. When a child's problematic behavior doesn't change, we've overlooked an unmet need. The teaching needs to change. Behavior is always communication. In a vast majority of instances of challenging behavior, once the root cause for behavior has been met, compliance will follow as the net effect. Learn to be a good behavior detective.

Designated teacher

Where there is more than one adult in the classroom, designate only one to give instructions for each task or project. Students with autism or Asperger's yearn for routine and consistency; many voices create opportunities for misunderstanding and challenge their already overtaxed auditory systems. Follow these tips for verbal instructions.

- Use the fewest words possible. Instructions that are too wordy will be lost in translation, as will instructions repeated by more than one adult but with slight variations.

- If the child appears not to understand the instructions, rephrase using fewer words. If that still doesn't work, move to a nonverbal communication method.

- Phrase instruction in positive terms. Some children with autism or Asperger's hear only the final verb. Example: A child is climbing too high on the playground equipment and jumping off. The child may hear only the last word of "Don't jump!"—and jumps. Say instead, "Please climb down."

Small group versus large group

Break classroom activities into small groups wherever possible. The child with autism may find the whole-group classroom intimidating or overwhelming, lessening her inclination to participate. The same child might succeed with the same material in a smaller group, where each child has a defined role and responsibility. Mixed ability groups mean everyone learns from each other, too.

Play to your child's interests

If your little collector owns enough Matchbox or Hot Wheels cars to simulate rush hour traffic (we know a child who did just that, every evening, down the main hallway of the house), be ever vigilant for ways to weave his interest into all areas of learning. Use those cars to:

- Combine tactile sensory with pretend play: Set up a shaving cream "snowstorm" and have him plow out stuck cars.
- Teach left from right or listening to directions by playing with the cars on a road-map children's rug or plastic floor map. "Go two blocks past the large tree and turn left."
- Make a memory game using a set of double prints taken of 24 of his favorite cars.
- Five red cars plus five blue cars = a custom tic-tac-toe game.

Shrek's social card

Have your students create evaluations for characters in a favorite book or movie. They can rate the skill level of the characters in various social arenas: helping others, empathy, self-motivation, daily interpersonal skills, manners, etc. The goal is to motivate children to consider the thoughts, feelings, and actions of others.

Privacy screen helps focus

Visual and auditory stimuli can often be distracting when trying to focus on an in-class assignment. Create a portable desktop or floor-standing privacy screen students can use whenever they need to shut out the rest of the class. All students can use the screens, not just those with autism or Asperger's.

Standing station

Make a podium-like space available in the classroom, where the child can go to work if he needs a break from sitting. (You may find your other students asking to utilize this spot as well.) Or the reverse may be true. Provide a mat or carpeted area where a child can read or do work lying down. Full-body contact with a firm surface may aid concentration.

Hand fatigue

Struggling to write is relatively common among students with autism. All that determined effort can result in hand fatigue from an inappropriate grip, a tight grip, or inefficient writing posture. Occupational therapy catalogs offer unusual grippers and ergonomically designed pens/pencils to help with handwriting. Some simple hand exercises done before, during, and after the writing session further alleviate hand fatigue.

> **QUICK IDEA**
>
> Visual processing challenges can make writing letters along a line a difficult task. Try using raised-line paper. Available through Magical Toys and Products: MagicalToysAndProducts.com.

- Rubbing palms of hands together briskly
- Shaking or flapping hands
- Clasping hands together then releasing; repeat
- Stretching fingers wide apart, then making a fist

Body warm-up for classroom work

Children with hypoactive senses need alerting input to be ready to learn. A body warm-up is a good whole-class activity to wake up sluggish senses. Spend a few minutes doing these exercises at the start of class:

- Deep pressure stimulation: Have children press the thumbs of each hand into their opposite palms. Tell them to "put ten dots on each palm," pressing deeply and firmly all over. Next, squeeze the arms and shoulder by crossing the arms and squeezing the right side with the left hand and the left side with the right hand.

- Skin sensation: Have students rub-b-b-b-b the palms of their hands together, then the backs of their hands, then rub in between their fingers. Have them "give themselves a hand!"—clap loudly! Then have them "give themselves a pat on the back"—*pat, pat, pat, pat, pat*—and then a pat on the tummy … the head … arms and shoulders.

- Muscle sensation: Children will now "put on their writing gloves." These are long, tight gloves. Pu-u-u-ull the glove up to the shoulder with firm pressure strokes. Repeat several times. Get out all the wrinkles in each finger of the glove!

- Joint compression: Have students press their hands into the desk. Next, they press their hands into their thighs trying to press their feet into the floor.

The routine works just as well at home. Do it with your child and see if you don't feel more alert.

Houston, we have no problem with transitions

Help your little spaceman or spacewoman transition to the next activity by "blasting off." Have him kneel, crouch, or sit on the floor with you behind him. Start counting down: "T minus ten and counting—nine, eight, seven, six—we have ignition—five, four, three, two, one—we have liftoff!" Lift him off the floor and send him on his way to nap, bath, story time, chores, or whatever his next activity will be.

The bridge to circle time

Teachers can help children switch from one activity to the next by using a physical task as a bridge. Inside of just calling children to circle time, have them negotiate a physical task or obstacle to get there. It could be going up and down some low steps, crawling or wiggling under a table, following footprints or stepping stones/shapes, going under or over a limbo bar. This activity has the double benefit of providing calming input for the movement seekers and alerting the movement avoiders of impending input.

Tips for successful circle time

Teacher calls for Circle Time and here come all the little bodies running for their place on the floor. All except your kiddo, for whom circle time presents major sensory and social challenges. The floor is hard and cold, the kids sit elbow to elbow, there are no personal boundaries, and he is unsure what he is supposed to do once he gets there. The songs are too loud and the oral directions evaporate in the air like steam before he can process them. It's no wonder that common reactions to circle time for children with autism include running away or simply glazing over. Neither of those behaviors promotes successful learning, but with gentle acclimation, your student with autism can join the circle. Ease him in with this incremental plan:

1. Let your student do a quiet activity, such as coloring, at a table near the circle. His chair should face the circle.

2. Little by little, over time (days or weeks), move the chair away from the table and closer to the circle. Replace the quiet table activity with a quiet lap activity, such as a squeeze toy.

3. Transition from chair to floor by providing a seating arrangement with clear boundaries for the student. This might be a cushion, camp chair, cardboard square, or colored tape outlining a square on the floor.

4. Allow a squeeze toy or other sensory calming item, such as a rubber chew necklace or weighted bean bag, as the child sits in the circle.

5. Give the child a job that allows him some movement and focus during circle time. He might pass out items or hold items for you. He might change or point out items on the calendar or the weather chart. Does he have a special skill that might ease him into the circle activities? He might lead or demonstrate stretches or yoga poses, or be the rhythm sticks leader. Have a clear signal to let him know when the job is done, and clear instruction as to what comes next: "Thank you for being our weather person today. Now, would you like to sit on your cushion or in a chair?"

6. Reward and reinforce his success at every increment, not just for participation and job-well-done, but for making good choices along the way. Reward and reinforce in a visual as well as oral manner so he can see his progress. Charts, calendars, and stickers are several common ways to do this.

Integrated play groups

Young children with autism or Asperger's need assistance in developing play skills. Integrated Play Groups is a structured instruction method developed specifically for kids on the autism spectrum. It entails play groups composed of three to five children, with a greater number of typically developing children involved than children with autism. The play groups generally meet at regularly scheduled times at least twice a week for thirty to sixty minutes, in settings like integrated school sites, after-school programs, recreation centers, or homes.

The Play Group Guide—a teacher or sometimes a parent—assists children through modeling and coaching, providing more support during the early stage of the group's formation than later. Initially the Play Group Guide may serve as a director, setting the stage for a performance—arranging play materials, assigning roles, setting up play events, and acting as an interpreter to help expert and novice players figure out each other's actions and words. At the next level the Play Group Guide moves toward the periphery of the play activity, posing questions, commenting on activities, and offering suggestions, but always modifying her behavior in response to the patterns of activity in the play group.

The goals of Integrated Play Groups are many: to expand social awareness and interest in other children, to increase reciprocal social interaction and symbolic representation through cooperative pretend play, and to create genuine friendships either between children with autism and children without, or between two children with autism. Pamela Wolfberg, director of The Autism Institute on Peer Relations and Play, created this strategy. Learn more about it at *AutismInstitute.com*.

Ready or not—here I come?

Your child may be turning five before your school's deadline, but chronological age should not be the sole determinant of whether he is ready for kindergarten. It's a huge leap from preschool, daycare, or the home setting to kindergarten, with its longer, more structured day, larger class or group size, and focus shift from play to academics. If your child exhibits some of the developmental delays characteristic of autism, you may be wondering if your child is ready for kindergarten. You're wondering if perhaps he wouldn't benefit more from an additional year of play-focused growth and maturity before facing the more difficult social and academic requirements of school.

There is no single criterion that indicates readiness for kindergarten in any child. You must look at both your child's current capabilities, and at the school he will be attending. Many of the skills regarded as typical for children entering kindergarten are in areas that greatly challenge our kids with autism. Each school has its own expectations and requirements, but general indicators of kindergarten readiness are used as guidelines. Few children meet all these indicators. Try to determine the degree to which your child fits this profile, and discuss with teachers and administrators of any school you are considering. He or she should be able and willing to:

- Speak clearly *or* communicate needs in an alternative fashion
- Follow instructions
- Listen actively—if you read him a short picture-book story, can he follow along, then retell it in his own words?
- Interact amicably with other children and with adults: wait her turn, share, refrain from hitting, biting, etc.
- Participate in group activities
- Put on outer garments without assistance
- Use the restroom without assistance
- Manage lunch items (juice boxes, baggies, lunchboxes) without assistance
- Blow nose without assistance
- Handle pencil/markers, scissors
- Count to ten
- Be familiar with the alphabet
- Learn new things, shows some curiosity about her world

- Identify colors, shapes, body parts (some schools expect a certain level of knowledge in these areas)

- Recognize and respect authority

- Spend extended time away from parents

Evaluate all areas of your child's development. He may be ready cognitively but not emotionally. Or he may have good motor skills but poor language/communication or social skills. Educators tend to place more weight on cognitive development than on physical or social development in evaluating kindergarten readiness.

Observe the kindergarten in the school your child will attend. Note how typical kindergarteners behave and the types of activities included in the day. Can you picture your child being successful in this setting? Other factors:

- How large is the class and how much support does the teacher have? Are there assistants or volunteers in the class? Are they trained in early childhood education?

- What accommodations are made for the different paces at which children learn?

- Does the program seem developmental in nature, or is the emphasis academic? Many schools have pushed what used to be first-grade curriculum down to kindergarten. Forcing reading or arithmetic on a child who is not ready will not produce success.

Some educators feel that, as a parent, you should look for a kindergarten that is ready for your child, rather than whether your child is ready for kindergarten. Still, you can do much to help your child's entry into kindergarten go as smoothly as possible. Look at the skill set recommended above and use these at-home activities to build those skills.

- Read alphabet books. Teach him to recognize upper and lower case letters.

- Teach him to recognize numerals. Read number books and look for numbers in your travels around town. Practice self-help skills such as managing a coat, washing hands, blowing his nose. If he has trouble with fasteners such as zippers, buttons or shoelaces, give him only school clothing that has none of these.

QUICK IDEA

- Teach him left from right.

- Discuss spatial opposite terms: up and down, forward and backward, over and under, in and out.

- Discuss temporal terms: before/after, yesterday/tomorrow, last year/next year.

- Read wordless books. Encourage him to make up stories about what he thinks is happening in the pictures and what will happen next. (see **Wordless books** in Chapter 2)

- Teach the names of coins: quarter, dime, nickel, penny.

- Help him memorize his home phone number and address.

- Teach him basic colors and basic shapes. Apply the knowledge to objects in the home and in your travels around town.

- Take the time to speak to him clearly and with limited jargon and slang, and remind him to do the same when he speaks to you.

- Do simple cutting, gluing, writing, and coloring activities, and incorporate these skills into everyday tasks, such as gift-wrapping.

- Incorporate gross motor activities into your family's days: walking, running, shooting hoops, playing catch, skipping, swimming, dancing.

- Tell your child what you and/or his other parent do for a living. Point out people's occupations in your travels around town.

- Expose him to as broad a range of experiences as he can tolerate comfortably. Children with autism frequently stick to a narrow range of interests and require much repetition and exposure to many different experiences before a new one "takes."

If you do decide to delay your child's entry to kindergarten for a year, experts are nearly unanimous in recommending that you do not keep him home, but

A desktop or floor-standing easel with adjustable writing angles may help with both motor skills and hand-eye coordination. Make your own lined paper if the child requires wider spacing than on commercially available products.

enroll him in a structured program such as a part-time or full-time pre-kindergarten or junior kindergarten for that year. Developing independence and peer-interaction skills should be the focus.

Off to kindergarten? Plan ahead

A child's first day of kindergarten class brings new teachers, new kids, new routines—lots of places for mishaps and miscues to occur that can quickly erode your child's self-esteem. Help your child pre-learn skills that will contribute to his daily success right from the start.

Ask your child's teacher for a "map" of his school day, then practice at-home skills that might prevent unanticipated problems: taking off his coat and hanging it on a hook, using a pencil sharpener or eraser, concentrating when it's noisy, walking with a cafeteria tray, opening and closing a lunch box or bag, handling a sandwich baggie, juice box, or other implements, throwing the trash away properly, blowing his nose, fastening his shoes.

Visit the new school, the new teacher, and the new classroom before the first day. Take photos of his new surroundings: the classroom, the gym, the playground, the lunchroom. Also take photos of the new people with whom he will come in contact: the classroom teacher and educational assistants, the principal, the school secretary, the librarian, the PE teacher, the music teacher, the resource teacher, the school cook, custodian, and the bus driver. Ask to see the class roster to identify a few friends who will also be in your child's class. Use the photos to construct a social story that emphasizes the things he noticed and liked on his visit: "I will get to play on the spiral slide." "Roger and Lisa will sit near me in class." End the story with an affirmation: "I will like my new school."

Beginnings and endings

Ward off potential behavior problems by communicating to your child or student a clear beginning and end to an activity. A task defined in nebulous terms, "Work on the project until the bell rings," or an activity that has no clear start/stop defined, "We have to run some errands" can create anxiety in the child from the get-go, compromising his focus and chance for success. Try these suggestions for placing easy-to-understand parameters on assignments and activities:

- Use two work baskets for hands-on tasks, one labeled Start and the other End. Teach the child to put work into the End basket as finished: instant visual recognition when the task is completed.

- Break a large job into smaller parcels. If the goal is to make twenty paper-tissue flowers for the school play, give the child materials to make just five at one time, depending the skill level of the child and the time frame. Many kids strive to perform well and are eager to please, but may not be able to mentally break tasks into smaller parts. One young man we know was given the task of stuffing one thousand envelopes. He refused to take a bathroom break, a lunch break or even engage in conversation until he had completed all one thousand of them—six hours of work!

  When scheduling homework or other long projects, incorporate break times as part of the task. For every half-hour of sitting, he must get up and walk around for five minutes—go to the bathroom, get a snack or just shake his limbs out and move. When a child drives himself too hard without breaks, he inevitably reaches a point of diminishing returns, and the project ends up taking longer and causing more stress than if he had taken those short, periodic breaks.

> ### QUICK IDEA
>
> Three-dimensional tracing of numerals and letters may help the student with space/ground difficulties. Form thick letters with white or colored glue and allow them to dry. Have the student trace each letter with his finger: starting point, direction, end point.

- Vocalize clear beginnings and endings. "Your room is cleaned when your bed is made, your toys are put in the toy box, and your dirty clothes are put into the laundry hamper."

- Be clear about quantity. "Work on problems 1-3 starting now. When finished, turn your paper over and wait for further instructions." Or use numbered lists on the blackboard to define tasks or activities with multiple components. For instance, "Today we will discuss five parts of the human body." List them on the board and as each discussion is completed, check it off. Or define a physical area, such as when asking your child to rake the yard.

- For a child who has an understanding of how to tell time, use it to define the start and end of a task. "The school walk will start at 1:00 pm and end at 2:00 pm." Use visual timers as needed.

- Use a visual schedule that illustrates start, middle components, and the end. For instance, use a picture of the child putting on his coat, then the dry cleaners, next the grocery store, then the child at home again.

The things-to-do-later bin

Interruptions are unavoidable. If work on a project or assignment must be interrupted (dentist appointment, dinner time, just plain fatigue), it goes into the Things-to-Do-Later bin—a specific place that visually reinforces that the child can or should return to it at a later time. For those days when planning runs amok, assign numbers to each item in the bin, designating which one to do first, second, etc. Use sticky notes; don't write on the actual assignment.

Think cultural, think socio

Allow extra teaching time to compensate for cultural or socioeconomic factors that further disadvantage a child with autism or Asperger's. If you are teaching keyboard skills to a child who does not have a computer at home, there is no outlet for home practice and you must arrange for more time at school or in an after-school instructional setting.

Partnership skills

Teaching children to work as partners involves more than putting two kids at a table together. For your student with autism, it takes a lot more. The social thinking skills inherent in reciprocal communication do not come naturally to him. Help your student become a stronger communication partner by breaking down this complex skill into its basic elements. Review these elements and teach or practice as needed until they become more natural to the child. Once he has been taught these skills, give him a visual support in the form of a small card or bookmark-shaped reminder list. This is a good whole-class activity; most students will benefit from extra coaching on how to be a good partner.

- Read the directions together. If we have questions, we can ask the teacher.
- Look at your partner when she is speaking to you.
- Listen to your partner.
- Think about your partner's ideas about the assignment.
- Tell your partner your ideas about the assignment.
- Take turns talking. We are each quiet when the other is talking.
- We stay on task. We do not talk about other things and we do not talk to other kids while we are working on our assignment. If we need help, we can ask the teacher.

Choosing a clinician

Whether speech language pathologist, occupational or physical therapist, psychologist, medical doctor, or tutor, a clinician's ability to connect with your child is every bit as important as whether he or she has sterling credentials and the recommendation of colleagues or friends. Ask to meet with professionals before engaging their services, and see if you can detect that connection with your child. Any therapy can drain your pocketbook as well as your child's energies, and it makes no sense to do so with a clinician who may be ineffective for your particular child.

Choosing an educational program

When choosing a program for your child, remember to look from results backward, not from theory forward. Start with a discussion of what you want your child to be able to do, then work backward to the instructional model or intervention method that best matches his learning style.

Review tests

Ask to see any tests administered to determine services for your child or used as a basis for grades in the classroom. Be comfortable that the test is really measuring what it claims to measure and speak up if you are not sure that it does, especially if it is going to affect placement or therapies rendered.

Example: A Functional Communication Assessment for a ten-year-old boy with autism noted that, in the Word-R Test, "he had the most difficulty when asked to change a semantic absurdity such as 'Mark quit the football team because he was a poor batter.'" This sentence is not a test of semantics, it is a test of sports knowledge. The child being tested had no background in or exposure to football. When the tester rephrased the sentence as, "Mark put his coat on to go swimming," the child responded with, "That's silly!"

School-bus safety

Ask the school district how much autism training your child's regular bus driver has received. The answer may be little to none. Yet the driver is responsible for your child under circumstances that are often high-anxiety and sensory-laden: the noise from the kids, the stops and starts, the hot and cold temperatures, the fumes, the bullies.

Parents or teachers can help make the ride easier for everyone by creating a Driver Tip Sheet that includes important information about a child and how best to communicate with him. Include his photo, a short positive description of the child, his likes (reinforcers) and dislikes, a list of simple strategies that work with him, warning about tactics that will backfire, and some activities to do on the bus that will keep the child's interest.

Auditory processing difficulties

To the untrained eye, the characteristics of a child with poor auditory processing can look similar to those of attention deficit disorder, but the two are not the same. It may look to you as if your student's eyes are wandering all over the room and that he is not paying attention. More likely, he did not comprehend what you just said and is looking to his peers for cues as to what to do next.

Often a teacher will move a student with autism to the front of the room to minimize visual and auditory distractions, and give him written or other visual instructions for schedules and tasks. That's helpful. A teacher may further promote success by making eye contact or getting his attention

> **QUICK IDEA**
>
> If your child is sound sensitive, ask for an upper locker at school, at the end of a row. A lower locker puts him directly in earshot level of kids above him slamming their locker doors.

another way before speaking to him directly. Carry that idea one step further when you're one step removed, i.e., speaking at the blackboard, overhead projector or other media. Make sure he can see your face at those times, not the back of your head.

Fire drills—red alert

For some children with autism or Asperger's, the sudden violent noise of a fire alarm can be extremely painful, and the resulting commotion can send them into full-blown meltdown. If your child has sensitive hearing, work with his teacher to determine how best to handle fire drills. Some children need to know exactly when the fire drill will occur. For others, knowing the time may cause them to obsess while waiting for it. This child may be better off with a more general warning: "Remember the fire drill we practice sometimes? We are going to get to do that again today but I am not exactly sure when." Whatever approach works best, plan for it ahead of time.

Teach one skill at a time

Mastering a mature pencil grip and learning how much pressure to apply when using a pencil are major tasks for sensory-challenged students. Learning to form numerals and letters at the same time is yet another difficult pairing. Break apart the skills and practice them independently. Offer alternative ways of learning related skills. For instance, let him practice numerals and letters with a felt pen (little pressure required), and practice pencil grip and pressure with shapes, squiggles and less precise requirements.

Reduce paper glare

Many white papers (those with brightness rating of 92 and higher) produce a glare that can be painful for light-sensitive eyes. Using soft gray, pastel-colored or off-white paper may help. Ditto for the ink color. Black may be too stark. Try a softer color.

Eyes wide open

Use exaggerated gestures and expressions when teaching a concept; it helps promote language comprehension. Stop! (hand extended, palm forward), Oops! (eyes wide, hand over mouth), Up, etc.

Participation plans

A Participation Plan is a one-page reference describing how a student takes part in a given activity. For example, a plan may explain how a nonverbal student participates in circle time using a video output device programmed by a peer. The plan includes where to position the device, what natural cues or prompts the student needs to communicate using the device, and what alternative strategies to employ if the device is unavailable.

A student may have several Participation Plans, depending on the number of daily activities that need modification. Each plan 1) describes the activity as it would typically unfold, 2) summarizes related IEP goals, 3) explains special preparation, strategies and materials, including where they are located, 4) shows how the student participates at each step, and 5) indicates accommodations, modifications, and alternative activities, if appropriate. (For explanation of the difference between accommodation and modification, see **Program accommodations and modifications** later in this chapter.)

Prioritize Participation Plans according to need, beginning with those for the most frequent or frustrating activities. Keep them well organized and easily accessible in a binder. Share plans with all staff who work with the child, especially substitutes, interns, or volunteers. Review and revise plans quarterly, or as the child's capability grows and new challenges arise.

Teaching concentration skills

One of the most useless and lazy verbal shortcuts we use to admonish our children is, "pay attention!" What we really mean is we want them to focus on listening to information we (or others) are giving them verbally, or showing/demonstrating for them. There is usually no tangible reward for paying attention; no money exchanged, no pay involved, and for concrete-thinking children with autism, the phrase can be meaningless. When the child then fails to "pay attention," we interpret it as non-compliance, when it may in fact be our own failure to communicate in a manner meaningful to him.

To "pay attention," a child must apply an assortment of skills required to focus and/or concentrate on a finite task successfully. Autism compromises a child's ability to do this in two central areas: language processing (how they process information through the auditory channel) and vision (how they process information through the eyes). Environmental insults to the child's other senses can further impede the child's ability to focus. Oh, how he would like to comply and "pay attention" only to your words and your voice, but an airplane is screaming by outside the window, it's too hot in the room (that's why the window is open), the scent from Trisha's shampoo is making him gag, Trevor is flipping his pencil over and over (oops!—he missed and jabbed himself, heehee) and there's a film booming from the room next door. With all manner of sensory invasions coming at him at once, he cannot sort out and distinguish what is important and what is a distraction.

The ability to focus and concentrate may not come naturally to your student with autism, but he can learn. When both you and the child understand

> **QUICK IDEA**
>
> Hearing sensitivity is the most commonly reported sensory processing difficulty for individuals with autism. Felt or tennis balls put on the legs of chairs and desks can help minimize noise within a classroom and at home.

how his brain processes sensory input, you will be able to help him implement strategies to improve his concentration skills.

- Talk to the child about focus and concentration. If you are going to use the phrase "pay attention," explain it thoroughly, then check for comprehension. Explain that "paying attention" may be easy for some children, but very hard for others. *It does not have anything to do with how smart a person is.* It is something we can all learn to do with practice. You will be helping him learn to "pay attention," and with his smart brain, you are sure he can do it!

- Having the right tools is essential for any task. Before asking the child to concentrate on a task or assignment, check that he has all the necessary materials at hand: pencil sharpened and with adequate eraser, clean paper, correct book(s). If he needs to see you during the task, ensure that his line of sight is unobstructed.

- Our visual sense is directly connected to concentration: what we see is what we think about first. For many children with autism, this is their strongest sense, and therefore can also be the first to become overloaded. Help your student learn to concentrate by reducing visual distractions.

  - Study carrels are effective for many students with autism. If you cannot set up a study carrel in your classroom, make a portable one with screens that can be placed on the student's desk when needed and removed when not needed.

  - Teach your student to place his materials in front of him, and direct his eyes to the book or paper on which he wants to focus. Teach him to put his hands up by the sides of his face so he is only looking at that one thing.

- Ask him to notice how people use their visual concentration skills in their daily lives. Athletes always keep their eyes on the ball. Drivers keep their eyes on the road. (Ahem … drivers are *supposed* to keep their eyes on the road.) Cooks keep their eyes on the knife and their fingers while chopping.

- Auditory distractions can interfere with concentration. A set of earbuds with the cord removed can be helpful in muffling ancillary noise.

- Auditory challenges can result in the child missing information or misinterpreting language, rendering focus and concentration nearly impossible. For instance, some children cannot process the hard edge of certain consonants, or are unable to discern foreground and background sounds. If you suspect these types of auditory issues, ask that a speech language pathologist work with your child to strengthen auditory processing.

- Start with short periods of concentration and work up. Five minutes seems like a long time to him at first. For every five minutes of concentration, build in a two-minute break wherein he gets up, moves around, looks at something else. Gradually increase the focus time as his skill grows.

- For older kids who have achieved some concentration ability: part of their preparation can be determining the parameters of the task. How many pages am I trying to read; how many math problems do I need to do?

- Acknowledge that tuning out distractions is hard work. The world is full of interesting new things to see, hear, touch, smell and taste. Every day, all day, we make choices about which of these things to "pay attention" to. We can learn to ignore some of them and not let them interrupt our work.

- Encourage your student to encourage himself. "You can do it" is great. But "I can do it!" is even greater

Cueing or prompting?

Cues and prompts are great teaching tools for our children with autism, and sometimes they are used interchangeably. But there is a distinction to be made, especially as your child's social awareness grows and he can interact more freely with his changing environment. A *cue* is information your child gets from what is happening around him that lets him know how he should react or what should happen next. A *prompt* is information the adult gives the child in the absence of or in addition to the cue. Prompts can be verbal, physical (hand over hand, signed, modeled), gestural, positional, or locational.

So, when a batter smacks the ball into the outfield, the runner on first base is *cued* to run to second base. If the runner does not run, his coach will *prompt* him, "Run, Chris!"

Many children with autism will need to be taught to cue off their environment, and prompts help us do that. It's not unusual to see all the kids in the class line up for recess while our student with autism stays in his seat, seemingly oblivious. So we prompt him in a manner that begins to teach him to cue: "You may line up for recess now, Carl. Whenever you see all the other kids line up, you can too." With repeated prompting and practice, Carl will begin to link his action to the environmental cue and, in doing so, lessen his dependence on the teacher. It's important for teachers to keep in mind that a verbal prompt, such as the one used above, is actually a two-step process being asked of the child: to line up *and* learn the social skill of cueing off his environment. For some children, especially those with more impaired social thinking skills, this will be difficult. In that case, use a nonverbal prompt at first, such as a physical or positional prompt, until the child achieves success, then add in the verbal element to foster his cueing skills.

Effective prompting

All prompts are not created equal, and the dynamics of prompting are as ever-changing as the learning process itself. Follow these guidelines when using prompting as a teaching tool:

1. In every situation, choose the modality to which your child or student is most likely to respond, knowing this may change from situation to situation and day to day. For instance, in times of stress, you may need to substitute a verbal prompt with a physical prompt because his language processing capabilities are being strained. Combining modalities can be effective (e.g., touching his shoulder and saying his name at the same time).

2. Beware both under-prompting and over-prompting. Observe closely so you will be able to determine just how much help your student needs. Too little prompting and your student will not have adequate information (or motivation) needed to complete tasks successfully. Too much

prompting and the child may become prompt dependent. This will impede him in learning to do tasks independently.

3. The goal is independence, so as your student's ability grows, you can phase out prompting. Begin fading this type of support by moving farther away from the student when you give the prompt. Then gradually replace physical and visual prompts with verbal prompts, working your way down to one-word prompts, then indirect verbal prompts. Eventually, the student will be able to execute the skills without prompting.

Types of prompting

- Gestural: Nodding or shaking head, fingers to lips, pointing, thumbs-up, other sign language or body language (think baseball signals).

- Indirect physical: Modeling the target behavior (zipping coat, putting napkin in lap, walking/not running, using tissue not sleeve).

- Direct physical: Body contact that either guides the behavior (turning his shoulder to face front, your hand over his hand while tracing, moving the child in front of a peer), or cues the behavior (touching shoulder or elbow).

- Visual: Cue cards, sequence cards, photographs, devices such as timers, hourglass, calendar, day planner.

- Direct verbal: "Line up for recess, Katie." Over time, the prompt can fade to "Recess line!" to just "Recess!" and finally, fade completely as Katie learns the routine and learns to cue off peers.

- Indirect verbal: Because children with autism tend to be concrete thinkers with at least some impairment to inferential ability, indirect verbal prompting is effective once a child knows a skill and needs only a gentle reminder or hint, such as "What comes next?" or "And the third step is … " Indirect prompts help a child learn to cue off the environment.

> **QUICK IDEA**
>
> For the child who is prone to drifting off-task, place a photograph of him working on-task on his desk as a silent reminder. This can also help him keep his desk or locker organized. Post a picture of the tidy desk or locker before it hits cyclone stage.

Is this a teaching moment?

In a perfect world, where brains function flawlessly and time is an abundant commodity, we might be able to capitalize on most moments when a teaching opportunity presents itself. However, in our imperfect world, it's important for parents, especially those new to autism, to understand that in the life of your preschool child, not every moment is a teaching moment. A teaching moment is a time when you can put aside whatever it is you are doing and create a successful learning opportunity for your child. That might mean you end the phone call you're on, you stop whatever you are doing and give the child your full attention, or you briefly consult your mental checklist of strategies before communicating with the child.

Moments of engagement

Teaching and engagement are equally important in the times you share with your toddler, but they're not the same thing. Engagement is helping your child explore her world in a way that is fun for her, exposing her to new things, helping create interest in social connections. Engagement is all about joining your child in play and creativity on her level and enticing her toward more. You get down on the floor and mimic the zoom-zoom sounds your child is making; you both laugh. You go to the beach and build a sand castle together. Stay engaged with your child as often and as much as time and her interest level will permit. If a teaching moment arises during engagement, and you can make it successful for her, go for it!

Pause and plan

Jim Ball, author of *Early Intervention and Autism: Real-life Questions, Real-life Answers*, tells us that one of the most frequent mistakes parents make in working with their children with autism or Asperger's is jumping into a teaching opportunity without a plan. Without a plan, a situation can quickly spiral out of control, despite the best efforts and intentions of parents. The interaction turns sour, both child and parent get agitated and you hear yourself saying things like, "stop that," "no," "why won't you listen?" The only thing that comes of such an interaction is the feeling, for both of you, that teaching and learning are no fun. That's both unnecessary and untrue.

What constitutes this all-important plan for success? Jim offers this advice:

1. Pause. Ask yourself if you can make this teaching moment successful for your child. If you can, proceed. If not, let it go. Practice engagement, not instruction.

2. Shift your mindset. Step out of the role of engaged parent and into the mindset of a teacher. Your goal is furthering your child's functional understanding or ability.

3. Decide what to teach. In any given opportunity, it's likely that several skills could be taught or practiced, or ideas shared. Focus on only one and make that your goal.

4. Choose your strategy. Will you use shaping, chaining, prompting, cueing, modeling, or a strategy of your own to guide your child to achieve success in the moment?

5. Be consistent in delivery. If you're working on learning to tie shoes or making a peanut butter and jelly sandwich, and you've got a practice sequence, stick to it. Deviations may seem creative to you, but can disarm the child with autism who lives by repetition and consistency.

6. Heap on the praise. Use exaggerated positive reactions to his attempts and his successes. Make trying and learning fun. Whether it's access to a high-interest toy or a high-five exclamation of praise, give him plenty of opportunities to associate his efforts with positive rewards.

Selecting a keyboard font

When teaching a child with autism to keyboard, a serif font (such as Times New Roman, the default font on most computers) is generally a better choice than a sans serif font (such as Arial). Serifs are the little tags or tails on the letters of certain type fonts. Sans serif fonts, with their clean straight lines may make it difficult for the child to distinguish between an upper-case I and a lower-case L. According to typographers, serif fonts are more readable, as they appear to lead the eye across the line of type.

Although Times New Roman is the default font on most computers, it is a condensed font and may be harder for your child to read than earlier standard fonts such as Courier or Bookman Old Style. If that's the case, you can adjust the character spacing options (size, letter spacing, kerning) in your font menu options, or reset your default font.

Tip

The most difficult-to-read text is that set in capital letters and is why it's used sparingly and only for short sentences or phrases. Our minds learn to visually process words not only by their individual letters, but also by the shape of the word itself. To read a word in capital letters, our minds need to slow down and process each letter, one at a time.

Also remember that in the world of e-mail and other electronic communication, text set in all upper-case letters is considered the equivalent of shouting, and may feel that way to your child.

What happened at school today?

It's the No.1 question parents ask their children. Too often, we receive either no response or get little in the way of useful, concrete information. A Communication Book that goes back and forth from home to school with the child each day bridges this gap. It tells Mom what went on at school that day and helps teachers and staff by letting them know what has happened at home since they last saw the student.

Keep the book simple and small enough to easily fit into a child's backpack. A half-page format works well. Create a form and photocopy pages, adding/replacing as needed. The parent fills out the Notes from Home page each morning; the teacher completes the Notes from School page just prior to the end of the school day. We've included a sample form here.

NOTES FROM HOME   Date:_____

LAST NIGHT I:
❏ slept well   ❏ didn't sleep well   Why?_____

TODAY I AM FEELING:
❏ happy   ❏ sad   ❏ sleepy   ❏ frustrated   ❏ just OK   ❏ well rested

Note from parent (special instructions, interesting experience):

_____

_____

Ask Julia about (something that happened after school that she wants to share):

_____

_____

Please call today. Phone number and best time to call: _____

NOTES FROM SCHOOL   Date:_____

TODAY AT SCHOOL I WAS:
❏ happy   ❏ sad   ❏ sleepy   ❏ frustrated   ❏ just OK

ACTIVITIES TODAY:
❏ library   ❏ PE   ❏ music   ❏ assembly   ❏ other: _____

Art: _____

Science/Social studies:_____

Math: _____

Books/reading: _____

This week we are studying/working on: _____

_____

Special Notes/Questions: _____

_____

Introducing new subjects to the child with limited interests ···························

He's interested only in trains and outer space; how do you engage his interest in curriculum areas outside his limited range, such as the human body, or the Oregon Trail? First, understand that his interests may be narrow because he clings to what is familiar and comfortable within the limitations of his sensory, social, and language deficits. Then use that understanding to help him expand his world.

- Expose the child to the new subject through his interest area. Start where self-motivation is high and he has already excelled.

  - Connect the two areas: What constellations would the pioneers have seen in the summer sky during the journey on the Oregon Trail? What engine types were used in the first transcontinental railroads? How did the building of the railroads affect the wagon trains?

  - Compare and contrast the two areas: In what ways are a journey on the Oregon Trail and a voyage to Mars different? In what ways are they alike? How are an engine and a human body alike or different— what are their parts, their fuel, how fast do they go, what sorts of illnesses do they get (boiler sludge versus chest colds)?

- Develop language objectives for the unit as well as content objectives. Don't assume a level of vocabulary he may not have: barrel, oxen, blacksmith and settler are not words commonly occurring in 21st century kid-conversation.

- Focus more on comprehension than on content. Understanding the impact of the steam engine on the country's development is more useful knowledge than is learning specific dates of various events that occurred along the way. Support with props, pictures, concrete objects.

- Show enthusiasm for the new subject! It's contagious. The child will sense if you are only mildly interested in the subject yourself.

The learning triangle

The Reggio Emelia approach to education contains many principles that are highly pertinent to teaching children with autism or Asperger's. The over-reaching philosophy is that the classroom environment is the child's third teacher, along with the parents and the teacher. (For more information visit *www.brainy-child.com/article/reggioemilia.html*.) The ideas that follow are suggestions for making the classroom environment friendlier for the child with autism and his peers too.

Bring the outdoors inside

Our occupational therapist does an exercise with staff and children in special education classrooms, asking them to describe a favorite memory from childhood, and draw a picture of it. She has found that almost all of the time, favorite memories occur outdoors. The class then builds on these memories to talk about the richness of the environment and its sensory experiences.

Teachers: Create a classroom environment everyone will love with these great ideas that bring the outdoors inside.

QUICK IDEA

Teachers can set up a Visitor's Board with pictures of people who will be visiting the class that day. This will help your student handle changes in the schedule, surprises, and fear of the unknown.

- Use natural, seasonal items for math manipulatives: acorns, pinecones, pebbles, seed pods. These items offer rich visual, tactile, and olfactory interest that plastic items cannot.

- Suspend a large branch from the ceiling as a natural canopy. Add found items, such as abandoned bird nests.

- Have nontoxic plants in the room. Large floor plants and hanging spider plants work well.

- Remove fluorescent lighting and replace with natural, full spectrum light tubes.

- Place a small indoor waterfall or fountain on a shelf or counter. Running water can be a soothing background sound.

- Frame children's artwork in simple natural-wood frames that the kids make themselves. Have kids break twigs into same sized lengths and glue them around the frames; use grapevine tendrils for a more artsy look.

- Hang pressed, laminated leaves mobile-style from the ceiling.

- Make leaf prints, flower prints or fish prints.

The kids in our occupational therapist's classroom named forts, spider webs and jungle huts as their favorite outdoor places. Their teacher constructed a jungle hut arrangement in a corner of the class. The kids could go there to hide (self-regulate) when they needed a break, and it opened an ongoing discussion about homes for both people and animals (the spider web being the spider's home). Interestingly, the class expressed no fear of spiders, just a pronounced fascination with webs.

Love your classroom

Setting up the environment for success is an idea that extends to educators as well as students. Teachers live in their classrooms as much as ten hours a day. Make it a place you like, with calming, soothing or invigorating options. (Do take into account, however, how your choices affect your student with autism.)

Reduce clutter

Rule #1: Reduce clutter. Rule #2: Reduce clutter. Rule #3: Reduce clutter. Teachers tend to be natural collectors. Because budgets are tight and replacement materials are hard to come by, it's understandable that you hang onto oodles of stuff because you might need it someday. Clutter and disorder is visually distracting for children with autism or Asperger's and makes it difficult for them to concentrate on assignments and move smoothly from activity to activity. Try to limit storage in the classroom to items used on a daily or weekly basis. Find another space for longer-term storage. If possible, keep non-essential classroom items behind doors, or in opaque bins with covers.

Minimize fluorescent lighting

Lighting has an enormous effect on children with autism, and fluorescent lighting has been shown repeatedly to be a major sensory irritant. It produces a low hum that can be very disturbing to hypersensitive hearing, and the pulsing nature of the light can distort visual perception, making objects and people in the room appear to be in constant motion. Modify the lighting in your classroom:

- Replace fluorescent tubes with newer, natural-light simulating tubes that reduce flickering.

- Fluorescent tubes that reflect toward the ceiling greatly reduce visual vibration.

- SkyPanels™ are decorative fluorescent light diffusers that replace existing diffusers in a quick, easy installation. Designed with images of skies and clouds, they create the feeling of looking up and out into the great outdoors, while reducing the harsh fluorescent glare. (*UsaSkyPanels.com*)

- Maximize use of daylight in the classroom, but watch for glare and sharp surface reflections. Blinds and shades can help direct light.

- Turn off some (half) of the overhead fluorescent lighting. It may still be enough for classroom work.

- Supplement reduced fluorescent lighting with incandescent desk and floor lamps. An incandescent desk lamp also reduces the flickering effect of overhead fluorescents.

The whole classroom

Children with autism can find such comfort in routine that they avoid open-ended activities and frequently get locked into using only certain physical areas of the classroom. If you notice this tendency in your student with autism or Asperger's, a twenty-minute study will enlighten you as to how to guide your student to experience the classroom space more fully. Have a parent or other adult assistant do the study. Make a quick drawing of the room and with a colored pen make an X to represent the child at his starting place. Then just draw a line indicating where he goes for the next twenty minutes. Do a second chart with a different colored pen for another child, or several children. You may see that the child with autism or Asperger's utilizes only a small portion of the room. Surprisingly, patterns might be similar to some of your other students'. Think about making changes to the room so children do multiple things at one location. Example: Place a block area next to a science area, with materials that children move or share between the two activities.

Move activity areas away from walls and the perimeter of the room. Doing so fosters exploration as kids walk through multiple areas during their day. Moving in something other than a straight path through the room stimulates their attention and awareness.

Make wall displays meaningful

Colorful posters, fancy character alphabets, and other generic classroom wall art may be cute but are often visually overwhelming for the child with autism or Asperger's. Limit wall displays to items that are truly meaningful to the students:

- Framed or matted artwork from each child (have a quote from each child under their art), changed on a monthly basis
- The week's vocabulary words
- Photos of the children doing various school activities
- A visual schedule of the day's routine
- Classroom rules

You'll know if your classroom displays are meaningful if a parent could walk into the room when no one's around and still get "echoes" of the children who bring that space to life during the day. It should feel personal and welcoming.

Paint walls a single, neutral color so as not to compete with or draw focus away from the information on the wall. Pastel blue and green tones are less energetic—helpful for students with visual processing difficulties. Show caution in using yellow—it's the color cited most frequently as negatively affecting individuals on the spectrum.

First-then rather than if-then

Use a first-then strategy to phrase instructions, rather than if-then. Example: "First we will put the paints away (or do our math problems), then we will go out to the playground." Rather than: "If you clean up your mess, then you can go to recess." First-then instructions suggest sequencing and appeal to the logical-thinking patterns of autism or Asperger's kids. If-then strategies imply a conditional attainment of a goal, often creating unnecessary per-formance-related stress.

Teach fluency/precision

Fluency strategies are designed to take an existing skill and increase accuracy and speed of skill performance. Example: a child may be able to tell someone his name ten seconds after being asked, but if he's already lost the attention of the person asking, the skill requires faster execution if it is to enhance his social success.

Teaching a skill to fluency brings the child to a point where he has mastered both accuracy plus speed. He has achieved 1) retention, 2) endurance—he can perform the skill at a particular level over time, and 3) application—he can com-bine elements of a behavior to create a more sophisticated behavior. Example: having a child repeat the colors of different circles in multiple rows, from left to right, and top to bottom, is early practice for reading. Pointing to the colors in a random way promotes joint attention.

Teaching a skill to fluency:

- Choose a specific target skill. "Teaching math" is too general; "teaching prime numbers" is specific.

- Define the goal. Your initial goal might be to have the child identify the prime numbers from 1-20.

- Teach the skill, allowing plenty of time and using strategies known to be effective for the particular child.

- Select a fluency target rate. Once the child has mastered the skill, select a rate of responding or performance standard that will help her achieve retention, endurance, and application. There are no norms for performance standards; they change over time and among learners. Fluency target rates are short for most skills (e.g., one response every second for fifteen to thirty seconds). Math skills can be targeted at rates ranging from eighty to one hundred digits per minute. Responses that take more sophisticated processing, like reading, can also be performed over one-minute intervals.

- Shorter response times can produce better results. In some cases, a ten-second fluency burst can be more effective than a thirty-second fluency burst, regardless of how many times the skill is practiced. Don't push the learner into fatigue with the number or length of fluency bursts.

Seeing time

Time can be a nebulous concept for children who think in pictures. Giving the child a timer is an effective, concrete way of letting him know the starting and stopping times for an activity or task. A kitchen timer, stopwatch, or wrist watch with an alarm works well. In the classroom or at home, try a device called the Time Timer®. The general principle is the same as a kitchen timer, but time is depicted with a red disc that diminishes as the time elapses, giving a visual indication. (Sound can be added.) By telling the child, "We will go to the library when the red is all gone," you interrupt the stream of anxious questioning and give him a measure of independence in monitoring and managing his own time. Wrist timers, watches, and computer timers are also available, using the same red disc principle. (*TimeTimer.com*)

Program accommodations and modifications ···················

Many children with autism or Asperger's can participate successfully in general education classrooms when reasonable accommodations and modifications to the curriculum or program are incorporated. What is the difference between the two? An accommodation is a physical or environmental change that allows a child to participate. It may include a different way of delivering information, taking tests, use of assistive technology, etc. A modification is a change in the program or curriculum standards or expectations of competency. Modifications entail a deliberate change to the achievement expectations and/or intellectual level of the coursework, for instance, a 4th grader doing 2nd grade math. Accommodations are good teaching practices for all students; they level the playing field and acknowledge learning differences. Modifications move the child onto a different playing field in a particular curricular area, but are often useful in keeping the child included with the rest of his peers.

> ### QUICK IDEA
>
> Sand timers are a great tool for helping children visualize and understand time concepts and develop patience. The timers come in a variety of sizes and times. Some children understand waiting "like a small timer" or "this is a big timer activity."

Examples of some common accommodations:

- Supplement verbal directions with visual cues and visual learning tools.
- Model the behavior or task to help her understand directions.
- Set up a quiet place for him to go to recoup when overstimulated.
- Adjust classroom work or homework.
  - Adjust math story-problems for relevancy. If Billy doesn't play soccer and doesn't eat chocolate, a story problem about selling candy bars for the soccer team has no relevance and may include an assumption of prior knowledge that doesn't exist. Change the problem to helping Mom choose oranges and bananas at the grocery store, or separating his marble collection into colors and sizes.
  - Highlight key vocabulary words on a test or homework assignment

- Draw boxes around individual math problems for students with visual processing challenges

- Make a keyboard (word processor, computer) available to facilitate written assignments if handwriting is cumbersome.

- Allow longer time for tests, or give tests in sections with a break or rest in between each section.

- Give tests in the resource room or another less distracting but familiar environment.

- Verbally coach a child through tests, repeating directions between each section.

- Offer the option of oral testing, with or without slight prompts ("What planet is closest to the sun? It starts with an M.")

Modifications involve changes to curriculum and/or testing and are usually agreed upon with parents and written into the child's IEP. Modifications include:

- Changing the grade level of the work the child performs within class to match it to his current cognitive needs. Example: The child works on addition and subtraction during math while the rest of the class practices solving equations. A child may be working at different grade levels for each subject. Such work may take place in a resource center setting rather than the general classroom.

- Using textbooks that offer information at an easier reading level and with fewer concepts introduced.

- Rewriting tests in a lower grade-level language that matches the child's cognitive level.

- Grading assignments on a different scale than used with the rest of the class.

Homework homeostasis

Monitor your child's homework; it should be challenging, not killing. Ask for accommodations. Many general education teachers do not understand the intrinsic language and processing challenges faced by many students with autism. Continually assigning reading or math materials, or longer-form projects that are above his ability to complete in a reasonable amount of time will defeat, not encourage him. Build these homework accommodations into his IEP.

But don't do his homework for him. Yes, he is frustrated, it's late, and you are both tired. But his teacher needs to be able to gauge his abilities, not yours. Do help him organize his schedule, his materials, and his workspace so he can make the most of the time he does spend on his homework. Then work with the teacher to adjust assignments as needed.

Appropriate IEP goals

Whether it's a single teacher or several, the person providing instruction to a child with autism or Asperger's is an invaluable team member in designing and implementing an education program that will reap benefits. All teachers should ascertain that goals and objectives are meaningful to the child, measurable and quantifiable, and aligned with the child's learning style.

> **QUICK IDEA**
>
> Parents can bring another person with them to the IEP meeting to take notes, be there for support, or to advocate on their behalf for educational services.

- *Inadequately stated goal:* Chris will sight-read third-grade spelling words.
- *Defined, quantifiable goal:* Chris will sight read third-grade spelling words from the Dolch Word List both 1) in isolation and 2) in context 225 out of 250 attempts, as reviewed quarterly at the end of each grade period.
- *Inadequately stated goal:* Jordan will initiate play with a peer.
- *Defined, quantifiable goal:* Jordan will initiate play with a peer with adult verbal prompting three out of four times on a daily basis, as recorded by staff observation with quarterly review and random probes.

IEP jargon

Parents and caregivers, if you don't understand any part of the discussion at an IEP meeting, speak up and ask for an explanation. School personnel often use acronyms, terminology, refer to test scores or assessment results in jargon that can be confusing at first, or may be new even to a seasoned parent. Ask questions whenever you're not 100% sure of information being discussed, and keep asking until you understand the explanation given.

Paraeducator-pro

Good paraeducators are worth their weight in gold. But not all of them arrive to the classroom fully educated in autism spectrum disorders or teaching skills. All parties benefit when the school administration takes steps to assure that the paraeducators they hire have the skills required to meet the child's needs.

- Start with a survey of needs that includes an assessment of the paraeducator's skills in relation to the duties of the position and the role he or she will take in the classroom. Is the paraeducator's knowledge of autism or Asperger's sufficient to work with the student(s)? Is further education required in any areas?

- Conduct an initiation and orientation to the school. To whom does the paraeducator report—the teacher, the Autism Specialist, the school administrator?

- Discuss the school's policies, procedures, lines of authority and chain of command, dress codes, emergency procedures, etc.

- Review the class setting.

- Define the paraeducator's tasks. Is he a one-to-one aide for a single student, or a teacher's assistant, too? Is clerical work expected? How will he divide his time among responsibilities?

- Review a typical day's routine with both the paraeducator and the class teacher.

- Review the child's IEP with the paraeducator. Does he or she understand the goals and objectives from a functional perspective?

- Review the positive behavior support plan in place for the child and/or the school's guidelines for handling behavior problems and crises.

- Review how best to get the child's attention.

- Review the child's reinforcer list.

- Familiarize the paraeducator with the child's primary communication system, especially with a nonverbal child (e.g., sign language, etc.).

- Discuss the child's social skills challenges so the paraeducator knows what to expect during interactions.

- Share the child's sensory sensitivities with the paraeducator and watch for new behavior issues that suddenly arise; they may have a basis in sensory issues (e.g., perfumes, grooming products, pet hair, etc.).

Help for the substitute teacher

A Student Profile for each child with autism or Asperger's in your class gives a substitute teacher a helpful snapshot understanding of the students. You might include:

- A photo of the student
- Strengths and challenges
- Dominant learning style
- Special learning needs or assistive equipment
- Brief summary of major IEP goals currently being worked on
- Key contact information

Keep all the Student Profiles in a binder, along with the daily class schedule, a map of the school, the discipline policy, emergency response plan and any other pertinent or helpful information. Check your school's policies on confidentiality of student information before implementing this.

Teachers' rights in special education ·······························

Teachers are the mainstay of education. As more and more students with disabilities are fully or partially included in regular classrooms, it behooves regular education teachers to not only know about the educational rights of students who need supplemental services, but to also familiarize themselves with their own rights in providing educational instruction.

Changes in special education law in the past decade hold not only administration staff, but also teachers, personally liable for lack of a good-faith effort in providing the needed educational services. It is imperative that general education teachers not only know their rights, but can exercise them freely for the benefit of every child they teach.

- Right of teachers to participate in a self-evaluation of the school district. The self-evaluation examines the policies, practices, and procedures relating to students with disabilities, and provides the opportunity for teachers to raise questions and receive answers that address their concerns.

- Right to seek assistance for a student in a classroom who is not receiving benefit. The program for a child with autism or Asperger's just isn't working. Teachers have a right—and a responsibility—to make a referral or request an evaluation where assistance is needed.

- Right to act as a child advocate. The Americans with Disabilities Act (ADA) recognizes teachers as advocates, and outlaws retaliation, intimidation, or reprisals for teachers who advocate for children.

- Right to have the child fully evaluated. The child has a right to evaluation in every area that might adversely affect educational performance. This is not limited to academics, but includes speech-language, sensory issues, social skills development, leisure and recreation, play skills, daily living skills, and numerous other areas.

- Right to receive any training needed under the Comprehensive System for Personnel Development. If the key to serving the student appropriately is teacher training, the teacher has the right to request and receive that training.

- Right to participate in the IEP process that develops the plan for a student in their class. Federal law includes "the child's teacher" as a participant in the IEP meeting. All questions a classroom teacher might have regarding curriculum modifications, methods of teaching, positive behavior supports and systems, delivery of services, etc., must be asked and answered before the child comes into the classroom.

- Right to receive the related services outlined on the IEP. If services agreed upon and written into the child's IEP are not provided, it violates the teacher's, student's, and parents' rights. As a teacher you are not only responsible, but accountable, for the delivery of services that will confer benefit to the child.

> **QUICK IDEA**
>
> If you disagree with a portion of your child's IEP, parents can sign the IEP at the meeting and attach an addendum that outlines the parts to which they do not agree.

- Right to be recognized as an advocate for all children in the classroom. A classroom teacher has a duty to all the children in the classroom—those with disabilities and those without. The law is adamant about placing children in the least restrictive environment possible, recognizing that the interests of typically developing children, and the ability of the teacher to teach the classroom, need to be balanced with the right of a child with special needs to be in that general education classroom.

- Right to participate in assessing the effectiveness of the program. Once the IEP is implemented, the teacher must have a role in assessing whether the IEP is working, and if it is not, reconvening the IEP team to make appropriate modifications.

- Right to be treated as a professional. Teachers are not just subordinate employees expected to carry out orders without questions. They are educated professionals with, in most cases, a sincere desire for all students to learn and excel.

It is clear from legislative history that Congress viewed the teacher as an important participant in the delivery of special education services—just as important as the parent or the school administrator. When regular education teachers learn and live by the rights afforded them, all the children they teach can learn and grow to their full potential.

Appropriately trained staff

Parents have the right under the No Child Left Behind Act to request a written response to questions about the credentials, qualifications, and training of personnel who are going to be in contact with their children. If you feel a staff member doesn't understand your child's autism or Asperger's and could benefit from more formal training, or the educational program set up for your child is not incurring benefit, ask about the autism-specific staff training. It may be time for a refresher course, an in-service workshop, or the help of an outside autism specialist.

Peer power

Young children are naturally inquisitive and are usually willing to help a classmate navigate her day if they have some basic knowledge about the child's learning style and challenges, suggestions for ways to help. We asked several students who had friends with autism or Asperger's for their advice; here are some of their responses.

- Don't be afraid of them. Sometimes they act differently but they're still kids like the rest of us.

- Ask them to do things with you or a group. They know a lot of things and are interesting.

- If it looks like they don't know how to do something, show them what to do rather than telling them. It helps when they can imitate your actions.

- Offer to help when they look like they need it, but don't just do things for them. They have to learn just like the rest of us.

- Don't tease kids with autism. If you see someone else teasing them, tell them to stop.

- Make sure you get their attention when you want to tell them something. Otherwise, they might miss what you say.

- Treat them the same way you treat your other friends. They can be cool too.

- Sometimes they don't respond right away—they need more time to think about their answers. Be patient and don't rush them.

- Learn more about their autism, from their parents, or a teacher, or from the internet. Ask about ways you can help.

- If you see them acting weird, remember they can't help it. Sometimes their bodies act in funny ways because they're stressed out or anxious.

- Say something to them when they do good things. Give them a high-five, or just say "great job." They like compliments too.

- They have trouble with all the social stuff, so give them hints, or talk them through situations if you think it might help.

- Many kids with autism have sensory problems. They get stressed out in loud, noisy places where there are lots of people or things going on. If you see your friend getting upset or nervous or hyper, suggest you both take a break for a few minutes and go someplace quieter.

Art therapy

Art can be a wonderful, expressive medium for children with autism or Asperger's, especially children with limited or no verbal communication abilities. The various mediums promote tactile development, fine motor control, and hand-eye coordination. Producing a visual, tangible product fosters self-esteem.

Teachers and parents can motivate children with autism or Asperger's to explore their artistic side with these useful tips from an art therapist/ paraeducator:

- Joint drawings can introduce detail a child might not otherwise think of. The adult can start the drawing—say, the house—then the child and adult take turns adding details like windows, door, grass, flowers, a weathervane, chimney, birds, the mailbox, clouds, a bike in the driveway. Let it go on as long as the child maintains interest. Then come back to it another day and add yet more details. Pair verbal language with each detail as it's drawn; practice spelling, pronouns, or imagination. The educational options are endless.

- Model drawing the object the child is trying to produce. Our art therapist says, "When a fabric mural was being created with an artist-in-residence, my student was to choose an animal to depict. It helped to have a picture of the real animal he chose but still his drawing was not a recognizable ant. Then I drew the ant as he watched. I left him alone and he drew an ant that looked much like mine—a believable ant."

- Step-by-step drawing is also helpful. This can be a whole class activity with the teacher leading.

- Art can segue into writing. Daily journal writing was painstaking for one little second-grade boy. Each day he would draw a train car with the single sentence, "My train is good." When pressed to write a second sentence, he would add something generic like "It is cool." His paraeducator noticed that while the writing was static, the drawings were taking on ever more detail: cars became either boxcars or flat cars with added features on the wheels, more cars were added to the train, people began appearing in them. The drawings continued to progress, even as the writing stayed stagnant—until the following year, when the floodgates opened and the child began writing a screenplay!

- Art can open the door to communication for children who are nonverbal or who cannot express their feelings otherwise. In one heartbreaking example, a paraeducator worked on a clay project for weeks with a nonverbal child. The school suspected child abuse, suspected the father, but couldn't prove anything. Week after week, the child worked soundlessly away on a sculpture of a dark, gaunt figure. One day, the silence broke. He noticed another child watching him and said, "My mom is mean to me."

- Art is a great a visual medium for story creation. Children can create characters and several drawings depicting their characters in various situations. We can teach concepts like sequencing and predicting using these visual representations.

Beginning art for the photo-oriented child

For the child whose level of representation is at the photograph stage, illustrations and abstract art will not yet make sense. Introduce her to drawing by placing a clear laminate piece, taped in place, over a photograph and having her trace it, using a felt pen that wipes or washes off easily (like those intended for overhead projectors). This helps her learn about edges, shapes and concrete objects, and she can be successful with the finished tracing.

Student teacher for a day

If your child has a favorite book he knows inside out, ask the teacher if he can teach it to the rest of the class or to a smaller reading group. He can lead the group in reading it, then ask questions he has written down ahead of time (with the help of teacher, therapist, or parent) about the main characters, setting, and sequence of events. Adapt questions as necessary for a nonfiction book.

Variation: Ask if he can be a guest speaker, visiting his former kindergarten classroom to read his favorite book to the younger kids.

Color walk

Tie or tape a piece of solid-colored paper or tape around your child's wrist, then go for a walk around the house, the neighborhood, or the mall, looking for things that are that color. When she finds one, reinforce with language: You found a red book. You found a red jacket. You found a red wheelbarrow.

Phonics hike

When the lesson plan involves learning new sounds for each letter of the alphabet, take a tour of the neighborhood or school grounds to find objects that start with that sound. Record the words in a journal or on a clipboard for later use: hallway, heat duct, Stony Hill School, history book, hoagie bun, hand dryer, door handle, door hinge, wall hanging, happy face sticker, hat, health room.

Variation: If you do the hike indoors one day, do it outdoors the next time. Children spend so much time indoors; take every opportunity to get them moving in the fresh air.

Language yes/no game

This game teaches full-sentence responses, a requirement in many written school assignments. Give your child or student ten small items he likes— nickels, stickers, or marbles. He must answer all your questions that day without saying yes or no. Each time he doesn't, he gives you back one of the items. If you ask, "Did you turn in your spelling homework?" he cannot say "yes" or "no." He must say, "I put it in your homework box," or "It is still in my backpack." Initially, it might help to hold up the favorite item as a visual cue to remind him that a yes/no response will cause him to forfeit one item. Use your judgment and cut him some slack while he adjusts to the game, and make the game reciprocal. If you answer one of his questions with yes or no, he gets to take back one of his confiscated items.

Name that classmate

Your child's social interactions with his classmates may be complicated by the fact that he can't remember all their names. Ask the school for a class photo or photos of all the children, along with their names.

- Post the photo(s) on your refrigerator or bulletin board. Practice each child's name.
- After she has learned all her classmates' names, take it a step further. Talk about who has short blonde hair and who has long black hair. Oh look, he's wearing glasses; she has such a pretty smile.
- Then go another step further and talk about something the classmate is interested in: Carson loves to draw comics, Shawna plays the piano.

- Compare and contrast the children. Do any of them have the same name? How many of their names start with the letter K?

Photo reminders

Provide a photo for any school or home situation where a gentle reminder might help. At school: sitting properly in circle time, walking in line, putting lunch trash in the bin, where to hang up his coat, are some school applications. At home: setting the table, hanging up his towel, brushing his teeth, and putting clothes in the laundry hamper. This approach facilitates positive behavior before the fact rather than criticizing improper behavior after the fact.

Pair a preferred item or task with something less-than-desirable

If she hates tooth brushing, read her favorite story while she brushes, or play some favorite music. Let him chew gum while he picks up his toys or writes out his spelling words.

Concept formation

The thinking pattern of most individuals with autism or Asperger's is specific to general, opposite that of neuro-typical thinking, which tends to be general to specific. This makes concept formation a difficult skill to acquire, but one that can be taught in hundreds of ways, starting while a child is young. Promote concept formation by making a game of putting objects into new categories. Put a number of objects on a table and start with simple sorting concepts: by color, by shape, by material, or the initial letter of the object's name. As abilities develop, encourage the child to invent new categories. This step will be much more difficult and require assistance on your part. Example: What can you do with a cup? You can drink from it, it can become a pencil holder, a vase for flowers, you can use it to measure out another substance, or more abstractly, as a paperweight, a plant holder, or a door prop.

Keep it fun. Your child needs a great deal of repetition before he learns to think flexibly and visualize concept categories.

A-hunting we will go

A major difference between the autism way of thinking and the neurotypical way of thinking is the manner in which brains categorize information. The neurotypical brain automatically sorts incoming information into categories and sub-categories, cross-referencing as it goes. For many children with autism, it is quite the opposite: their brains do not readily sort information, and they are not able to generalize specific information until taught do so.

Scavenger hunts are a fun, active way to promote categorizing and generalizing skills. At school, home, or in the community, there are infinite ways to scavenge, all of them valuable to your child or student on many levels. Hunt indoors, outdoors, in magazines or books. Hunt solo, in pairs, in groups. Animal, vegetable, mineral. Colors, shapes, sounds. Check items off a list, photograph items, cut out images from magazines, or collect actual items. Here's a list to get you started.

- Phonics: Look for items with certain letters or letter sounds
- Colors: Look for items in differing shades of the same color
- Geometry: Look for shapes and angles
- Rhyming words: Door, floor, apple core, Mrs. Moore, student store, etc.
- Sounds: Listen for animal or nature sounds, machinery sounds
- Smells: Need we explain?
- Occupations: Look for jobs people are doing
- Transportation: Look for ways people and animals get around
- Alphabet: Look for objects beginning with each letter, A – Z
- Safety: In the home or outdoors, is it dangerous?
- Materials: Look for items made of plastic, wood, metal, fabric
- Ongoing: A hunt needn't be limited to the usual thirty minutes. Kids can start a scrapbook, a collage, or a treasure box of items as part of an ongo-

ing hunt that spans a period of days, weeks, or months. This is particularly fun for seasonal items, such as autumn leaves, cones, nuts, etc.

Safety first: whether your hunt is indoors or out, set clear boundaries for the area in which children are allowed to search. Adult supervision should be ongoing at all times.

And keep it fun. If the purpose of the hunt is educational or developmental, forget any competitive aspect, such as dividing kids into teams and naming a winner based on who finds the most items. Emphasize cooperation and discovery.

What's your name?

Let your child's teachers know exactly which names your child will or will not answer to. If you have always called her Candace, she may not answer to Candy; likewise, Benjamin may not realize his teacher is talking to him when she calls on Ben. And beware asking a concrete-thinking child, "what would you like to be called?" We know a boy named Richard who answered that question with "Mike." The teacher was confused and called the mother. Mom asked Richard, whose reply was that he liked the name Mike better and that's "what he would like to be called." He was merely answering the teacher's question.

Mirror, mirror

Try having a child use dry-erase markers on a mirror to practice writing her name, address or phone number, spelling words, tic-tac-toe, or artwork. It may add just enough interest to keep her going beyond her usual attention span. The markers clean up with glass cleaner.

Teach success

One of the simplest ways to build self-esteem in children is to incorporate an already mastered level of skill into a novel or difficult task. Example: alternate new vocabulary words with mastered vocabulary words in a flash card drill. The idea can be incorporated into almost any teaching situation.

Is it okay to visit?

In our best-intentioned efforts to learn as much as we can about our child's day at school, many a parent will visit the school class or cafeteria unannounced to the child. Before you do, discuss your plan with the child, and ask his permission to be at school or join him for lunch. Some children with autism view a parent's lunchtime visit as an unacceptable breach of routine, and Mom's participation during class events as not-so-welcome interference. Respect your child's wishes. An interruption that violates his need for routine can color the remainder of the day in a unhappy way.

Designed with Asperger's in mind

While some children with Asperger's Syndrome can learn and thrive in a general education classroom, others need a more controlled environment and more structured supports. A student's IQ level may be high and language may be functional, but the social and sensory challenges of Asperger's can interfere to the point that a smaller, more contained setting might be more appropriate. The school's special education class may not offer a student with Asperger's the academic challenge he needs, nor the opportunities to learn from peers who exhibit socially appropriate behaviors. Some schools are responding with classrooms designed specifically for the Asperger's student. Characteristics of the class might include:

- A ratio of about eight students to one teacher
- Classroom located in the neighborhood school in a quiet part of the building
- Same academic curriculum as general education students
- Sensory-sensitive environment
- Social skills training included as part of the curriculum: etiquette, friendship skills, body language, etc. Social activities and social thinking exercises included as homework
- Strong routine built into the daily schedule that includes private time for students

- Alternative physical education options if needed: miniature golf, dance, outdoor walks, frisbee, bowling, use of nearby fitness club
- Curriculum add-ons that include things like extra practice on note-taking, task analysis, drawing conclusions, noticing implications, character motives, etc.

When, when, when?

If your student is asking repeatedly when the next activity will occur, place a card with a representation of a clock on her desk. The clock should look like the one in the classroom, with hands pointing to the appropriate time for the next activity. Go one step further and write "9:20 PE Gym" under the clock face; you will further reinforce time-telling skills.

Practice makes perfect

Instill in your child an understanding of the necessity of practice in learning any new skill, whether academic, social, athletic or self-care, and how this applies to everyone, even though some people make it look easy. Athletes and musicians look great on the court, the field or the stage, but behind their performances are untold hours of mind-numbing repetition. Point out or make a list detailing the many skills he has already mastered in his life through practice: walking, running, talking, feeding himself (as applies: dressing self, toileting, reading, riding a bike/trike, throwing a ball, swimming, singing, etc.).

Help your child visualize all he has already learned. The family photo album and videos are natural documents of his progress. By keeping a box of his schoolwork from year to year, he can look back and see how much he's achieved. Putting a selection of the best of these items in a scrapbook each year makes for handy reference, nostalgia, and encouragement.

The right write stuff

One child may like the control and pressure needed to use colored pencils. Another child may prefer the ease of felt pens—instant color without needing to use pressure. Crayons may be more difficult; it is harder to control the edges, and pressure is needed to get good color. Paint is even harder to control, and has the additional complication of the messy factor. Both art and writing projects have to be achievable and make sense. Otherwise, the task may get done but with an obvious disconnection—ergo, no benefit.

Easy sports and PE adaptations

While team sports may present a difficult menu of challenges for some autism or Asperger's kids, others naturally gravitate toward one type of team sport or another. Maybe it starts as an interest within the sport; baseball players and stats are more interesting at first than actually playing the game. But somewhere along the way your son or daughter decides being out on the field is something he or she really wants to do.

Adapted physical education specialists are teachers trained in making modifications to equipment and curriculum so that children with supplemental needs can participate in general education PE classes with their peers. PE can be a confusing mix of motor skills, rules, and the social complexity that goes along with the concept of teamwork and competition, offense and defense. However, being able to participate with peers goes a long way toward erasing yet another distinction that may separate the child with autism from his contemporaries.

Most of these adaptations are things you can also do at home to help your child become more skilled at common sports activities.

1. Vary the size of the equipment: a larger or smaller ball, a heavier or lighter bat, a larger racket head with a shorter handle, a golf club with a larger head.

2. Allow two hands for typically one-handed actions: dribbling the basketball, rolling the bowling ball, handling the tennis or racquetball racket.

3. Decrease distances: between bases, from the tee to the hole, from the mound to the plate. Stand closer to the net to serve; lower or eliminate

the net. Stand several steps over the foul line at the alley. Adjust as skills increase.

4. Slow the pace of the activity down. Lengthen or shorten times as needed.

5. Provide oral or visual prompts or cues. Do not expect your child to remember rules if he is focusing on learning a motor skill. Visual aids are always a plus!

6. Speaking of rules, take care to explain them to the child in a manner he understands, even those that at first glance might seem obvious or simple. One child we encountered loved baseball. Coach assigned him to right field. When the ball came toward the boy, he didn't understand that he might need to run one way or another, forward or backwards, to catch it. He just stood there waiting for it to come exactly to his spot. Mom and Dad worked with him, and at the next game he was back in right field. The next hit headed midway between center and right field—a situation they had neglected to go over. Who runs for it? Team sports are highly complex. Even the most obvious rules, like running to the next base, usually involve many options.

7. Support from a peer partner or buddy may be more readily accepted than instruction from an adult. Choose a buddy whose skills are good but not so elevated as to make your child feel inadequate or discouraged.

8. Allow frequent rests if needed.

9. Use a tee for softball, baseball, tennis, golf.

10. Allow extra bounces in volleyball, tennis, racquetball, basketball.

11. Allow drop serves in racket sports.

12. Do the activity in an area with minimal external distractions.

13. Halt the activity if you sense your child's frustration building. Take a break or have the child engage in a calming activity and then try again, or end the session and move onto something else.

14. Keep instructions short and clear. Do not use sports lingo unless you are sure the child understands the terminology.

15. Allow your child to choose an at-home activity: "I'd love to play with you after dinner. Shall we jump rope or toss the frisbee?"

16. Have the school's PE teacher and/or adapted PE teacher send you a weekly note or email regarding what the week's activities will be or have been. Reinforce at home, not just with the activity itself, but also in talking about it, asking questions about it, reading or looking at books about it.

A tricycle by any other name

Three-year-old Michael's mom wanted him to learn to ride a tricycle, but he was afraid to take his feet off the ground ("gravitational insecurity"). His occupational therapist confirmed he was very coordinated and there was no physical reason he couldn't do it. His teachers noticed Michael always chose books about machines: tractors, cement mixers, combines, loaders. They began referring to the tricycle as a "machine," and having him acclimate to it gradually. First, he would just touch it. Then, sit on it briefly. Within a short time, he was pedaling away. Sometimes just changing the name of the item is an inroad to interest and skill development.

Acclimating to group work

If your student seems to work well one-on-one with a peer, give him as many opportunities as possible to do so. When he seems comfortable and confident, add a third person. Gradually increase the number in the group.

A quick reference guide to successful inclusion

With appropriate supports and services, many children can be fully or partially included in general education classes. Successful inclusion requires attention to the environment, curriculum, teaching methodology, and daily modes of interaction.

The following quick reference guide for teachers outlines some of the salient points in making inclusion work for everyone in the class: the child, his peers, and the teaching staff. Copy it, clip it, and post it on your desk as a helpful visual reminder.

Teaching methodology

- Use visual tools:
    - A daily/weekly visual schedule and a monthly visual calendar
    - Visual cues during instruction
    - Posted classroom behavior rules
    - Visual representation of time
- Discuss changes in the schedule ahead of time with the student; be specific.
- Teach flexibility and change as part of the normal routine.
- Define a clear beginning and end to each activity; make the activity reasonable for the time limit and the child's functioning.
- Give student opportunity for repetition, repetition, repetition, in both academic and social skills.
- Emphasize positive behaviors. Show the child what to do, as opposed to telling him what not to do.
- Stay calm when behaviors escalate.
- Assess reinforcers at least once per month.
- Teach classmates about autism or Asperger's, and offer concrete suggestions for how they can help their classmate.

Language and communication

- Check for comprehension often. Beware of mere echolalic recitation.
- Supplement verbal instructions with written instructions and/or pictures.
- Keep instructions simple and straightforward; avoid idioms, metaphors, figurative speech.
- Phrase requests in the positive.

Social skills

- Education is more than just academics; teach social thinking and social skills.

- Model and role-play social situations incorporating appropriate behaviors.

- Create opportunities to practice social skills for upcoming social events.

- Compile a social skills notebook with stories of correct and incorrect social behaviors.

- Encourage perspective taking: Discuss how ideas, attitudes and opinions differ among people, and the social consequences of behavior.

Accommodations

- Be sensory sensitive: sounds/smells/visuals/touch/motor.

- Offer a quiet place to work on assignments.

- Incorporate test accommodations: a silent room, extra time, alternative formats.

- Allow keyboard access rather than requiring handwriting.

- Provide a safe place the child can retreat to when needed.

Curbing perseveration

Some children will perseverate on objects or ideas, or engage in other behaviors that can hinder academic progress during the school day. Trying to extinguish this type of behavior without identifying and addressing its source is not the answer, but placing a time limit on such behaviors can help.

As soon as the child begins to exhibit an inappropriate, perseverative behavior, set the timer for a predetermined amount of time. Teach the child that as soon as the timer rings, she must rejoin the rest of the class in the current activity. Then reduce the time limit gradually over a period of weeks.

Child on the run

If your student is a "runner" (movement seeker/perpetual motion machine), he will dehydrate more quickly than his more sedate classmates will. Allow trips to the drinking fountain or let him keep a water bottle on his desk. The water bottle may also serve as an oral-motor calming device.

Take it apart

Many of our kiddos love to take things apart, often to our dismay. We weren't done with that DVD player, toaster or radio! Taking things apart is a wonderful learning opportunity as well as a chance to practice fine motor skills. So take this worrisome proclivity and turn it into something positive. Incorporate take-apart activities as an incentive, reinforcer, or choice time activity. Keep a stash of broken or used up items from which they can choose. (Obviously, no dangerous components or chemicals.) Garage and rummage sales are ideal locations to find items. Teachers, ask parents to donate stuff.

Down with "up"

Actively empathize with your child or student; it goes a long way in helping him cope with difficulties and the feelings of isolation that frequently accompany his work. Tell him about your own struggles in school and life and describe how you overcame them. Acknowledge that it's hard, whether "it" is math, making friends, learning to hit a ball—but that you believe he can do it. Don't offer him meaningless platitudes, which include just about any phrase ending in "up:" cheer up, buck up, suck it up, chin up.

Down with "down"

Make your home and your classroom No Put-down Zones, and that includes your student putting himself down. Don't ignore "I'm stupid," or "I'm never gonna get this." They are flags for deeper feelings of inadequacy that your student with autism may not be able to express. He is different, and children in general don't like to feel different. His difficulties make him feel angry, frustrated, and isolated.

- Talk about how everyone has strengths and weaknesses, using yourself as an example.

- Point out his strengths and interests—how you admire them and how they are an important part of the family and his classroom community. Nurturing of these strengths will bolster him when difficulty strikes in other areas of his life.

- Identify the source of any outside put-downs and put an immediate stop to them. Frequently it is a top-down phenomenon, with older students and/or older siblings initiating the insults. Look at your own language too. Even nicknames that you might use affectionately, (goofball, space ranger) may have negative connotations to your concrete-thinking child with autism. Using these nicknames suggests it is appropriate for other children to mimic, as they so expertly do.

- Money talks. Some families have successfully used a cussing cup (see **Profanity** in Chapter 2) to curb profanity, and the same principle can work for put-downs, too.

  - Set a fine amount that children must contribute to the cup when caught in a put-down. If they do not have money of their own, they can pay the fines in time given up for privileges or with extra chores.

  - You can even increase the fines for second, third, and fourth offenses within a day, week, or month.

  - Or use a reverse fine: each child gets ten nickels, dimes, quarters, or privilege tokens at the beginning of each week or month. They forfeit one for each put-down, but they get to keep anything remaining at the end of the period.

WHAT IS A PUT-DOWN?

When establishing a No Put-down Zone in your home or school, define clearly to both children and adults what constitutes a put-down. A put-down is any negative remark, accusation, or name-calling that insults a person's appearance, abilities, family, or interests.

Environmental learning preferences

You can find plenty of advice on strategies to help your spectrum child handle homework. But often we neglect to take into account the individual environmental learning preferences that can make or break a child's study session. Margaret prefers absolute quiet, while Mark does best with some music playing in the background. Josh likes to sprawl out on his bed while reading an assignment, but Julia focuses better while seated at her desk.

Parents and teachers can help the spectrum child learn best by noticing the environmental factors that help or hinder learning. Don't assume your child's style matches your own, or that of classmates or siblings. Discuss with him factors such as sound, light, temperature, seating, and watch what conditions your child or student naturally gravitates to while doing homework or class work. Then plan the environment accordingly.

Bridge the gap between schoolwork and "real life"

Emphasize relevance of the school curricula at every opportunity. Slaving over a page of math problems may be torture for him, but when he understands that telling time and exchanging money are skills needed to check the movie schedule, buy a ticket, and get change back from the popcorn, you will see his interest skyrocket.

Use individual interests to promote math skills

Make a custom set of math manipulatives utilizing the child's personal interests. This could be little barrettes, plastic ponies or dinosaurs, Matchbox cars, baseball cards, shells, rocks, or doll shoes. If the items don't all match, so much the better—they can be sorted, compared, patterned, and made into story-problems.

Teach math kinesthetically

Many children on the autism spectrum stumble over the language of math (borrowing, carrying, into, minus, "times," one-half, two-tenths, etc.), let alone the abstraction of numbers and symbols on a page. A three-dimensional, hands-on approach may be much more successful. To teach math kinesthetically:

- Use manipulatives wherever possible. Go one better, have the child make his own manipulatives in a manner that interests him.

- Music, especially very rhythmic music, can encourage patterned thinking. Marching, jumping rope, or playing drums or rhythm sticks is a good way to practice arithmetic tables, or counting by twos, fives, tens, etc.

- Couch problems in active terms. Instead of presenting $10 \div 2$ on a piece of paper, have the child divide ten pretzels into two piles, or cut a banana or piece of play clay into ten pieces and separate them into equal piles.

More math tricks

- Your student with autism is usually visually oriented. Color-coding his math problems may help differentiate operations for him: orange pen for addition, green for subtraction, purple for multiplication, red for division.

- Have your child or class engage in a day- or week-long math scavenger hunt. Math is all around us, and the way to get good at math is not to listen to someone talk about it, but to do it, practice it, and play with it every chance we get. Help your child or students keep a running list of all the ways we use math in our lives: cooking, telling time, filling the gas tank, checking the weather, paying for groceries, playing cards, keeping score, measuring, weighing.

Teach spelling kinesthetically

Your student with autism learns more readily by seeing and touching than by listening.

- Teach letters and words using tiles, flashcards, word strips, letter magnets.

- Some children will learn letters more readily by tracing them with their fingers.

- Kinesthetic learners need to move. They actually concentrate better during movement. Allow them to stand, lie down, or move around the room while contemplating letter or number manipulatives.

- Roll modeling clay into ropes or shape into thin slabs to form letters.

- Use plastic alphabet cookie cutters to form letters in play-dough.

- Bake 6-8" alphabet pretzels; fun, instructional and yummy!

- Cut giant letters out of cardboard appliance boxes; let kids decorate them in whimsical ways.

- Thread beads onto a long string and use it to shape letters; make a bead alphabet.

- Glue pasta pieces, popped popcorn, cereal, or old buttons in a letter shape on a piece of paper.

- Create a Nature Alphabet: Create letters by gluing items found during your nature walk: acorns, leaves, twigs, blades of grass, flower petals, etc.

> ## QUICK IDEA
>
> If she constantly falls behind in homework because of forgetting to bring home her textbook, ask that an extra one be issued to keep at home. If the school cannot issue one, look for a used copy online.

My report card for teacher

Former New York mayor Ed Koch was famous for his quip, "How'm I doing?" As parents and teachers, we ask ourselves this question frequently—but rhetorically, and it may not ever occur to us to ask our children and students. If we did, what we might learn!

Veda Nomura, MS, OTR/L shared with us the idea for a report card that can help older elementary and middle school students tell their teachers how they feel about their work. The suggestions that follow can, and should, be modified according to the ToM, perspective-taking, and the vocabulary/language abilities of your child. For younger children whose skills are just developing, you can fill out the report card together, reading the possible responses to the child, and further exploring his answers and probing for more detail.

Note: as with all materials for children with autism, the text will be more effective if presented with visual backup. Boardmaker, a family of software programs based on picture communication symbols, is helpful in creating support materials. Gear the type of visual you use to your child's or student's level of representation. Some students relate well to line drawings like those found in Boardmaker programs, while others require photographs or more detailed artwork illustrations. (For example, some concrete-thinking children won't like Boardmaker symbols that feature a unisex child with a bald, distinctly egg-shaped head. Your child probably does not have any classmates who look like this!)

MY REPORT CARD FOR TEACHER

MY _____ WORK/ASSIGNMENT

I think I did:
❏ a great job   ❏ good enough   ❏ bad   ❏ I couldn't finish the assignment

I think this work/assignment was:
❏ boring
❏ okay
❏ fun
❏ confusing
    ❏ I didn't understand the instructions
    ❏ I understood the instructions but didn't know how to do the work

❏ cool
❏ too hard
❏ too long
❏ too easy

It would be better if:
❏ an adult helped me
❏ a peer helped me
❏ I had more time
❏ I could work by myself
❏ I could work in a different place
❏ I could do the assignment with a group

❏ I could show you what I know in another way. I could:
    ❏ tell you about it
        ❏ in private
        ❏ in a speech to the class
    ❏ write about it
    ❏ draw, paint, or show you with manipulatives
    ❏ type my thoughts about it
        ❏ on the computer, to be printed
        ❏ in an email
    ❏ show you on the computer another way
    ❏ act it out

Something else I want to tell you about is: _____

_____

Summer's over: Back-to-school strategies

Help prepare your son or daughter for the back-to-school transition with these ideas designed to ease them into the school routine again.

- A few weeks before school starts, begin shifting bedtime to the school year routine to get them used to waking up at a set time again.

- Simulate homework routines before the start of school. Have your child do quiet activities at a specific time and place every day. Guard against having your child perform preferred activities at this time; it's designed to set the stage for homework.

- Review your child's preferred reinforcers and be creative about finding new ones if needed.

- School clothes: If your child has to wear a uniform to school, wash it several times to break it in. Have your child wear it at least several hours prior to the first day of school to get used to it, and determine if any sensory issues arise. The same sensory issues can apply to new clothes in general.

- To help your child adjust to new people or new surroundings when transitioning to middle school, purchase a school yearbook. Then go over peoples' names and faces with the child before summer ends.

- Record your child walking through the day's schedule at school before school starts; let him review it often at home.

- Refresh your child's memory, if needed, with photos and names of people he will encounter on a daily basis: school personnel such as cafeteria workers, the school nurse, office staff, bus drivers. These can often be found in school yearbooks.

- Do a test run or two, even with familiar routines, like putting clothes out the night before, getting breakfast, the route to walk to school, the parent or bus pick-up location after school, putting backpack by the door, etc.

- Set up a few social gatherings, especially with a peer buddy before school starts. That positive social relationship set up ahead of time will be helpful in those early stress-filled days of school.

- Review back-to-school conversation starters and group social skills to help him get through the first couple of days. "How was your summer?" "I like your new shirt." "Wow, you cut your hair!"

The effective advocate

The Rolling Stones wrote a lot of songs about raising a special needs child, didn't they? "I Can't Get No Satisfaction" and "You Can't Always Get What You Want" were anthems of the 1970s. But don't forget the rest of the song: if you try sometime, you just might find, you get what you need.

Government agencies, school districts, individual schools within the same district—each operates differently. And so do parents, so each experience advocating for a special needs child will be different. What remains constant, however, is the value a parent derives from 1) knowing the law, and 2) understanding the social, emotional, and organizational politics at play. Knowing and practicing the elements of effective advocacy can save time, tempers, and money spent on lawyers, mediators, and other intervention specialists.

> **QUICK IDEA**
>
> Keep copies of all correspondence and e-mails with your child's school in a Special Education binder, arranged in a chronological format.

- Know your rights. State and federal agencies administer special education and other services for which your child may be eligible. All must provide you with written materials regarding 1) evaluation and determination of eligibility for services, 2) through what means and entities those services will be delivered, and 3) the mechanisms for filing complaints or appealing decisions. Working your way through the bureaucracy is challenging enough without finding out that you've spent countless hours fighting for something that is not handled by the agency, or covered under the law.

- Know the law. Do not assume the personnel involved in an agency— or even the school system—know or correctly interpret state and federal special education legislation. Many a parent has walked away from a negotiation trusting the information offered as accurate, only to find out later that it was misleading or incomplete. Sadly, no school or agency can do everything for your child. School personnel do not always receive training in special education law. On every parent rests the responsibility of knowing the law and what they are entitled to request.

- Be assertive, not aggressive. If you are not sure of the distinction between the two, check a few dictionary definitions. Assertive is generally defined as being resolute and confident, whereas aggression is defined as hostile or destructive behavior caused by frustration. Assertive means being informed, focused, tenacious, firm but respectful. It's much more likely you'll be heard when communicating in this manner than when you're in the attack mode, where the listener's natural tendency will be to tune out/avoid/defend and/or engage in similar reciprocal behavior—none of which will be productive.

- Know what you want and come prepared. Effective advocates are clear about their child's strengths and challenges, the child's learning style, and what strategies may be more effective for helping him learn and grow. If needed, present professional assessments or recommendations as back-up to the services or options you are negotiating. Anticipate information you may need to present to make your case, and come prepared with it.

- Leave your emotions at the door. Advocating for your child is not an exercise in becoming well liked or in establishing friendships with school or agency personnel. Your job is to do your best to secure individualized and appropriate services for your child. You should be professional, cordial, and respectful and keep in mind at all times that you are involved in a negotiation, working toward a partnership where all parties feel positive about the outcome. Body language, voice tone, eye contact, language—all affect how successful you will be as an advocate. Don't let your emotions lead the conversation.

- Allow adequate time for meetings. Schedule meetings allowing enough time for adequate discussion of the issues, or schedule several shorter meetings. Rushing through too many items in too little time increases opportunities for misunderstanding and dissatisfaction, and almost guarantees that future meetings will be necessary. One professional negotiator put it this way: "You may have the watch, but I have the time. I can drink as much tea or coffee as the next person."

- Keep good written records. Keep all IEP documents in a chronological binder. Keep notes from phone conversations in a binder or folder, and mark each one as soon as you end the call as to date, time, to whom you spoke, what you requested, actions promised, or conclusion reached. If you are not a good note-taker, consider getting a phone recorder to record conversations. (You must inform the other party you are recording.) Bring a voice recorder to face-to-face meetings.

  Don't trust your memory on this, no matter how sharp you think you are. Phone calls and details pile up, and you may need to refer to specific details of these conversations at some point, especially if services promised do not materialize.

- Address issues specifically: "Amy's IEP calls for paraeducator assistance during reading and math time. She tells me an aide came for the first two weeks and hasn't been back since. How do you plan to reinstate this assistance and when?"

- Follow through and follow up. Always supply what is asked of you in an efficient and accurate manner. When following up on action promised by others, be persistent but reasonable.

  - When a promised callback doesn't come, allow a reasonable amount of time, then you call. "When we spoke on Tuesday, you were going to fax me the meeting times. I know how busy you are, but I am anxious to address these issues and really want to get those dates on my calendar."

  - Electronic communication: our motto is, technology is great until it isn't. Email and texting are not perfect communication tools. Emails get lost or diverted into spam files, and many people are buried in email and cannot answer it all efficiently. Text messages are especially easy to ignore. If your emails and text messages are getting no response, attach receipt tags to them. Keep messages as succinct as possible; we've all opened messages so lengthy that we just sigh and move on.

- Paper letters. This old-fashioned method may work where electronics fail, especially if you include a self-addressed stamped envelope for the reply.

- When all this fails, escalate—politely. Go to the next level of administration with a respectful request: "I've made several attempts to schedule these meetings, with no response. Can you advise me as to how we can get the process moving again? I will call you tomorrow to get your thoughts."

- Reach out. Joining a support group, starting a mom's or parents group, blogging, contacting your representatives in local, state, and federal government—all these activities will put you in touch with others who are going through similar experiences and help you create a pool of ideas and support from which to draw.

  Always remember that there are no stupid questions if you don't know the answer, and that most people like to help others. Ask caseworkers, doctors, teachers, family members, neighbors, and friends for information, support, suggestions, help with tasks. There is rarely any harm in asking for help (the worst anyone can say is no, and even then, you've lost nothing), and even more rarely any advantage in trying to handle your child's autism alone.

Help with understanding the special education maze. The special education process and the federal laws governing it are a maze of new terminology, regulations and procedures. It can be mind-boggling for parents of a child newly diagnosed with autism or Asperger's. Luckily, there are resources that can help.

- Parent Training Information Centers (PTIs) are organizations that offer parents advocacy, training, and information on their children's educational rights

- Protection and Advocacy agencies (P&As) are federally mandated in each state and territory to protect of the rights of persons with disabilities through legally based advocacy.

- Local/state chapters of nonprofit organizations, such as the Autism Society of America, Easter Seals, and United Cerebral Palsy exist in every state, with services ranging from training workshops about special education issues, to providing advocates to accompany parents into IEP meetings. Find referrals in your state at the Resource section of the Autism Society of America's website, Autism-Society.org.

- Wrightslaw is an excellent web source of information on special education issues for parents, educators, advocates, and attorneys. Founders Pete and Pam Wright offer articles, books, DVDs, explanations of court cases, blogs, and professional referrals on the site, as well as host multimedia e-training opportunities and in-person conferences around the U.S. (*Wrightslaw.com*)

- Many states and state organizations sponsor IEP Partners Programs or similar coaching-type support that matches advocates with parents in need.

Mediation alert! ·

The benefits of formal mediation are many. There is no cost to the parent and the resolution time is much shorter than the months or years that could be involved in a hearing. Parents could walk away at the end of a proper mediation with a "done deal," as opposed to a hearing, where the losing party can appeal in court and keep the process going.

But there's also a downside, one often not explained to parents. Parents who voluntarily enter into mediation and then go on to accept a written agreement waive their rights to all claims made to the school up to and including the date of the signed document, *whether or not they were addressed* in the agreement.

While mediation can sometimes be a useful tool in obtaining needed services, parents should be aware of what they give up when accepting an agreement through mediation. Generally, it will benefit parents more to refuse mediation when offered and pursue other grievance mechanisms first.

Ask these important questions

Wouldn't it be ironic if, in diligently teaching your child how to gain information through asking questions, you neglected to do so yourself—about the very school to which you are entrusting him each day? Moving to a new home is an obvious time to ask questions of school personnel. But even if you are not moving, you owe it to your child to ask the questions the answers to which will determine whether he is going to be in an environment that supports all efforts to meet his full potential, or whether it's time to start shopping for an educational setting other than the nearest neighborhood school.

- What is the school's overall culture in terms of dealing with bullying and teasing? Zero-tolerance is the only policy you should accept. If you hear "kids will be kids, and we let them work it out themselves" approach, know that your child has neither the language nor the social skills to be able to hold his own in that atmosphere.

- What is the school's policy on parent visitation to the classroom? Schools may require that you sign in and wear a name tag, but beyond that, are you welcome to drop in any time? Can you visit with a day's notice? Or will you have to jump through hoops of fire to be able to observe your child's classroom? If your phone calls and e-mails are not returned in a reasonable timeframe (within 24 hours), if the teacher has an endless stream of reasons why "that day wouldn't be good," if you get verbal agreement but the body language is telling you otherwise, speak to the principal at once.

- In what ways are parents involved in the school? Are there parent representatives to site councils or advisory committees? Does the district or school offer parent development workshops? Do parents teach after-school classes, coach sports teams, maintain the school garden, coordinate the auction or the food drive, plan the field trips, staff the library?

- What is the average tenure of the general education teaching staff? What is the average tenure of the special education staff? Low turnover generally indicates a positive working environment.

- Where is the resource room located? In the mainstream of the school, or tucked away in a little-seen corner?

- Does the district offer regular or ongoing in-service training, itinerant consulting or other professional support specific to autism for general education and special education teachers?

- How are IEP goals measured and quantified? IEP goals must be measurable and dictated by the child's needs as evidenced by hard data collected in a clearly defined manner.

- Will the IEP be based on your child's actual needs or on resources currently offered or projected to be available?

- What is the school or classroom culture regarding inclusion in general and autism, specifically? A one-size-fits-all policy should raise your radar. Slotting your child into a special classroom without evaluating his individual needs is never appropriate.

- How will the school keep you apprised of your child's progress? A communication book that travels back and forth from home to school each day is one way, a daily or weekly email or phone call is another. You should expect a written quarterly progress report for each IEP goal, but there must be communication in between, or valuable time may be lost as problems fester.

Creating positive partnerships

Throughout this book, we've stressed the significance of strong, effective partnerships based on honesty, respect, empathy, and commonly shared goals and ideals. Parent-professional partnerships do have an emotional layer, and it can sometimes waylay even the best-intentioned participants. Creating and maintaining positive partnerships requires that parents, educators, private therapists, and service providers hold to these actions and attitudes:

- Commit to a team mentality, with a common goal of creating the best possible instructional program for the student.

- Resolving issues in a win-win format is essential to fostering a long-term positive relationship. Leave egos and personality differences at the door.

- Base decisions on the child's need, not in response to the personalities or interpersonal skills of team members.

- Familiarize yourself with both the rights of parents and the responsibilities of the school system with regard to the provision of services. Don't leave it up to someone else. Be personally educated and responsible.

- Arrive for meetings on time, organized, and prepared. Have questions ready.

- Be respectful. Present your opinions firmly, but politely. Avoid putting team members on the spot or consciously embarrassing them.

- Explain concerns clearly, without unnecessary jargon. Present specific examples; be able to back up your statements with facts. Check for comprehension often.

- Control your emotions: learn how to discuss, disagree, and reason with others to accomplish your goals.

- Accept that a team member may have a differing point of view, but still hold the child's best interests in mind. No one is always right or always wrong.

- Establish a rapport and maintain communication throughout the year. Share information freely. Return calls promptly, write notes often.

- Express appreciation for all efforts large and small.

- Parents must respect that teachers, administrators, and service providers are responsible for the educational programs of many other children besides your own. They may not always be able to respond to requests immediately. Professionals must set and adhere to reasonable response timeframes.

- Professionals must recognize the parent as the expert in understanding the child and how he functions.

- Be realistic about what constitutes a crisis. Only call an emergency IEP meeting when dangerous consequences are imminent. Parents have the right to call an IEP meeting at any time during the year but whenever possible, should keep scheduling demands reasonable.

- Parents who decide that due process is warranted must say so honestly, without using it as a threat, so that educators may respond in a manner that avoids such a step if possible.

- All team members must recognize that district policy or state law does not override federal law. Identify and discuss discrepancies.

- All team members should be proactive in seeking advice from other professionals, additional personal/professional training, or requesting further evaluations in areas of need or uncertainty. A child's program should be based on autism-specific expertise and individualized evaluation rather than generalized speculations and assumptions.

At the beginning of this chapter, we stated that the most important thing parents and teachers can do for their student with autism or Asperger's is to create and sustain a productive working relationship. Respecting and valuing all individuals as individuals must be the cornerstone of all learning, throughout formal education and beyond.

Understand the gravity of the decisions being made about this one child. They will affect his success or failure not just this year, but for all the years ahead.

Endnotes

From Chapter 1 – Sensory

Introduction. *Ten Things Every Child with Autism Wishes You Knew* by Ellen Notbohm. Future Horizons, 2005.

Vision and Seeing. Some material adapted from *EnVISIONing a Bright Future* by Patricia Lemer. Optometric Extension Program Foundation, 2008.

Walking on Tippy Toes. Copyright © Lindsey Biel, OTR/L, co-author of *Raising a Sensory Smart Child*. Originally published in *Autism Asperger's Digest*, July-August 2009 issue.

From Chapter 2 – Communication and Language

When Speech Gets Stuck. Adapted from "Finding the Words … When it's Hard to Find Your Voice!" by Marge Blanc. *Autism Asperger's Digest*, January-February 2006.

Visual Strategies. "How to create a visual schedule" adapted from information appearing on Linda Hodgdon's website, *www.UseVisualStrategies.com*.

Tips for Using Your Visual Schedule. Adapted from "Schedules, Schedules, Schedules: Tips for Teaching, Tips for Using" by David Freschi. *Autism Asperger's Digest*. July-August 2003.

Jump-start Literacy for Concrete Thinkers. Adapted from "Real Animals Don't Talk: Nurturing a Book Lover When Fantasy Isn't Part of Their Reality" by Ellen Notbohm. *Autism Asperger's Digest*, March-April 2004.

Make Reading Fun. Copyright © Michelle McConnell. Originally published in *Autism Asperger's Digest*, July-August 2009.

Beware of Idioms. Instructions for the Go Fish Idioms Game adapted from *www.glc.k12.ga.us.*

The Four Steps of Communication. Adapted from "The Social Communication Dance: The Four Steps of Communication" by Michelle Garcia Winner. *Autism Asperger's Digest,* May-June 2008.

From Chapter 3 – Behavior

From Bad to Worse: How to Avoid Escalating a Skirmish. Adapted from L. Albert's *A teacher's guide to cooperative discipline: How to manage your classroom and promote self-esteem.* Ags Pub., 1989.

Deals and Contracts. Adapted from "Deals and Contracts" by David Freschi. *Autism Asperger's Digest,* September-October 2003.

Watch What You Reinforce. Adapted from "10 Everyday Teaching Bloopers & How to Avoid Them" by David Freschi. *Autism Asperger's Digest,* March-April 2004.

More about Enabling Behaviors. Adapted from "The Enigma of Autism Behaviors:

Enabling Success & Finding Solutions, Part 2 – Parent Behaviors. By David Freschi. *Autism Asperger's Digest,* May-June 2006.

From Chapter 4 – Daily Living

Just Take a Bite. Adapted from presentation by Lori Ernsperger (Utica, NY. 2004) and also contained in *Just Take a Bite: Easy, Effective Answers to Food Aversions and Eating Challenges* by Lori Ernsperger, Ph.D. and Tania Stegen-Hanson, OTR/L. Future Horizons, 2004.

Uncommon Gifts for Uncommon Kids. Adapted from "Uncommon Gifts for Uncommon Kids" by Ellen Notbohm. *Autism Asperger's Digest,* November-December 2004.

Home Safety for Escape Artists and Acrobats. Ideas adapted from material on the Special Needs Children's Network website, *http://archive.specialneedschildrennetwork.com/archive/sncn2.html.*

Medications: Be Thorough. Adapted from "Medications and Informed Consent" by Luke Tsai, M.D. *Autism Asperger's Digest,* January-February 2002.

So Many Books, So Little Time. Adapted from "So Many Books, So Little Time," *The Autism Trail Guide: Postcards from the Road Less Traveled* by Ellen Notbohm. Future Horizons, 2007.

Guiding Your Child with Autism to Adulthood. Adapted from "Independence Day: Guiding Your Special Needs Child to Adulthood" by Ellen Notbohm. Originally published in *Parenting New Hampshire,* June 2006.

From Chapter 5 – Thinking Social, Being Social

Perspective Taking. Adapted from material in *Think Social! A Social Thinking Curriculum for School-Aged Students* by Michelle Garcia Winner. Think Social Publishing, 2005.

Friend to Friend. Adapted from material on the Friend 2 Friend Social Learning Society website, *www.friend2friendsociety.org.*

When "Sorry" Seems to Be the Hardest Word. Adapted from "Learning to Say Sorry" by Ellen Notbohm. Originally published in *Child* magazine, Australia, 2008.

Everyone Makes Mistakes. Adapted from "Rule Number One: Ask for Help" by Ellen Notbohm. *Autism Asperger's Digest*, March-April 2009.

From Chapter 6 – Teachers and Learners

Teaching Concentration Skills. Adapted from "Teaching Concentration Skills" by Ellen Notbohm. *Children's Voice,* September-October 2009.

Pause and Plan. Adapted from "Building a Firm Foundation: Errorless Learning" by James Ball, Ed.D., BCBA. *Autism Asperger's Digest*, March-April 2009.

Teachers' Rights in Special Education. Adapted from "Regular teachers' rights in Special Education" by Reed Martin. *Autism Asperger's Digest*, March-April 2004.

Designed with Asperger's in Mind. Adapted from "Is There a Continuum of Alternative Placements for Students with Asperger Syndrome?" by Gretchen Mertz. *Autism Asperger's Digest*, July-August 2004.

Creating Positive Partnerships. Adapted from "Creating A Positive Partnership Between Families and School. PDD Network newsletter, June 2002.

Index

J

About
the Authors

Ellen Notbohm

Three-time ForeWord Book of the Year finalist Ellen Notbohm is author of one of the autism community's most beloved books, *Ten Things Every Child with Autism Wishes You Knew.* She is also author of *Ten Things Your Student with Autism Wishes You Knew* and the Eric Hoffer Book Award finalist, *The Autism Trail Guide: Postcards from the Road Less Traveled.* Her articles, commentary and  book excerpts have appeared in hundreds of magazines, newspapers, academic journals, training manuals and websites around the world. Ellen welcomes reader feedback and newsletter sign-ups through her website at *ellennotbohm.com.*

Veronica Zysk

Veronica Zysk has been working in the field of autism since 1991. She served as Executive Director of the Autism Society of America from 1991-1996, and then joined Future Horizons, moving into an editorial position within the company in 1999, as Managing Editor

and visionary for the first national magazine on autism spectrum disorders, the *Autism Asperger's Digest*, winner of multiple Gold awards for excellence. She continues in that position today. In addition to her writing collaborations with Ellen Notbohm, she has co-authored and/or edited 14 other books on autism and Asperger's, working with noted authors such as Temple Grandin (*Unwritten Rules of Social Relationships; The Way I See It*), James Ball (*Early Intervention and Autism: Real-life Questions, Real-life Answers*), Jean Duane (*Bake Deliciously Gluten & Dairy Free*), and Michelle Garcia Winner (*Think Social!; Thinking About You Thinking About Me; Socially Curious and Curiously Social; A Politically Incorrect Look at Evidence-based Practices & Teaching Social Skills*). Veronica makes her home in the beautiful western mountains of North Carolina.

More award-winning titles by Ellen Notbohm!

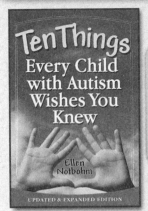

Winner of an iParenting Media Award and Honorable Mention in the 2005 ForeWord Book of the Year Awards! Every parent, teacher, social worker, therapist, and physician should have this succinct and informative book in their back pocket. Framed with both humor and compassion, the book defines the top ten characteristics that illuminate the minds and hearts of children with autism.

The unique perspective of a child's voice returns to help us understand the thinking patterns that guide their actions, shape an environment conducive to their learning style, and communicate with them in meaningful ways. It's the game plan every educator, parent, or family member needs to make the most of every "teaching moment" in the life of these children we love. Winner of an iParenting Media Award and Finalist in the 2006 ForeWord Book of the Year Awards!

"Do not go where the path may lead, go instead where there is no path and leave a trail." —Ralph Waldo Emerson.
In a cohesive compilation of her best articles, Ellen offers advice on concrete issues such as math homework, video games, and tricky behavior, and also tackles the more abstract concepts of parenting: trusting parental instincts, when to take risks, how to hang on, and when to let go. Finalist in the 2007 ForeWord Book of the Year Awards and finalist in the 2008 Eric Hoffer Awards, this book is absolutely invaluable to all who are "on the autism trail."

> **Ellen captures the major issues of autism and makes them understandable and usable, even to those new to spectrum disorders ….**
> Nancy Cale, Vice President of Unlocking Autism

Available in bookstores everywhere!